PIMLICO

512

FLIGHT FROM REALITY

David Stafford is the author of several books on intelligence history, including *Britain and European Resistance, Churchill and Secret Service, Roosevelt and Churchill: Men of Secrets* and *Secret Agent: The True Story of the Special Operations Executive*. He is Project Director at the Centre for Second World War Studies in the Department of History at the University of Edinburgh.

FLIGHT FROM REALITY

Rudolf Hess and his
Mission to Scotland, 1941

———————

Edited by
DAVID STAFFORD

PIMLICO

Published by Pimlico 2002

2 4 6 8 10 9 7 5 3 1

Selection and introduction copyright © David Stafford 2002
Individual essays copyright © each author 2002

First published in Great Britain by
Pimlico 2002

Pimlico
Random House, 20 Vauxhall Bridge Road,
London SW1V 2SA

Random House Australia (Pty) Limited
20 Alfred Street, Milsons Point, Sydney,
New South Wales 2061, Australia

Random House New Zealand Limited
18 Poland Road, Glenfield,
Auckland 10, New Zealand

Random House (Pty) Limited
Endulini, 5A Jubilee Road, Parktown 2193, South Africa

The Random House Group Limited Reg. No. 954009
www.randomhouse.co.uk

A CIP catalogue record for this book is available from the British Library

ISBN 0-7126-8025-X

Papers used by Random House are natural, recyclable products
made from wood grown in sustainable forests; the manufacturing processes
conform to the environmental regulations of the country of origin.

Printed and bound in Great Britain by
Mackays of Chatham PLC, Chatham, Kent

Contents

Illustrations vii

Preface ix

David Stafford
Introduction 1

Lothar Kettenacker
Mishandling a Spectacular Event: The Rudolf Hess Affair 19

John Erickson
Rudolf Hess: A Post-Soviet Postscript 38

Warren F. Kimball
The Hess Distraction: A Footnote from America 61

James Douglas-Hamilton
Hess and the Haushofers 78

Peter Longerich
Hitler's Deputy: The Role of Rudolf Hess in the Nazi Regime 104

Len Deighton
Hess the Aviator 121

Roy Conyers Nesbit
Hess and Public Records 139

Hugh Trevor-Roper
Hess: The Incorrigible Intruder 153

Notes on Contributors 173

Index 175

Illustrations

Hess speaks at the laying of the foundation stone of the Adolf Hitler Canal, May 1934 (*AKG London*).

Hitler and Hess at the 1937 Nuremberg Party Congress (*AKG London*).

Hitler, Goering and Hess at the 1938 Nuremberg Conference (*AKG London*).

Hess and Hitler on a forest ramble (*photograph by W.G. Fitzgerald; collection of James Douglas-Hamilton*).

Hitler, Hess and Leni Riefenstahl (*photograph by W.G. Fitzgerald; collection of James Douglas-Hamilton*).

Hitler inspects one of Hess's early aeroplanes (*photograph by W.G. Fitzgerald; collection of James Douglas-Hamilton*).

Rudolf Hess and Professor Karl Haushofer (*copyright Haushofer family*).

Albrecht Haushofer (*copyright Haushofer family*).

The Duke of Hamilton, as the Marquis of Clydesdale, leaving for the Mount Everest Flight Expedition in 1933 (*copyright © The Times*).

Hess with Hitler and Goebbels at the Sportpalast Berlin, on the 8th anniversary of the Nazi seizure of power (*AKG London*).

Hess the aviator prepares for a flight in his Messerschmitt 110 (*photographer unknown; collection of James Douglas-Hamilton*).

Hess in Vienna after the *Anschluss* (*AKG London*).

The front page of the *Daily Record*, 13 May 1941 (*AKG London*).

The local soldiery poses next to the wreckage of Hess's Messerschmitt (*Hulton Getty*).

'He must have been mad': cartoon by David Low, 15 May 1941.

Sir Alexander Cadogan, Sir John Simon and Sir Anthony Eden in 1933 (*Hulton Getty*).

Kim Philby in 1955 (*Hulton Getty*).

Churchill, Roosevelt and Stalin at the Yalta Conference in 1945 (*Hulton Getty*).

Hess in the dock at Nuremberg (*AKG London*).

Interrogation of Hess at Nuremberg (*AKG London*).

Every effort has been made to trace and contact copyright holders. The publishers will be pleased to correct any mistakes or omissions in future editions.

Preface

Most of the chapters in this volume originated in a special symposium on Rudolf Hess organised by the Centre for Second World War Studies at the University of Edinburgh in May 2000 – the fifty-ninth anniversary of his dramatic flight to Scotland. For financial assistance in making possible that event I am grateful to Dr Frances Dow, Dean and Provost of the Faculty of Arts at the university; and for advice and help with other aspects of the symposium I am indebted in particular to Dr Paul Addison and Dr Jeremy Crang, Director and Deputy Director of the Centre for Second World War Studies, respectively. My agent, Andrew Lownie, patiently dealt with contractual issues, Cristina Collejo helped organise the manuscript for delivery to the publisher, and Lord James Douglas-Hamilton kindly lent photographs and other valuable assistance. My editor at Pimlico, Jörg Hensgen, skilfully guided the text into print. Above all, I am profoundly grateful for the commitment and willing co-operation of the several authors which made this venture both possible and enjoyable.

David Stafford
Centre for Second World War Studies
Department of History
University of Edinburgh
June 2001

DAVID STAFFORD

Introduction

Shortly after 11 p.m. on 10 May 1941, a Scottish ploughman spotted a parachutist floating to the ground on a field at Floors Farm, just a dozen miles south of Glasgow. He ran out to find a burning twin-engined Messerschmitt BF 110 bomber and an injured German officer wearing the uniform of a captain in the German Air Force. The aviator identified himself as 'Captain Albert Horn' and asked to be taken to see the Duke of Hamilton for whom, he claimed, he was carrying an important message.

In reality, 'Captain Horn' was none other than Rudolf Hess, Deputy Führer and veteran comrade-in-arms and right-hand man of Adolf Hitler himself. Hess, with his membership card number 16, was one of the earliest members of the Nazi Party, he had been imprisoned with Hitler in the Landsberg fortress after the abortive Munich Beer Hall *Putsch* of 1923, had helped him write *Mein Kampf*, and served as his private secretary until the Nazis seized power. After Hitler became Chancellor of Germany Hess took over the running of the Nazi Party and it was he who regularly introduced the Führer to the mass Party rallies at Nuremberg, events that mesmerised and seduced the German people in the 1930s. Hess was probably the only Nazi who addressed Hitler by the intimate '*du*'(you) rather than the more formal '*sie*'. He adored Adolf Hitler and was his most subservient follower.[1]

His arrival in Britain thus defied all credulity. The Prime Minister Winston Churchill, who was told the news while indulging in one of his favourite night-time relaxations, watching films, famously captured the mood after being left almost speechless. 'Well,' he declared once the news had sunk in, 'Hess or no Hess, I'm off to watch the Marx Brothers.' After the war he summed up the breathtaking impact of Hess's arrival this way: 'It was as if my trusted colleague, the Foreign Secretary [Anthony Eden] who was only a little younger than Hess, had parachuted from a stolen Spitfire on to the grounds of Berchtesgaden.'[2]

In the sixty years since Hess's extraordinary arrival on British soil, controversy has raged over this episode, which still stands out as one of the most bizarre chapters in the history of the Second World War. Much of the discussion has been wild speculation based on rumour and fancy, and a clamorous multitude of colourful and sometimes contradictory conspiracy theories have jostled for attention. The press and television have enjoyed a field day with ever more extravagant and outlandish theories vying to catch the headlines and raise the ratings.

Among the most spectacular claims are those that argue that it was not Hess at all who flew to Scotland, but a double; that Hess was secretly carrying out the wishes of Hitler as his personal emissary to negotiate with a powerful 'peace party' in Britain; that the massive assault by German bombers on London that same night, during which the Houses of Parliament were severely damaged, was a diversionary attack by the Luftwaffe to assist the mission; that for part of his flight he was accompanied by Reinhard Heydrich, head of the Reich Security Main Office, Himmler's deputy, key actor in the 'Final Solution', and, as 'Protector' of Bohemia and Moravia, the feared 'Butcher of Prague' who was eventually assassinated by Czech patriots in May 1942; that the Royal Air Force and British Home Defence forces were mysteriously ordered not to attack his plane; that the Duke of Hamilton and Hess were personal friends and that the Duke was deeply implicated in the affair; and that Britain's Secret Intelligence Service, MI6 (or its Security Service, MI5), were behind the whole business and had cleverly inveigled Hess into making his flight in the first place. A book published in Britain even as this one goes to press proposes not just that there was a conspiracy and a massive post-war cover-up, but that the royal family, and particularly the King's brother, the Duke of Kent, were heavily involved in the plot, not to mention that the prisoner who died in Spandau was not the real Rudolf Hess, but a double. Written by a team of authors which includes lecturers on the paranormal and religious conspiracies, this might be termed the mother of all conspiracy theories – were it not, perhaps, for the website entitled 'The Omega File: Rudolph Hess and Secret German Space Base', which claims that the real Rudolf Hess was murdered because he held the file on German space plans in the Antarctic.[3]

Nor do conspiracy theories end with Hess's life sentence in Berlin's Spandau prison handed down at the post-war Nuremberg trial of top Nazi leaders in 1946.* His death more than forty years later in 1987, at ninety-three, was officially declared to be suicide – the last in a long sequence of attempts by Hess to take his own life. Yet his son, Wolf Rüdiger Hess, who campaigned long for his release from years of solitary confinement, remains convinced that this was a cover-up for official murder by two SAS men on the orders of the British government.

More disturbingly, among neo-Nazi elements in modern-day Germany and elsewhere, Hess has even emerged as a 'martyr'. This represents an extraordinary transformation for the man who was so roundly denounced by Hitler when the news reached him of Hess's flight. 'It's to be hoped he's crashed into the sea', a shaken and furious Hitler was heard to say, and he personally insisted that the word 'madness' featured in the official communiqué first broadcast to the German people by radio to explain the affair. To a hastily convened meeting of Nazi Party functionaries at the Berghof two days later, as described in the recent authoritative biography of Hitler by Ian Kershaw, a still shaken Hitler declared baldly that Hess had betrayed him.[4] Soviet-like, all references to him, including portraits and photographs, were immediately expunged from the Third Reich.

Ultimately, in their desperate and ever more extravagant search to unearth some 'rational' explanation for the mysteries of Hess's

---

*After his ill-fated flight Hess was kept in prison in Britain until his transfer to Nuremberg in 1945 to face trial with other members of the Nazi elite. Here he was convicted of committing crimes against peace and the planning, preparation, initiation and waging of aggressive war. He was acquitted of war crimes and crimes against humanity. After 1966, when Albert Speer and Baldur von Schirach had served their twenty-year sentences, Hess remained the only prisoner in this Allied prison in West Berlin. Following his death, the prison was demolished.

flight, the conspiracy theories become not merely absurd but banal. They also reduce the figure of Hess to a mere cipher, a hapless and unwitting tool in some greater plan, a passive victim of forces beyond his control or ken. In reality Hess was no such person. He was fully and willingly complicit in the misdeeds of the Third Reich prior to his flight, including the comprehensive and disastrous anti–Semitic legislation that condemned the Jews of Germany to pariah status and opened the door to the Holocaust. That in itself makes his flight to Britain far more intriguing than any of the increasingly convoluted and far-fetched theories hold.

So dominated by conspiracy theories has the Hess affair become that some important questions about his mission have been largely ignored. One of the most intriguing is this: what did Churchill, Stalin and Roosevelt make of his flight to Britain at the time, and how did they and their governments react to it? Hess appeared in Britain waving the banner of peace at a most critical stage of the war, before either the United States or the Soviet Union were officially belligerents, and when Britain was still struggling to hold its own in the Mediterranean. Just over a month later Hitler launched Operation Barbarossa against the Soviet Union and thus sealed his ultimate fate. In those crucial weeks during the spring of 1941, what calculations were made in Washington, London and Moscow about the meaning of the Hess mission? How – if at all – were policies and the course of international affairs thereby changed or modified? The issue touches significantly on the politics, strategy and diplomacy of the Second World War. It provides the starting point for many of the explorations in this book.

The authors contributing to this book are mostly trained historians and scholars accustomed to the hard-headed examination of documentary and archival evidence. Sceptical by training and experience, they agreed to collaborate on this volume, sharing the view that the Hess flight to Scotland was best explored outside the framework of any conspiracy theory. While by no means agreed on every issue relating to the flight of Rudolf Hess, they remain firmly of this view. Yet some of their conclusions throw intriguing new light on the Hess controversy by revealing how and why the most persistent of these conspiracy theories originated and have endured.

The most endemic view, which appears in many variations, is that Hess's flight was part and parcel of some Byzantine operation run by British Intelligence. This theory was most strongly and effectively publicised in two books on Hess by British authors that appeared in the 1990s. One was written by the late controversialist John Costello, entitled *Ten Days that Saved the West*, the other by the respected historian and biographer Peter Padfield under the title *Hess: Flight for the Führer*. This is not the place to refute their views in detail, save to say that Costello's book was so riddled with elementary errors about the response of the Royal Air Force to Hess's flight that it completely discredits his thesis of a deliberate decision to let his Messerschmitt fly unhindered to Scotland. Padfield's arguments, while far more serious and substantial, are considerably challenged by the fact that files recently opened in the British Public Record Office fail to support his prediction that they would substantiate his theory of British Intelligence involvement; and that, on his own admission, a key informant allegedly substantiating his theory of a British Intelligence plot refused at the last moment to deliver the crucial evidence. When allegedly vital proof continually keeps slipping away like this, any sceptical reader must wonder how credible the basic thesis is.[5]

If we stick with the evidence that exists, what is of far greater interest and fascination – and what this volume so clearly reveals – is how and where this theory of a British Intelligence conspiracy began in the first place. The short answer is that it started in 1941 with Stalin and the KGB, and has been running strongly ever since. In one way or another, all subsequent theories alleging an active British Intelligence connection with the flight of Rudolf Hess can be traced back, even if indirectly and unwittingly, to this one highly suspect source.

We can even put a specific name to it – Kim Philby, the notorious MI6 officer and Soviet mole who after years of betrayal finally defected to Moscow in 1963. As the chapter by John Erickson reveals, it was Philby, operating with the codename 'Sonnchen' under the control of the legal NKVD *rezident* in London, Anatole Gorske, who first reported Hess's arrival in Scotland to Moscow. What Philby himself knew, however, was imprecise and gleaned largely second-hand from a friend of his in the Press Department of the Foreign Office. This did not of course hinder Philby in offering his own personal view to Moscow that while *no* Anglo-German peace talks were afoot, as the time was not ripe, *later on* Hess could become 'the centre of an intrigue' serving both 'the peace party' in Britain and Adolf Hitler. Philby's speculative and malicious assessment struck home with Stalin and the notion lingered. Over a year later, in the summer of 1942, Stalin even accused Churchill of 'keeping Hess in reserve'.

Despite Philby's insidious observation, however, Stalin quickly came to the view himself that Hess *was* the focus of some immediate peace deal between London and Berlin that would leave Hitler free to strike in the east. The Hess flight came at a crucial juncture in the Second World War, when Soviet Intelligence was (accurately) reporting a huge German build-up along the Soviet border. But did this, wondered Stalin, presage an actual attack – or was it merely designed to back up new demands from Hitler that could be negotiated over? As Stalin contemplated talks with Hitler – who was, after all, still his nominal ally since the infamous Nazi–Soviet Non-Aggression Pact of August 1939 – the Hess flight proved enormously convenient. Intelligence reports reaching his desk from Soviet agents across Europe were deeply confused about whether or not Hess had arrived in Britain as an official emissary of Hitler, or whether his flight was a significant sign of some deep divisions about future strategy within the top Nazi leadership. Stalin grasped at the second interpretation because it gave him room for hope that a Nazi attack might yet be prevented by negotiation. By the same token, he clung firmly to his suspicious and even paranoid view that the British, through their alleged Intelligence Service manipulation of Hess, were trying to embroil Berlin and Moscow in a war – an attitude strengthened when the British passed on evidence from their own Intelligence sources (mostly 'Ultra') indicating a German build-up on the border. When war finally came with Hitler's massive onslaught on 22 June 1941, it merely confirmed in Stalin's mind 'an inextricable link' between that event and Hess's flight. Subsequently, whenever Moscow wished to embarrass Britain, it would wheel out the Hess affair – 'an all-purpose alibi,' writes John Erickson, 'to be unco-operative or overweening as was their wont'. The habit persisted long after the war and even lies behind the widespread rumour that Hess's death was not suicide but murder by the British.[6]

But what, in the first place, encouraged Stalin and the Kremlin to come up with their theory of a British Intelligence conspiracy? It is clear from Erickson's evidence that Soviet Intelligence reports to Moscow on the affair consisted almost exclusively of speculation and second-hand gossip, and that they had virtually nothing concrete to go on. Yet it was not as though on other issues Soviet Intelligence could not deliver the goods. So why so much hollow if fervid speculation in this case?

The answer lies in the official British response to Hess's flight, one that was carefully and deliberately calculated in the hope of achieving a particular diplomatic goal. Unfortunately, as Lothar Kettenacker convincingly demonstrates, it was a sadly *mis-*calculated manoeuvre that ended in a catastrophic own goal.

Churchill and his government had no prior knowledge of Hess's flight. After he recovered from the initial shock, Churchill wanted simply and directly to tell the British people what had happened, and to use the hapless figure of Hess for anti-Nazi propaganda. The facts, he believed, would easily discredit Hess, and were not to be feared. But he was firmly resisted by the Foreign Secretary, Anthony Eden, and his Permanent Under-Secretary, Sir Alexander Cadogan. In Hess's arrival they saw a unique and unexpected opportunity to further British diplomacy at this critical stage of the war when rumour was rife about Hitler's designs on the Soviet Union – and about Stalin's likely response. The British were desperate to prevent a Soviet–German *rapprochement*, and to improve Anglo-Soviet relations. They, like Stalin, interpreted Intelligence about a build-up of forces along the Soviet border as most probably a prelude to moves by Hitler to force more concessions from Moscow.

So Cadogan and other high Foreign Office officials devised a complicated and subtle plan. They would *deliberately* misrepresent the facts about Hess to suggest that there was a real possibility of peace negotiations between London and Berlin. This would so worry Stalin, they calculated, that he would then abandon any hopes of his own talks with Berlin and become more amenable to British overtures. Cadogan was the Foreign Office link with MI6, and once this disinformation strategy was approved instructions were issued on 23 May 1941 to SIS stations to launch a global 'whispering campaign' of rumours. Wrapped up in a blanket of deliberate ambiguity and accompanied by an *official* silence on the Hess affair, its object was to send 'a clear warning to the Soviet government to beware of Hitler's present offers of collaboration and friendship' and was 'designed for Russia only and to be spread only through channels leading direct' to the Soviets.[7] The 'whispers' were quickly picked up by the world's press, diplomats, and Intelligence services and, as planned, taken as truth.

But Cadogan and his colleagues, calculating this strategy in the ivory tower of the Foreign Office, had been too clever by half. Stalin certainly took the bait – but then digested it and spewed it out in a manner totally unanticipated in London. Far from persuading him to forget his hopes of negotiation with Berlin and thus being receptive to overtures from London, the rumours simply confirmed his ideological paranoia about British intentions (and perfidy), strengthened his simplistic conviction that Britain's ruling class had indeed produced a party for peace, and thus hardened his line of sitting tight and hoping for the best from Hitler – a disastrous misjudgement on his part.

Stalin was not the only one to be fooled by this miscalculated and far too clever campaign of British disinformation. The story of a British peace party and the notion of some substantial chance of peace talks between London and Berlin have disfigured the historical landscape ever since. Hess's flight to Britain was, as Kettenacker so aptly writes in reminding us how barren his supposed peace terms really were, 'a flight from reality'. So, too, has been the subsequent myriad conspiracy theories, constructed as they are on the insubstantial foundation of some distant disinformation campaign. This should occasion no surprise. History is littered with examples of disinformation campaigns being mistaken for reality.

Hitler was furious, Stalin anxious, and Churchill bemused by the bizarre flight of Hess. Across the Atlantic, what did that other major international player, President Franklin D. Roosevelt, make of it all? In late May 1941, a few days after Hess's arrival in Scotland, Roosevelt was dining at the White House with his close adviser Harry Hopkins and Sumner Welles, the Under-Secretary of State, who the previous year had met the Deputy Führer in Germany. After Welles expanded on his unfavourable impression of Hess, the President paused and then mused aloud: 'I wonder what is *really* behind this story?'

To the suggestible, Roosevelt's rhetorical question predictably invites suggestions of mystery, even conspiracy. Indeed, along with Stalin's conviction of a sinister British plot, it has recently prompted yet another book arguing the case for some deep-laid British plot to lure Hess to Britain.[8] Yet the most intriguing question arising from Roosevelt's response is why he so quickly lost interest in the affair and ceased to ask questions at all – a point overlooked by those in search of unnecessary complication.

The chapter by Warren Kimball, the United States' leading historian on Roosevelt and his wartime relationship with Churchill, demonstrates from the surviving documentary record that despite his May 1941 response to Welles, Roosevelt was soon very fully informed about, and apparently satisfied by, the facts surrounding Hess. At first, like both Churchill and Stalin, he hoped to use the Hess affair to his own advantage. In his case, to strengthen his domestic argument against the anti-interventionists by revealing Nazi expansionist ambitions in the Americas including 'commerce, infiltration, military domination, encirclement of the United States, etc'. In response to Roosevelt's request for more detail, Churchill sent him a reasonably full account of what Hess had so far revealed under interrogation. However, none of it contained any material of propaganda use to Roosevelt, and all mention of Hess disappears from his extensive correspondence with Churchill for over a year.

This did not mean, however, that Roosevelt was kept in the dark. He may well *not* have been told about the British dis-information plan (understandably so, as the United States was not yet a belligerent), but he was almost certainly *verbally* briefed about further Hess interrogations over the summer of 1941. At the Atlantic Summit Conference between Roosevelt and Churchill that August, Sir Alexander Cadogan recorded in his diary that he had given Sumner Welles 'some dope about Hess'. We can be sure that Welles passed this on to Roosevelt, but what it consisted of is anybody's guess. What is not speculation is that Roosevelt very quickly lost interest in the Hess affair and displayed no inclination at all to pursue any 'mystery'. Kimball concludes that the most likely reason for this was that he received transcripts of the various Hess interrogations, at least after the launch of Barbarossa (which rendered redundant the British disinformation campaign). Nothing in the files left by Roosevelt or his aides, stresses Kimball, indicates that Hess gave away any specific indication of an impending Nazi attack on the Soviet Union, as often alleged.

True, on 5 November 1941 Brigadier-General Raymond E. Lee, the American military attaché in London, sent a report to G-2 (Military Intelligence) in Washington saying that a reliable source in London had revealed that Hess *had* warned of such an attack. A similar report, based on the same source, reached Stalin from Soviet Intelligence. The source was Desmond Morton, Churchill's close friend and personal Intelligence adviser. On the surface this seems conclusive evidence, from a cast-iron source, that Hess actually did reveal to the British plans for Barbarossa, a fact consistently denied in official British accounts of the affair. It would thus seem to substantiate the notion of some British cover-up and, hence, a conspiracy to hide.[9]

In reality, however, the 'Morton Report' is far from conclusive. First, it should be noted that despite being Churchill's Intelligence adviser, Morton was steadily sidelined as his confidant over the course of the war by Sir Stewart Menzies, the chief of MI6, and was not always as well informed as he wished. He could be garrulous and boastful, eager to demonstrate to others that he knew far more than he actually did; some of his documented 'private' recorded wartime statements are both bizarre and wildly misleading, and he simply cannot be regarded as a reliable source.[10] Secondly, in any case, his claim does no more than repeat what Hess had told Sir John Simon in his interrogation of Hess about Hitler's plans for Russia – a vague intimation of what a lot of people were guessing anyway, and one devoid of any significant or revealing details of the timing and strategy of Barbarossa.

So much, then, for the reactions of Churchill, Stalin and Roosevelt to Hess's flight of fancy.

Yet, amidst the cascade of speculation, is there *anything* more to suggest any involvement by British Intelligence? In particular, is there evidence of a British Intelligence dimension *prior to* Hess's flight to Scotland?

In *Hess: The British Conspiracy*, two British authors, John Harris and M.J. Trow, claim to have made a significant discovery. It has long been known that MI5 (the British Security Service, which included its Second World War deception and double-cross division) used a post office box in Lisbon for some of its operations. Also established for some time has been the fact that Albrecht Haushofer, a close German friend of Hess, used a Lisbon box number to send at least one letter to the Duke of Hamilton in September 1940. The letter was addressed to a 'Mrs Violet Roberts', an old family friend of the Haushofers.[11] What Harris and Trow have discovered is that Violet Roberts was not just an anonymous elderly widow living in Cambridge, England, but that she was closely related to a leading figure in Britain's secret wartime 'black propaganda' agency, SO1 (Special Operations 1), which later became the Political Warfare Executive (PWE). Violet Roberts's nephew, it transpires, was a man named Walter Roberts, a member of SO1.

To have uncovered what may have been the fingerprints of British black propaganda on the Haushofer–Hamilton link is certainly interesting. The evidence, however, does not bear the weight of interpretation placed upon it by the authors, who have instantly leapt to a grand conspiracy theory replete with the all-too-predictable plot of Hess following Hitler's orders to meet a peace party in Britain followed by a massive official cover-up in Britain.[12] Yet the monumental disarray and disagreement between Churchill and the Foreign Office over how to handle Hess's arrival in Scotland stands as overwhelming evidence against any such theory about some carefully plotted conspiracy. For why, if it was so cunningly prepared, was there no strategy in place to exploit it?

What *does* now seem possible, although undocumented and far from proved, is that from the autumn of 1940 the British were running a disinformation campaign that quite accidentally caught Hess in its net. The goal of this campaign was probably to help dissuade Hitler from attempting an invasion of Britain; although he had called off his 1940 invasion, London feared he might try again in the spring of 1941. SO1 would help deter him by suggesting that he could win by simply being patient and waiting for a (mythical, non-existent) peace party to topple Churchill from power. By surreptitiously feeding such beliefs in Berlin, where eager recipients such as the naïve Hess were already disposed to accept them, the British hoped to ward off attack at a particularly desperate stage of the war when, along with the Dominions, they stood alone against Hitler. But even here there is not one iota of evidence to suggest that SO1 was deliberately plotting to lure Rudolf Hess to Britain.

If not SO1, what about MI5? Could its Section B1A, responsible for deception, have tried to manipulate the affair in some obscure way? Theoretically, once MI5 learnt of the Hamilton–Haushofer link, it might have exploited it. But any operation could only have begun once the Duke had been thoroughly investigated and proved reliable. Although by March 1941 this had been done and Intelligence feelers put out to the Duke, nothing came of them. As T.A. Robertson, the head of B1A, later explained, any possible deception project was, from the beginning, a non-starter and far too risky – especially when MI5 was already running other highly valuable double-cross operations.[13]

So why did Hess make his flight? The question takes us back to Hess himself, the often all-too-forgotten and determined actor in this drama. Here Hugh Trevor-Roper, himself a veteran of Britain's Intelligence war, offers a speculative but highly convincing explanation for Hess's actions. In the summer of 1940, despite the collapse of France, Churchill refused to contemplate a negotiated peace. Eager to free his hands for the war he was already planning against the Soviet Union, Hitler decided he had to get rid of Churchill by fomenting an internal coup in Britain. This task he assigned to Hess, who was not only his oldest and most intimate friend but also fervently shared his belief that failing to neutralise Britain had been the greatest failure of Germany's leaders in 1914. To argue this, however, is far from saying that Hitler either knew or approved of Hess's flight. It was one thing, argues Hugh Trevor-Roper, to commission Hess to feel his way towards stimulating a coup in Britain. But is it remotely conceivable that the arch-realist Hitler would have sent Hess, a political *ingénu*, physically into the depths of Britain 'to waste his naïve rhetoric on unknown politicians in that enigmatic island'? Obviously not. Unknown to Hitler, a frustrated and desperate Hess finally decided to dispense with all intermediaries and take on the historic task of saving Germany from a two-front war himself.

Who were these intermediaries? As made clear by James Douglas-Hamilton, the essential key to unlocking the Hess riddle lies with the Haushofers, father and son. Professor Karl Haushofer was a potent intellectual influence on Hess and the father of twentieth-century German geopolitics, a theory which under-pinned much of Hitler's thought on international affairs, and on which Haushofer held a chair at the University of Munich. His son, Dr Albrecht Haushofer, was a friend of Hess, a senior adviser to the German Foreign Office, and an ardent believer in German friendship with Britain and its Empire – a pillar of Hitler's international vision as laid out in *Mein Kampf.* In the 1930s Albrecht, who spoke fluent English, befriended the Marquis of Clydesdale, who became the Duke of Hamilton in 1940, after Clydesdale, then a Member of Parliament, visited the Berlin Olympics in 1936.

In September 1940, after the fall of France, and while Hitler was making preparations for an invasion of Britain, Hess urgently summoned Albrecht to Bad Godesberg for a lengthy discussion on the possibilities of a compromise peace with Britain. In the course of the discussion, Haushofer mentioned the possibility of a meeting on neutral soil with 'the closest' of his English friends – the young Duke of Hamilton. Hess then said he would consider the whole matter thoroughly and get back to him. Two days later he wrote to Karl Haushofer suggesting that peace feelers should not go through official channels, but via a letter 'to the old lady, with whom you are acquainted'. This was the by now well-known Mrs Roberts, and James Douglas-Hamilton provides extensive details of the Haushofers' dealing with Hess on this matter. Significantly, though – and a fact all too often overlooked by the conspiracy theorists – Albrecht thought – as he told his parents – 'the whole thing is a fool's errand'. He also frankly told Hess that 'there is not the slightest prospect of peace'.

Hess was undeterred, however. Haushofer's letter to Hamilton was never answered, having been intercepted in Lisbon by British Intelligence and then (possibly) put to the service of the (still) obscure British misinformation campaign. As a result, after several months Hess decided to undertake a special mission himself to meet Hamilton, thus setting off the chain of events discussed in this volume. The tragic effect of all this on the Haushofer family – Albrecht's imprisonment by the Gestapo, his lengthy interrog-ations, and finally his murder, and the suicide of his father and mother in 1946 – is closely documented by James Douglas-

Hamilton. It makes crystal clear that Albrecht Haushofer at least regarded Hess's mission as the single-minded folly it was.

Single-minded? Folly? Almost certainly, even if Hess and Hitler did talk lengthily about seeking peace with Britain in September 1940.

Peter Longerich is a German expert on Hess and the Nazi Party and is fully conversant with its voluminous files. He makes clear that while Hess had once been extremely close to Hitler, remained important in Party affairs, and took an active part in aspects of domestic policy such as the anti-Semitic and racial legislation, by 1940 he was no longer in the inner circle of decision-making. 'Overcoming the distance,' writes Longerich, '(and thereby re-establishing his absolute loyalty to his idol, Hitler) via an extraordinary independent initiative' may well have motivated his mission. But Hess should not, insists Longerich, be caricatured either as some lunatic or as someone desperate to distance himself from Nazi policy through illness or hocus-pocus.

Hess was not insane, but he was certainly eccentric, held fast to certain fixed ideas, and believed that he could interpret Hitler's will. In his post-war interrogation by Allied officers prior to his appearance in the dock at Nuremberg, Albert Speer described Hess as 'one of the great cranks of the Third Reich'.[14] One of Hess's most tenaciously held opinions was the view expressed by Hitler in *Mein Kampf* that an understanding with Britain should form a central pillar of Nazi foreign policy. The belief that Britain would do almost anything to preserve its Empire, especially against the growing might of the United States, and that this would impel it into dealing with Germany, represented a pervasive and fatal Nazi misperception of Britain which has been brilliantly explored elsewhere.[15] In the autumn of 1940, after the fall of France and as Hitler threatened to invade Britain, Hess and Hitler discussed Churchill's refusal to make peace. 'What more can I do?' asked Hitler in exasperation. 'I can't fly over there and beg on bended knee.'[16] But if Hitler could not do it (and how, indeed, could his beloved Führer be expected in war to approach the British?), and if the Duke of Hamilton did not respond to Haushofer's overtures, then *he*, Rudolf Hess, would have to assume the task. And what more dramatic way to highlight its importance and urgency than to fly single-handedly to Britain?

Present-day readers who take for granted the ease of international air travel may be forgiven for underestimating the significance of this dimension to Hess's mission – namely *flight*. It was not only, as Len Deighton reminds us so forcibly, that Hess was an impassioned and skilled aviator with the means at his disposal to obtain the necessary aircraft with the modifications it required to reach its target. Nor that his ability, which had seen him win the prestigious 1934 *Zugspitze* air race flying a Messerschmitt M 35, more than qualified him for his self-imposed mission.

It was also that making dramatic and highly publicised flights for peace had exercised a powerful pull on the popular imagination since the early 1930s. It was still barely thirty years since the Wright brothers had pioneered the first machine-powered flight and only thirteen since Charles Lindbergh had mesmerised the world with his historic solo flight in the *Spirit of St Louis* across the Atlantic. So awestruck was Hess by this feat that he tried – unsuccessfully, as Len Deighton points out – to get funding to repeat the venture in the reverse direction, from east to west. In the 1930s flying was still novel, daring and perilous, and those who triumphed in the challenge received popular acclaim of almost mystical dimensions. Hitler himself regularly exploited the dramatic impact of flight in his regular descents on Nuremberg for the great Party rallies. And, as Europe had held its breath over the Czechoslovak crisis of 1938, the elderly British Prime Minister, Neville Chamberlain, had boldly flown from London to Munich to bring back 'peace in our time'. Could not Hess emulate Chamberlain, flying from Germany to Britain to restore the peace so tragically lost after Munich? It is more than coincidence that the man in Britain on whom Hess mistakenly pinned his awesome faith was the Duke of Hamilton. For as the Marquis of Clydesdale he had led the highly publicised first flight by plane over Mount Everest – a feat in 1933 as bold as space flight in the 1990s. Hess had never met Hamilton, but he knew him as a bold and brave pioneer of flight and on his bedside table kept Clydesdale's photographic record of his expedition, *The Pilot's Book of Everest*.[17] Could he, Hess, not emulate him and put his rare skill in flying at the service of his Führer and peace? Would his personal flight to Britain be, perhaps, as suggested by Len Deighton, 'Hess's

Everest'? In such flights of fancy, or indeed fantasy, did Hess conceive his mission to Scotland. The rest, while often fascinating or intriguing in detail, is essentially peripheral.

The facts about Hess remains firmly with Hess, and nowhere else. The endless prediction that Foreign Office or MI5 files would finally reveal otherwise, and that there still exists some deep-laid conspiracy awaiting discovery, have been confounded. As Roy Nesbit's article on the Public Records on Hess clearly demonstrates, they merely confirm the view that the decision for the flight to Scotland was made solely by Hess. Interestingly, one of the items in the MI5 files consists of the British codebreakers' interception of a telegram sent by the Japanese ambassador in Rome, General Hiroshi Oshima, to the Foreign Minister in Tokyo, just a week after Hess's flight. In it, Oshima reports on remarks made to him by Hitler's Foreign Minister, Joachim von Ribbentrop, during a visit to the Italian capital which make it clear that the Nazi regime was putting the best spin possible on the event. Hess, declared Ribbentrop, had become worried over the fact that 'he was cutting little ice in the present war'. And although his action had been eccentric, his intentions had not been treasonable, but excellent. A further item in the MI5 file, reporting on a German secret service investigation of the case immediately following Hess's flight, confirms that 'Hess had flown to UK on his own initiative, notwithstanding Hitler's orders to the contrary'.[18] This is also borne out in the immediate post-war interrogations of captured Nazis or others close to Hess. Albert Speer, who was present at Berchtesgaden with Hitler at the time of the Hess flight, believed he undertook it because he was 'very sore and embittered at having been side-tracked by Hitler'; while Hess's secretary, Laura Schroedl, claimed that no one except Hess's adjutant knew of the plan.[19]

'There is no denying I have failed,' wrote Hess to Albrecht Haushofer after his capture. 'But there is no denying that I was my own pilot. I have nothing to reproach myself with in this respect. At any rate I was at the helm.'[20] From a British prison he also wrote a letter to his four-year-old son explaining his reason for the flight, quoted by Roy Nesbit: 'There are higher . . . let us call them divine powers. . . which intervene, at least when it is time for great events. I HAD to come to England [*sic*] to discuss an agreement and peace.'

This, at least, sounds like the authentic Hess. As so often, the truth is stranger than all the fiction.

Notes and References

1 Ian Kershaw, *Hitler 1936–1945: Nemesis* (London, 2000), p.369; James Leasor, *Rudolf Hess: The Uninvited Envoy* (London, 1962), p.13; and see Peter Longerich's chapter on Hess in this volume, passim.
2 Winston S. Churchill, *History of the Second World War*, vol. 3, *The Grand Alliance* (New York, 1962), p.43.
3 Most of these conspiracy theories are clinically and effectively dealt with by Roy Nesbit and Georges Van Acker in *The Flight of Rudolf Hess: Myths and Reality*, especially ch. 8. *Double Standards: The Rudolf Hess Cover-Up* (London, 2001), floats the Duke of Kent/royal family involvement.
4 Kershaw, *Hitler 1936–1945*, p.375.
5 For Costello's many egregious errors of fact, see Nesbit and Van Acker, *The Flight of Rudolf Hess*, pp.131–4; for Padfield, see his *Hess: Flight of the Führer* (London, 1991) especially p. 349, for his suggestion that the closed files would reveal Secret Service involvement. After they failed to do so, Padfield graciously conceded in his *Hess: The Führer's Disciple* (London, 1995) that 'there were no revelations'. But in the latest (2001) edition of his book he still argues the case for a mysterious Secret Service link. This time, however, it appears that his key informant, the person who would unlock the riddle of Rudolf Hess, has failed to deliver the promised and decisive proof.
6 Peter Padfield, *Hess: The Führer's Disciple*, 2001 paperback ed. p. 347. Hess's son and others supporting his view, writes Padfield, 'were obvious tools for a KGB campaign to foment trouble between West Germany and the NATO allies'. The Hess affair has been exploited on many occasions for such ends.
7 Gabriel Gorodetsky, *Grand Delusion: Stalin and the German Invasion of Russia* (London and New Haven, 1999), p. 265. See also Rainer F. Schmidt, 'The Marketing of Rudolf Hess: A Key to the "Preventive War" Debate', in *War in History*, 1 (1998), pp.62–83, another scholarly study of the Hess files ignored by conspiracy theorists.
8 John Harris and M.J. Trow, *Hess: The British Conspiracy* (London, 1999).
9 See especially Costello, *Ten Days that Saved the West*, who makes much of the Lee report and its Morton sourcing. In the light of John Erickson's evidence in this volume about the published KGB files on

Hess, it is of considerable significance that Colonel Tsarev, their editor, was a principal collaborator in the Costello book.

10 For a particularly egregious example of Morton's wild talk, see David Stafford, *Roosevelt and Churchill: Men of Secrets* (London, 1999), pp. 235–48, where among other accusations Morton says Churchill's relationship with Roosevelt was 'almost homosexual'.

11 See James Douglas-Hamilton, *The Truth About Rudolf Hess* (Edinburgh, 1993), especially pp. 119, 128.

12 It is unfortunate that the authors feel obliged to inflate the significance of their discovery by claiming that SO1 was 'one of the most secret and unfathomable organisations of the British Secret Service'. Unfathomable perhaps, but the PWE files, including a wealth of SO1 material, have been lying open in the Public Record Office since 1973. The origins of SO1 lie in the creation of the Special Operations Executive (SOE) by Churchill in 1940. SO1, responsible for propaganda, became PWE in 1941 and SO2, the sabotage and subversion wing, assumed the general title SOE.

13 See Hugh Trevor-Roper's chapter in this volume, pp. 153–71.

14 Quoted in Richard Overy, *Interrogations: The Nazi Elite in Allied Hands, 1945* (London, 2001), p. 119.

15 See Gerwin Strobl, *The Germanic Isle: Nazi Perceptions of Britain* (Cambridge, 2000).

16 This was according to Otto Dietrich, Hitler's press officer, who was present. See *Hitler's Henchmen: The Deputy: Hess*, ZDF television documentary broadcast on Channel 5 in 2001.

17 For an account of Clydesdale's expedition, see his son James Douglas-Hamilton's *Roof of the World: Man's First Flight Over Everest* (Edinburgh, 1983).

18 See Roy Nesbit's chapter in this volume, pp. 139–52.

19 Overy, *Interrogations*, p. 120.

20 Letter to Haushofer quoted in Gorodetsky, *Grand Delusion*, p. 253.

LOTHAR KETTENACKER

Mishandling a Spectacular Event: The Rudolf Hess Affair

Despite the many speculations and insinuations surrounding the spectacular flight of Hitler's Deputy to Scotland on 10 May 1941 it can be stated with some certainty that 'The Facts about Rudolf Hess'[1] are, by now, well known. The only questions which invite further debate are firstly that of Hess's motives, and secondly, how the British government's reaction to his arrival is to be interpreted.

One caveat might, perhaps, be permitted. It was assumed at the time, as established by Lord Simon on 9 June, that Hitler had, as Hess himself always maintained, no prior knowledge of his Deputy's plans. Here certain doubts may be raised. It is very unlikely that Hess had Hitler's advance approval for his audacious and in many ways rather lunatic mission. He was not 'Hitler's last emissary' as Ulrich Schlie insists.[2] It is possible, however, that Hess *had* advised Hitler of his plans to attempt an extraordinary bid for peace. Why else should Hitler, without consulting Goebbels, the chief spin doctor of the Third Reich, issue a statement two days after Hess's spectacular arrival in Britain explaining *inter alia* that he was the 'victim of hallucinations' and had been expressly forbidden by the Führer to use an aeroplane 'because of a disease which has been progressive for years'?[3] Balfour assumes that this formula was to acquit Hess of treachery and make the British distrust him.[4] The clue to this mystery, i.e. the letter by Hess addressed to his master, and passed on to Hitler by his adjutant, has not yet surfaced. We can safely assume that Hess had assured Hitler of his unswerving loyalty coupled with the pledge not to give any military secrets away. Moreover, it is more than likely that by distancing himself from his Deputy Hitler had acted on the recommendation of Hess and on the assumption that the mission had failed. Hitler and his entourage were convinced that 'Party comrade Hess crashed' and could not have reached his destination alive, but this was wishful thinking. At midnight the same day the British issued a brief statement, drafted by Churchill and Eden, confirming the arrival of the Führer's Deputy in Britain.

As to his motives, Churchill was probably right to stress Hess's diminishing influence at home, due to his eclipse from power within the circle of Hitler's closest advisers, and his desperate attempt to regain his master's trust and confidence.[5] After all, Hitler's 'peace offensives' following the defeat of Poland and the fall of France had failed abysmally. It would have amounted to an unparalleled triumph had Hess succeeded where everyone else had failed. His zealotry got the better of him. It may well have been a combination of his esoteric inclinations and his well-meaning dilettantism in matters of diplomacy which contributed to his growing isolation.

In the evening of 10 May 1941 Hess took off from Augsburg, southern Germany, in an Me 110 fitted with extra fuel tanks on a secret peace mission to Dungavel in Scotland expecting to meet the Duke of Hamilton whom he considered to be a friend of Germany. This day incidentally marked the climax of German terror bombing over London: more than 500 bombers dropped 711 tons of explosives and over 2,000 incendiary devices resulting in the death of 1,212 people. Hess and the Duke had, in fact, never actually been formally introduced and may merely have exchanged glances at a dinner party during the Olympic Games. How Hess therefore should have arrived at the conclusion that he would be welcomed by the Duke with open arms is a mystery, unless we give credence to the assumption that the British Secret Service supplied him with misleading information about a peace party in Britain. This is the questionable contention of Rainer F. Schmidt, author of a book on Rudolf Hess[6] as well as an article in the respectable *Vierteljahrshefte für Zeitgeschichte*.[7] He argues that MI5 led Hess, as it were, up the garden path to Scotland – a somewhat implausible allegation which has been convincingly refuted by Ted Harrison, a British expert on this episode, who sees in Schmidt the latest victim of the persistent myth of an almighty and scheming British Secret Service.[8] But it is the very involvement of British Intelligence agencies which had led some to read more into the whole affair than is perhaps wise. What, then, happened in the lead-up to Hess's solitary flight into fantasy?

According to British sources, Albrecht Haushofer, a close friend of Hess and the son of his Munich academic tutor, had paid frequent visits to Britain between 1935 and 1937, in the course of which he had established many intimate connections, among them the Duke of Hamilton, then Lord Clydesdale.[9] Since then Haushofer, like his father an adherent of geopolitics, had been regarded in Germany as the greatest expert on the British Empire. He tried to exercise a restraining influence on the regime and fell from favour after Munich when the proud Empire nation seemed to cave in to the dictator. Hess saw Albrecht Haushofer while staying in a health resort in upper Austria in early September 1940 and talked to him for two hours about the chances of a peace mission. According to Haushofer's report, his own analysis of the situation in Britain regarding the prospect of peace under the prevailing circumstances was not encouraging.[10] He later referred to the flight, in a letter to his father, as 'a fool's errand'.[11] However, for the time being he seems to have been prepared to arrange for a meeting between Hess and the Duke of Hamilton in Lisbon, possibly with a view to dissuading Hess from any more dramatic and reckless action. Thus, HMG Censorship Department later that month intercepted a letter by Haushofer to the Duke of Hamilton – inside a letter addressed to a Mrs V. Roberts – suggesting a meeting in Portugal and signed 'A'. Otherwise the letter of 23 September 1940 was noncommittal and unrevealing. There was certainly no indication that Hess could be behind the move. It was only much later, after Hess had arrived in Scotland carrying with him the Haushofers' visiting cards, that Hamilton realised the person he was meant to have met in Lisbon was none other than the Führer's Deputy seeking to negotiate a peace deal. Since this did not work out Hess must have come to the conclusion that there was only one alternative left: to undertake himself the secret mission to see the Duke in Scotland. As it happens, British

Intelligence authorities were considering sending Hamilton to Portugal and running the case 'as a possible double-cross' in the hope of eliciting information regarding German intentions. However, the Duke was not excited about this prospect and demanded that various high-level personalities should be informed or give their explicit approval.[12] Naturally, Hamilton was also annoyed that the crucial letter should have been withheld from him for nearly six months. Eventually the whole idea of sending the Duke into unknown territory was dropped.

The circumstances of Hess's reception in Britain do not at all suggest that his mission had been engineered by MI5 or that he had been expected. At the time the Duke of Hamilton was not waiting for him in his mansion near Dungavel Hill, which Hess was aiming for, but was on duty observing that part of the eastern coastline where the lonely pilot was to penetrate British airspace. A fighter plane sent up by Wing Commander Hamilton was four miles away in hot pursuit when Hess bailed out. The rest of the story is well known and has been described in some detail in various books: how he was first picked up by a farmer and handed over to Lieutenant Clarke of the Renfrewshire Home Guard, how he was then escorted to Maryhill Barracks in Glasgow long after midnight, that he first identified himself as Captain Alfred Horn carrying an important message for the Duke of Hamilton, etc. The latter saw the prisoner on the following day at 10 a.m. In his presence Hess revealed his true identity and explained that he had hoped to arrange a meeting with the Duke in Lisbon. In his official report about the interview Wing Commander Hamilton stated: 'He went on to say that he was on a mission of humanity and that the Führer did not want to defeat England and wished to stop fighting. His friend Albrecht Haushofer had told him that I was an Englishman who, he thought, would understand his (Hess's) point of view.'[13] Hamilton came to believe that the prisoner was indeed Hess himself and concluded his report by saying: 'Until this interview I had not the slightest idea that the invitation in Haushofer's letter to meet him (Haushofer) in Lisbon had any connection at all with Hess.' The Duke then decided to report to Churchill, whom he saw the same evening. The PM was at Ditchley Park and apparently unwilling to be disturbed while watching the Marx Brothers. The following day Hamilton saw Eden in the presence of Sir Alexander

Cadogan, Permanent Under-Secretary of State at the Foreign Office. Then and there it was decided that Sir Ivone Kirkpatrick, once first secretary at the British embassy in Berlin, should be dispatched to Scotland to gather more information about this strange emissary and his true intentions: Kirkpatrick knew Hess personally and could address him in German. In the course of the following days he conducted a series of interviews with the prisoner, three in all, which established the identity of Hess as well as the emptiness and futility of his mission. Naturally Hess was disappointed that he had been debriefed by a minor official and not invited to unburden himself to someone in authority. Therefore it was hoped that it might be possible to prise further secrets out of Hess if he were approached by high-ranking members of the British government. In June, Lord Simon, the Lord Chancellor, conducted an extensive interview with the Deputy Führer which is recorded verbatim in the British files,[14] to be followed in September by a shorter interrogation by Lord Beaverbrook, minister for aircraft production.[15] That members of the government should have gone out of their way to see Hess was for a long time, even after the war, regarded as the most sensitive and potentially damaging aspect of the whole episode.

Hess did not claim that he had been sent by Hitler with a specific purpose. His argument was that this was not necessary since he knew what the Führer had in mind. But what he was actually putting forward was basically the old worn-out offer made by Hitler after each successful campaign: Germany should be given a free hand in Europe in exchange for graciously leaving Britain in sole command of her Empire. The German Wehrmacht and the Royal Navy would rule the world. 'Other minor conditions', as Churchill put it in his memoirs, 'were the return of the German colonies, the evacuation of Iraq and an armistice and peace with Italy.'[16] Hess had no more specific terms to offer than those which Hitler had last outlined in his victory speech on 19 July following the defeat of France. Here he prophesied that a great empire would be destroyed: 'An empire which it was never my intention to destroy or even to damage.'[17] His conscience dictated, Hitler claimed, that he appeal once more to England to see sense and abandon the war which she was bound to lose. This was exactly the same language which Hess employed in his interviews with

Kirkpatrick and government ministers. He represented himself as the voice of humanity, hoping to bring to an end the unnecessary slaughter and hardship of war. In fact, he made things worse by stipulating that these proposals would only be considered on the understanding that Hitler would not have to negotiate with Churchill and his government. 'If this chance were to be rejected it would be the Führer's duty to destroy Great Britain utterly and to keep this country after the war in a state of permanent sub-jection.'[18] None of the various peace feelers which had reached the British government since the autumn of 1939 contained such threats, or, for that matter, the demand for a change of government in London.[19] It was, as Harrison says, a typical Nazi peace offer: make peace, or else we destroy you![20]

In other words, Hess had nothing of any substance to offer, nor did his interrogations suggest that he was privy to or would divulge any operational secrets. He did not, for instance, come up with the proposal of an Anglo–German alliance against Bolshevik Russia. He emphasised that though Germany had certain demands on Russia, there was no truth in the rumour that the Führer was contemplating an early attack on the Soviet Union. However, when interviewed by Lord Beaverbrook in September, Hess handed him a long memorandum in which he warned against the Bolshevik danger and argued that Great Britain should support Germany against Russia.[21] By that time Germany had, of course, engaged Russia for more than two months and had learnt that the country was not just a walkover. His long-winded exposition of Anglo–German relations, with which he bored the Lord Chancellor for two and a half hours on 9 June 1941, reads like any Nazi propaganda tirade by a provincial Party stalwart.[22] He boasted that Germany was able to produce any number of U-boats and more tanks and fighter planes than Britain and the United States put together. Unsubstantiated boasts like these were bound to damage his credibility even further. Above all, there were clear signs of paranoia. Simon reported to Churchill: 'He repeated to me his fears of being poisoned. He thought he might be assassinated . . . He hinted that it was an unseen hand in the kitchen he was afraid of. At meals he insists on being served out of the common dish and sometimes exchanges his helping with the Commandant. He is certainly hypochondriacal and mentally unstable and, to my mind, not at all in a condition where he could keep up a "bluff" of acting independently when really acting on instructions.' Even before the interview with the Lord Chancellor Churchill was told by Desmond Morton, one of his close advisers, that Hess had come to Britain without Hitler's prior knowledge, that he was not in the inner council of Hitler and his generals, and that, though he was not mad in a medical sense, he was 'highly neurotic and a very stupid man'.[23] Clearly he had been misled about the morale of the British people and had no idea how Britain was governed if he thought he could bring about a *rapprochement* between the two countries single-handedly where others had failed without being in a position to make any substantial concessions.

From a German point of view Hess gave nothing away, although he did cause his government a great deal of embarrassment. He was, no doubt, a faithful devotee of Hitler and throughout his captivity he never let him down, which contrasts sharply with the Führer's own behaviour – he hastened to distance himself from his Deputy, and to put Bormann in charge of Party affairs. Hess has always been depicted, both during and after the Third Reich, as a Nazi idealist of a somewhat naïve cast of mind. Hess's mind-set was one-dimensional, based on preconceived ideas which were by then more representative of ordinary Party faithfuls than of the hardcore powerbrokers in Hitler's entourage. He clung to Hitler's early ideas about the desirability of an alliance with 'England', expressed both in *Mein Kampf* [24] and in his so-called *Second Book*, where the latter elaborated on Britain's true interests, i.e. building up and maintaining her overseas Empire and not meddling in Europe's affairs.[25] Traditional concern for the balance of power was only a means of safeguarding the Empire and not an article of faith. The British elite would be led by their pragmatic instincts. If Germany did not threaten Britain's maritime and commercial interests because her aims were confined to the Continent, there was no reason to fight each other. Hess had helped Hitler with the writing of *Mein Kampf* and was therefore well acquainted with his political thinking. Hitler was a great admirer of Cecil Rhodes. In embarking on an imperialist war of expansion to acquire *Lebensraum* he looked up to Britain as a model and was therefore psychologically unprepared for the fact that times had changed and that the British were somewhat less jingoistic in the late 1930s than during the Boer War. Hess, equally blinded to the realities of the twentieth century, hoped to persuade the British that by abandoning the war with Germany they would be able to resume the pursuit of their true interests. This kind of thinking was typical of the doctrinaire approach to power-politics and foreign policy prevailing among the national conservative elites in Germany at the time: they thought they understood the dictates of Britain's colonial interests. Did not Britain's empire building benefit greatly from the alliance with Frederick the Great when the latter pushed Prussia's frontiers eastwards?

Within a few days of Hess's arrival the British government had come to the conclusion that the only possible gain to be made from this spectacular affair was its value for propaganda purposes. Indeed, this aspect remained, right from the beginning and up to the present day, the most debatable issue of this extraordinary event. However, within the government, counsels were divided on how to exploit this news to maximum effect. Churchill's chief concern was to strengthen home morale and reassure Britain's allies. He preferred to come clean and give a factual account of what had happened, in other words admit that Hess had indeed come to make peace, thereby more or less confirming the version the Germans had put out. In his memoirs Churchill claims that he never attached 'any serious importance to this escapade' since 'it had no relation to the march of events'.[26] Churchill, himself the government's most important propaganda asset, was no great believer in psychological warfare and in dressing up the facts. In this instance his gut feeling suggested he was moving in the right direction. He felt that reproducing a summary of the most outrageous statements made by Hess would be the best way of reassuring the world that Britain's determination to pursue the war was not waning. His draft statement which he read to the cabinet contained the following sentences:

Germany and Herr Hitler should become the unquestioned master of Europe. In support of these ideas [Hess] stated that the German production of U-boats and aircraft was such that, apart altogether from invasion, the British Isles would soon be starved out and that American aid would be cut off or arrive too late. He further stated that if after the surrender of Britain the British

Empire and the United States endeavoured to continue the war this would be of no avail because Herr Hitler would continue the blockade by U-boat and aircraft until either a general peace was made or the last Englishman had starved to death.

Moreover, Churchill wished to stress that Hess was held as a prisoner of war 'who had bailed out in this country in uniform', and that he was also regarded as a potential war criminal 'whose ultimate fate must be reserved for the decision of the Allied nations when the victory has been won'.[27] A day later Churchill wrote to Eden: 'He [Hess] should be treated with dignity as if he were an important general who had fallen into our hands.'[28] In his memoirs Churchill does not mention the draft statement which would have done him nothing but credit. Instead a short statement was issued from Downing Street at 11.20 p.m. on 12 May, just mentioning the bare facts.[29] This resulted in innuendo and speculation for months and even years to come. What had happened?

The Cadogan diaries, edited by David Dilks, are perhaps the best source for reconstructing the internal decision-making process. Churchill wished to make a statement in Parliament for which he had prepared the above mentioned draft. Cadogan objected: 'This won't do – looks like a peace offer and we may want to run the line that he has quarrelled with Hitler.'[30] After so many reverses in the war Whitehall mandarins were only too pleased that Hess had landed them with a propaganda coup. The temptation to be too clever by half was simply overwhelming. On 15 May Cadogan noted in his diary: 'Cabinet at 12. P.M. in v. good form – has got over his tantrum and admits our view correct.'[31] Within two days Churchill, against his better judgement, had been talked out of his initial response not to fool around with this news. However, on 13 May the Dominion High Commissioners had received a report of what had happened which was both factual and in line with Churchill's spirit: 'He [Hess] said, speaking for himself, that German morale was unbreakable, that Germany was immensely strong and that German victory was absolutely certain.'[32] He advocated a settlement 'on the all too familiar lines that Hitler wished to live in harmony with the British Empire provided he were given a free hand in Europe. Hess appeared to be completely calm and collected and gave no sign of insanity.' The Dominions were asked to treat this information as secret. So was Roosevelt who was put in the picture by the Prime Minister four days later on the basis of the three interviews conducted by Kirkpatrick: 'He [Hess] will not be ill-treated but it is desirable that the press should not romanticise him and his adventure.' He concluded: 'Mr President, all the above is for your information. Here we think it best to let the press have a good run for a bit and keep the Germans guessing.'[33] Clearly, the government's intention was to unnerve Hitler and to undermine German morale. In fact, Goebbels was relieved that the British seemed to be so restrained in their propagandistic exploitation of the affair. According to his assistant Rudolf Semler he mused: 'One has only to think of the false statements and views with which he could have been made to discredit Hitler, statements which might have wrecked our friendship with Italy and Japan without our being able to put up any defence.'[34]

At the same time Americans and Russians were also kept guessing. On 19 June the acting British Consul-General in New York informed the government that various pieces of news 'have combined in the public mind to create out of the Hess case a series of steps towards a negotiated peace'. The most serious impact had been the doubt of some industrialists 'as to the advisability of vast plant extension lest this rumoured peace negotiation should prove a reality'.[35] Friendly governments wondered whether Hess was not being kept in reserve for ulterior purposes. How else could the official silence be interpreted? As it happens, the government was pursuing a kind of dual-track policy not easily understood at the time. That ministers in Parliament remained taciturn on the Hess affair did not mean that no use should be made of this extraordinary event in order to confuse or unnerve the enemy. The propaganda line was: 'A. Hess is sane. B. He has given important information on various subjects. C. He is anxious for peace because he has lost his confidence in a German victory. D. He is not an idealist or refugee, but a Nazi who has lost his nerve and his faith in Hitler.' None of this was true, as Con O'Neill, an official in the Central Department of the Foreign Office dealing with German affairs, pointed out in a memorandum which recommended a new approach. Hitherto only newspapers and selected radio stations were allowed to disseminate these distortions. But O'Neill felt that more could be done to inflict maximum damage on the enemy's morale. What mattered, in his view, was that the truth should not be distorted in a way that could be detected and thereby embarrass the government. He submitted a draft public statement which encouraged the government to tamper with the truth in the service of propaganda. Even though Sir Alexander Cadogan admired O'Neill's ingenuity his advice to Eden was nevertheless to rely on covert means such as 'whispers and radio stations' rather than to proceed with official statements based on distortions of the truth. Eden agreed: 'I should not be willing to make such a statement, despite its possible immediate advantages. Therefore we must proceed within the limits Sir Alexander lays down.'[36] Distortions of the truth were a matter for propaganda experts, not ministers of the crown. Goebbels was not to be taken as an example.

Not surprisingly the Russians were most suspicious about the official secrecy surrounding the Hess mission. This was not unintentional as far as the British government was concerned. It was trying desperately to cut off the supply lines between the Soviet Union and Nazi Germany. And there were no qualms in Whitehall about stoking up Russian anxieties. On 23 May the Foreign Office sent a directive on Hess to Stockholm, New York and Istanbul designed to reach Russia, only 'as a whisper through covert channels'. According to this deliberately misleading instruction, Hess's flight indicated 'a growing split in Party and nation about Hitler's collaboration with the Soviets' inasmuch as Nazi purists allegedly resented Hitler's betraying of Nazi faith'.[37] In the end Hitler would be forced to turn against the Soviet Union after making maximum use of Russian deliveries of raw materials. It is very unlikely that such rumours made Stalin more favourably disposed towards the country which he believed to be most anxious to involve him in a war with Nazi Germany. Gabriel Gorodetsky has exposed Britain's publicity blunder *vis-à-vis* the Soviet Union on the eve of Barbarossa. Why Rainer F. Schmidt should then come to the opposite conclusion ten years later in congratulating the government on their handling of the Hess affair is difficult to understand.[38] One explanation may be that he did not sufficiently consider the overall impact of this episode on Anglo-Soviet relations over a longer period. The British government's silence over the Hess affair tallied with previous threats by Stafford Cripps, the British ambassador to Moscow, regarding the possibility of a separate peace in his frantic efforts to wean Stalin from collaborating with Nazi Germany. Gorodetsky concludes: 'Though not a well-thought-out policy, Cripps's threats, Hess's flight and the use made of it were deflecting the Russians towards a faulty and tragic evaluation of German intentions.'[39] In the end Stalin's mistrust in Britain's ulterior motives was greater than that in Hitler's immediate plans.[40] In their Intelligence assessments both the Soviet and the British governments were captives of their respective systems of belief: the ideological outlook suggested that it was to be in Britain's true interest to come to an understanding with Hitler-Germany whereas British common sense assumed that Hitler would only stage a show of force in order to ensure Russia's total collaboration. They both got it wrong and they would both go on making similar mistakes in analysing each other's intentions.

The haste with which Stalin pursued an alliance with Britain after 22 June 1941 only shows that he remained in constant fear of a separate peace. Throughout the war the spectre of an understanding between Germany and the Western powers loomed large in his mind. In his conversation with Lord Beaverbrook on 30 September 1941 Stalin indicated that he thought that Hess had come 'not at the request of Hitler but with the knowledge of Hitler', a theory with which the British minister seemed to have agreed.[41] Later on the Foreign Office came to the conclusion that this conversation may have given Stalin 'the wrong impression as there is not in fact any evidence that Hess came with the knowledge of Hitler'.[42] Stalin could not quite persuade himself that Hitler should have been so stupid as to attack the Soviet Union without a prior agreement with Britain. The dictate of an ideological perception of international relations is not always necessarily at odds with a rational assessment of the situation. If Stalin has always been depicted by British Intelligence as an arch-realist and Hitler as an arch-opportunist then this only shows the limits of common sense in understanding the mind-set of ideologically motivated dictators.

The Hess affair reverberated throughout the war and the diplomatic fallout cannot be restricted to the summer of 1941. The Foreign Office was most upset when *Pravda* played up this incident in October 1942 by insinuating that London was offering 'refuge to Nazi gangsters'. In connection with the unilateral initiative of the Western Allies to set up a United Nations Commission for the Investigation of War Crimes, the Soviets insisted on the immediate trial and punishment of war criminals such as Hess, who should not be allowed to enjoy diplomatic immunity.[43] Churchill was outraged and instructed Eden that 'no concession to this behaviour' was to be made. The Foreign Secretary at once expressed the government's indignation to Soviet ambassador Maisky, and declared in Parliament on 21 October that Hess had been treated, right from the day of his landing, as a prisoner of war, without any diplomatic privileges.[44] Theoretically, it is just feasible that the government was not too unhappy about Soviet apprehensions regarding Hess. It might have suited British diplomacy to instil some uncertainty in Stalin's mind, so that he would not take the alliance for granted. The idea that the British had some means of communication with the Nazi government in reserve might have induced Stalin to be somewhat more restrained in his policy of demanding more material help. There is, however, no documentary evidence in the files to substantiate this hypothesis.

As to the Soviet government's position one can only speculate about the reasons which had motivated them to antagonise London in this extraordinary way. Three possible explanations come to mind: the West's unilateral approach to the investigation of war crimes which resulted in them upstaging the Soviet Union in the eyes of the smaller allies,[45] disappointment about British strategic priorities at the expense of the second front, and last but not least renewed fear of a separate peace. On 5 October *The Times* had reported on an article by a well-known Swedish newspaper that stated that the time was now ripe to lift the veil on Hess's flight to Britain, which was part of Hitler's well-considered policy always directed towards an alliance with England.[46] Naturally Hitler wanted to protect himself against a 'possible though improbable miscarriage of his plan'. Therefore Hess was to offer England a profitable agreement in the form of an alliance to make war on Russia. Germany was to receive the Ukraine and the Caucasus oil regions and Japan was to be given Siberia, the rest of Russia was to be split up into homogeneous states.

This may well have been a reflection of Hitler's thinking in the autumn of 1942, i.e. before the crucial defeat at Stalingrad.

Whether it was also the chief reason for Moscow's propaganda campaign against Hess is another matter. Whatever the true state of affairs, it was only now that the British government felt compelled to ask the Lord Privy Seal to compile a lengthy memorandum regarding 'The Facts about Rudolf Hess' which was circulated as a cabinet paper on 2 November 1942.[47] It was not to be published yet, but the Foreign Secretary was authorised to communicate the gist of it to the Soviet government along with a report on Hess's medical condition. As a matter of fact, Eden had earlier on been worried that if it were admitted that Hess was certifiable as a mental case, the government could possibly be called upon to repatriate him under the Hague Convention.[48] Such were the scruples of a liberal government in the midst of a genocidal war in the east! If traitors like Philby had knowledge about such considerations this would be an additional explanation for the Soviet government wanting to have Hess indicted and put out of the way. On 5 November the British ambassador Sir A. Clark Kerr had a meeting with Stalin lasting for two hours, in the course of which the dictator asked for the incriminating article published in *Pravda* the previous month, and having read it dropped it like a hot potato. He then wondered whether it was the intention of HMG to repatriate Hess after the war as was the custom with prisoners of war, and whether Goebbels would enjoy the same courtesy should he arrive in Britain under similar circumstances.[49] Soon the Soviet government tried to made amends by communicating that the article in *Pravda* did not contain any attack on the British government but 'took up a position against certain British public men' with unacceptable views. Even if this was a cheap excuse it settled the matter for the time being.

During the course of the war Stalin realised that his ways of dealing summarily with captured enemies was not appreciated in the West. In Tehran he suggested, to the horror of Churchill, that the whole German general staff, some 50,000 officers, ought to be executed.[50] A year later he had changed his mind on the matter of war criminals and, as Churchill wrote to Roosevelt on 22 October 1944, took 'an unexpectedly ultra-respectable line' by insisting on proper trials.[51] However, as far as Hess was concerned, he had not yet been convinced that he had been told the truth and nothing but the truth. He sincerely believed, he told Churchill, that Hess had been lured over by the British Secret Service.[52] Clearly, the Russian dictator must have acquired some bits of information which he then turned into a conspiracy theory. In the meantime the British government had divulged the last secrets about Hess to its own public in September 1943. Apparently the answer to a parliamentary question had been triggered off by a remark made in New York by Brendan Bracken who not only had dismissed Hess as an 'overgrown Boy Scout' but also disclosed some information which had hitherto remained confidential.[53]

Hess's mission constituted a flight from reality. This is fertile ground for the mushrooming of fanciful stories which appear to be much more intriguing than the plain facts: the messenger of peace touching down from the clouds in a terrible war must not be remembered by posterity as a halfwit. It is therefore not surprising that Hess has been elevated to the status of a cult leader by the neo-Nazis in present-day Germany. It makes more sense to follow another leader in his approach to war and peace. Churchill's attitude towards Hess mellowed considerably after the war. He was glad not to be responsible for his treatment at the hands of the Nuremberg Tribunal. He now referred to his mission as a 'completely devoted and frantic deed of lunatic benevolence' concluding: 'He [i.e. Hess] was a medical and not a criminal case, and should be so regarded.'[54] Kurt Pätzold and Manfred Weissbecker, to whom we owe the most recent and comprehensive biography of Hess, disagree with Churchill in this important respect: in their view he was not 'insane' in the sense of diminished responsibility.[55] This is arguably a matter of interpretation because he might have been both responsible for his words and actions and yet insane to a degree. But if Churchill's opinion were to be the last verdict of history it would be a fair judgement and certainly one that ought to make his new followers think twice about him, and for that matter about themselves and their cause which can also be seen as a flight from reality. Churchill's views on this misguided peacemaker reflect the 'moral' of his memoirs: 'In War: Resolution, in Defeat: Defiance, in Victory: Magnanimity, in Peace: Goodwill.'[56] The defiant and resolute warlord who had turned into a magnanimous victor hoped himself, once Prime Minister again in the 1950s, to become a peacemaker and to bring the Cold War to an early conclusion.[57] In this effort he failed no less than Hess; but this is all these two most unequal men have in common.

Notes and References

1 Cabinet paper by Sir Stafford Cripps, WP (42) 502, 2 November 1942, PRO: FO 371/30920/C10635.

2 Ulrich Schlie, *Kein Friede mit Deutschland. Die geheimen Gespräche im Zweiten Weltkrieg (1939–1941)* (Munich and Berlin, 1994), pp. 290–324.

3 Translation of text in: PREM 3/219/4. See also Max Domarus (ed.), *Hitler. Reden und Proklamationen* (Munich, 1965), vol. II, p. 1714.

4 Michael Balfour, *Propaganda in War 1939–1945. Organisations, Policies and Publics in Britain and Germany* (London 1979), p. 217.

5 Winston S. Churchill, *History of the Second World War*, vol. 3, *The Grand Alliance* (London, 1950), p. 44. This is also the view of Rainer F. Schmidt, *Rudolf Hess: 'Botengang eines Toren?' Der Flug nach Grossbritannien vom 10. Mai 1941* (Düsseldorf, 1997), p. 271–3. See also the contribution by Peter Longerich in this volume.

6 Schmidt, *Rudolf Hess*. It is in his book, not in his article (note 7), that Schmidt makes the allegations about MI5.

7 'Der Hess-Flug und das Kabinett Churchill. Hitlers Stellvertreter im Kalkül der britischen Kriegsdiplomatie Mai–Juni 1941', *VfZG*, 42 (1994), pp. 1–38.

8 Ted Harrison, '". . . wir wurden schon viel zu oft hereingelegt". Mai 1941: Rudolf Hess in englischer Sicht', in Kurt Pätzold and Manfred Weissbecker, *Rudolf Hess. Der Mann an Hitlers Seite* (Leipzig, 1999), Exkurs 1, pp. 368–92. This is the most reliable interpretation of the British documentary evidence refraining from all undue speculation.

9 Note by the Secret Service on Haushofer, 19 May 1941; also Swinton to Brook, 20 May 1941, PRO: CAB 118/56.

10 See Pätzold and Weissbecker, *Rudolf Hess*, p. 242; also *Akten zur Deutschen Auswärtigen Politik*, D/XI, p. 69.

11 Quoted ibid., p. 243.

12 For details see Harrison (note 8).

13 Quoted *in extenso* by James Douglas-Hamilton, *Motive for a Mission. The Story behind Hess's Flight to Britain* (London, 1971), p. 157–9.

14 Report by Lord Simon as requested by the PM and the Foreign Secretary, 10 June 1941, PREM 3/219/7.

15 See A.J.P. Taylor, *Beaverbrook* (London, 1972), pp. 483–5, as well as

Appendix 3 of Douglas-Hamilton, *Motive for a Mission*, pp. 237–41.

16 Churchill, *The Grand Alliance*, p. 49.

17 Domarus, *Hitler*, p.1558.

18 'The Facts about Rudolf Hess', see footnote 1. See also Douglas-Hamilton, *Motive for a Mission*, pp. 157–71.

19 See Summary of Principal Peace Feelers, September 1939–March 1941, FO 371/26542/C4216, published in Lothar Kettenacker (ed.), *The 'Other Germany' in the Second World War. Emigration and Resistence in International Perspective* (Stuttgart, 1977), pp. 164–87.

20 Harrison in Pätzold and Weissbecker, p. 375.

21 See Taylor (note 15). Beaverbrook handed Stalin this memo – to my mind a stupid thing to do.

22 Minute by Lord Simon, 10 June 1941, PREM 3/219/7.

23 Minute by Desmond Morton for PM, 9 June 1941, ibid.

24 Adolf Hitler, *Mein Kampf*, 241/45. (ed. Munich, 1937), pp. 697–700, where he explains that there were only two potential allies left for Germany: Britain and Italy.

25 Cf. Gerhard L. Weinberg (ed.), *Hitlers zweites Buch. Eine Dokumentation aus dem Jahre 1928* (Stuttgart, 1961), pp. 164–75.

26 Churchill, *The Grand Alliance*, pp. 43–4.

27 Draft statement by the PM to be made in Parliament on 14 May, PREM 3/219/4.

28 PM to Eden, 13 May 1941, PREM 3/219/7. Even though Churchill saw in Hess 'potentially a war criminal' he wanted to make sure that 'his health and comfort should be secured'. But 'he should see no newspapers and hear no wireless'. Later this was rescinded.

29 PREM 3/219.4.

30 David Dilks (ed.), *The Diaries of Sir Alexander Cadogan 1938–1945* (London, 1971), p. 377 (12 May 1941).

31 Ibid., p. 379 (15 May 1941).

32 FO 1093/6.

33 Churchill, *The Grand Alliance*, pp. 47–8.

34 Quoted by Balfour, p. 219.

35 Consul-General/New York to Ministry of Information, 19 June 1941, PREM 3/219/1.

36 Minute by Eden, 29 June 1941, FO 1093/7.

37 Special Telegram (Venom), 23 May 1941, FO 1093/6.

38 See note 7.

39 Gabriel Gorodetsky, 'The Hess Affair and Anglo-Soviet Relations on the Eve of *Barbarossa*', *English Historical Review 1.1* (1986), p. 414.

40 On Stalin's reaction to Hess's flight see the pertinent contribution by John Erickson in this volume.

41 Taylor is critical of Beaverbrook's inclination of agreeing all too easily with his interlocutors (see footnote 15).

42 Eden to Clark Kerr, 3 November 1942, FO 181/969/12.

43 Clark Kerr to FO, 19 October 1942, F0 371/30919/C10029. The following minute by Churchill, ibid.

44 Parl. Debates, House of Commons, vol. 383 (1942), col. 1943–4. See also Dilks (ed.), *Cadogan Diaries*, p. 484–5.

45 Clark Kerr was instructed to make every effort to discover what their real grievances were. One British theory was that they had first discussed the treatment of war criminals with the US government before putting the result of these deliberations to the Soviet government at the same time as to the other Allies in spite of the special treaty relations with Moscow. Telegram of 30 October 1942, FO 371/33036/N5566.

46 PREM 3/219/7 which contains other material on Hess. See also Schmidt, 'Der Hess-Flug', p. 1 (note 7).

47 See note 1.

48 Eden to Churchill, 20 May 1942. The place where Hess was imprisoned had been a mental hospital before it was taken over by the War Office. Eden kept the PM informed on Hess's medical condition, always referring to the prisoner as 'Jonathan'. A medical report on Hess by Brigadier J.R. Rees (29 September 1942) stated: 'He is a paranoid person of a psychopathetic type who has definite hysterical and hypochondrial tendencies . . . There is still the risk of futher attempted suicide.' PREM 3/219/7.

49 Clark Kerr to Eden, 6 November 1942, FO 181/969/12.

50 Cf. Churchill, *History of the Second World War*, vol. 5, *Closing the Ring*, p. 330. See also *Foreign Relations of the United States, The Conferences at Cairo and Tehran (1943)* (Washington, 1961), p. 554, as well as Keith Eubank, *Summit at Tehran* (New York, 1985).

51 Warren F. Kimball (ed.), *Churchill and Roosevelt: The Complete Correspondence* (Princeton, 1984), vol. III, p. 364 (C–801). Originally the British did not favour a military tribunal, least of all Churchill. See Lothar Kettenacker, 'Die Behandlung der Kriegsverbrecher als anglo-amerikanisches Rechtsproblem', Gerd R. Überschär (ed.), *Der Nationalsozialismus vor Gericht. Die alliierten Prozesse gegen Kriegsverbrecher und Soldaten (1943–1952)* (Frankfurt, 1999), pp. 17–31.

52 Churchill, *The Grand Alliance*, p. 49.

53 Cf. Balfour, *Propaganda in War*, p. 221. Goebbels had no explanation why a statement should have been made by the British government at this late stage.

54 See note 44.

55 Pätzold and Weissbecker, *Rudolf Hess*, p. 366–7.

56 Originally suggested by Churchill as an inscription for a French war memorial after the First World War. It was then used for his memoirs figuring as 'Moral of the Work' in each of the six volumes after the title page.

57 As to Churchill's hopes of overcoming the Cold War by agreeing to a unified but neutral Germany, see Klaus Larres, *Politik der Illusionen: Churchill, Eisenhower und die deutsche Frage (1945–1955)* (Göttingen, 1995).

JOHN ERICKSON

Rudolf Hess: A Post-Soviet Postscript

On 6 November 1941, with the Wehrmacht less than fifty miles away, in the bombproof, marbled Mayakovsky station of the Moscow Underground Stalin, chairman of the State Defence Committee (GKO), declared that Hitler's Blitzkrieg had failed. It had failed because the Soviet Union had not disintegrated, because the Red Army had not been destroyed and because the 'Hess mission' had not managed to enlist Great Britain and the United States of America as partners or even as neutrals in Germany's eastern venture. The 'Hess mission' haunted Stalin at the time and for many years after. In its multifarious guises, interpretations, fabrications, inventions, denunciations, suppositions and concoctions, it has continued to exercise an enduring fascination and an almost insidious allure for Soviet and post-Soviet historians and publicists.[1]

The sense of a wholly unsuspected, unimagined event, at first sight one so bizarre as to defy credibility, the very essence of sinister conspiracy, long pervaded Soviet versions and has by no means vanished from more recent post-Soviet accounts. The Hess tumbril rolls on, with the latest Russian accounts and documentary publications attending once again to the primary questions: what at the very beginning of the 'Hess mission' did Moscow know (or not know) and, if so, by what means? What effect did the affair have, principally upon Stalin, on his attitude to and interpretation of 'the threat' prior to June 1941? What was the basic Soviet verdict on the 'Hess mission', if indeed one ever existed? What role did British 'disinformation', the SIS exploitation of the Hess affair, play?

The 'Hess affair' is a story that has run for well over half a century and promises to run yet further. Each decade has produced its own gloss, the post–Soviet decade being no exception. Access to former Soviet archives has proved to be a decided advantage for Western historians, while Russian historians and analysts have readily availed themselves of the same facility. In 1997 Colonel Oleg Tsarev published *The Last Flight of Black Bertha* in the third volume of a projected six-volume history of Russian foreign Intelligence, *Ocherki istorii rossiiskoi vneshnei razvedki*, edited by M. Primakov. Documents pertaining to the 'Hess affair' were published in *1941 god. Dokumenty*, volume 2; the general editor of this impressive collection was Academician A.N. Yakovlev.[2]

Where did the first intimations of this unsuspected and unimagined event originate? Rudolf Hess took off from Augsburg in a Messerschmitt BF 110 (Me 110) at 5.54 pm, 10 May 1941. He parachuted from his aircraft over Eaglesham in Scotland after dark, wearing the uniform of a Luftwaffe captain. Passers-by duly reported a crashed aircraft near Eaglesham House at 23.12 hours, to the police and the Home Guard. When first apprehended the parachutist gave his name as Alfred Horn. It was only on the following day, 11 May at 10 a.m., on meeting with Wing Commander Hamilton, that Hess revealed his true identity.

The Germans were informed of Hess's flight by German radio at 8 p.m. on 12 May 1941. On learning of this announcement on German radio, Churchill, greatly excited, called Anthony Eden, urging him to 'issue some thing at once'. The British statement took the form of a press release from Downing Street at 11.10 p.m. in the late evening of 12 May, in the wake of the German announcement.

According to Colonel Tsarev, Soviet Intelligence received the first hint of Hess's arrival in Scotland on 14 May through a Soviet agent in London codenamed 'Sonnchen' (or 'Sohnchen', Russian *Zenkhen*); this was none other than Kim Philby. 'Sonnchen' reported that Hess, having landed in England (*sic*) declared that he intended above all else to turn to the Duke of Hamilton: 'Hamilton belongs to the so-called Cliveden set.'[3] Hess affirmed that he was carrying peace proposals, their contents unknown.

Tsarev assumed that Philby had garnered his information

between 11 and 12 May.[4] 'Vadim' (Anatole Gorske/A.V. Gorsky, 'legal' *rezident* of the London NKVD-NKGB *rezidentura*, known to Blunt, Burgess, MacLean and Philby as 'Henry') transmitted this material to Moscow on 14 May, confirming that Hess had been positively identified by 'Kirk Patrik' (Ivone Kirkpatrick), an official of the *zakoulok*, the 'back-alley', Soviet Intelligence codename for the British Foreign Office.[5] The mysterious new visitor was undoubtedly Rudolf Hess, Adolf Hitler's Deputy.

The news of his arrival, though there was no further elaboration on 'peace proposals', was sufficient to alert Soviet Intelligence to the danger of a possible 'understanding' between London and Berlin. Cipher telegrams of warning were dispatched to Berlin, London, Stockholm, Washington and Rome with instructions to clarify the likelihood of such an eventuality.

The warning telegrams sent to Soviet Intelligence operatives evidently had a galvanising effect. Tsarev cites a number of reports from America and Europe on the Hess mission. From America an agent reported that 'Hess arrived in England with the full agreement of Hitler in order to begin talks for a truce. Because Hitler found it impossible openly to suggest a truce in view of the damage this would inflict on German morale, he selected Hess as his secret emissary.' In a telegram from Berlin agent 'Yug' reported that Eisendorf, from the American section of the Propaganda Ministry, confirmed Hess's excellent health: 'he had flown to England on a specific mission and with proposals from the German government'. Referring to a conversation with a senior Wehrmacht officer, agent 'Frankfurt' reported that 'Hess did not flee, his action [was] undertaken with Hitler's knowledge to propose peace with England.' In the same vein agent 'Ekstern' also conveyed information from Berlin to the effect that 'Hitler sent Hess for talks on peace, in the event that agreement was reached with England, Germany would at once attack the USSR.'[6] The flood of reports concurred that this was not the act of a madman or an attempt to escape Himmler's intrigues.

In view of this 'flood of information' affirming Hess's flight as an officially sanctioned mission to present peace proposals, Moscow was puzzled as to why the British government appeared neither to accept nor to reject them. Colonel Ivan A. Chichayev, second Soviet *rezident* in London, head of the NKVD liaison mission to

SOE (the Special Operations Executive, charged with infiltrating sabotage agents into occupied Europe), and also responsible for contact with Allied governments-in-exile, supplied part of the answer in report No. 338 of 18 May. 'Vadim' could not as yet supply precise information about the aim of Hess's flight to Britain. According to 'Sonnchen' (Philby) in a personal conversation with his friend Tom Dupree, Deputy Head of the Foreign Office Press Department, the following was ascertained but not so far confirmed from other Intelligence sources. Up to the evening of 14 May Hess had not supplied any information of value to the English. In the course of a conversation with a British Intelligence officer Hess stated that he had come to England in order to conclude a 'compromise peace', the intention of which was to halt 'the growing exhaustion of both warring parties and prevent the final disappearance of the British Empire as a force for stability'. Hess affirmed his loyalty to Hitler. Beaverbrook and Eden had visited Hess though this was officially denied. In conversation with Kirk Patrik (Ivone Kirkpatrick) Hess stated that war between 'the two northern powers' was a crime. He considered that England nurtured 'a powerful anti-Churchill party', which with his (Hess's) arrival had received 'a powerful stimulus in the struggle to conclude peace'. On being asked by Philby as to whether an Anglo-German alliance directed against the USSR would be acceptable to Hess, Tom Dupree commented that in his opinion this was precisely what Hess aimed to achieve.

Philby reported that before arriving in England Hess had written to the Duke of Hamilton. The letter had been intercepted by British Intelligence and was in their possession for six weeks (*sic*) before being forwarded to Hamilton. Three days after the letter finally reached him 'Hamilton handed the letter over to intelligence'. In Parliament Churchill was asked which authorities – military or civilian – were holding Hess. Churchill replied: 'Hess – my prisoner', thus 'pre-empting any opposition intrigue with Hess'. The real thrust, however, one which did lasting harm to Anglo–Soviet relations, was Sonnchen's observation that at the present time peace talks were not yet afoot, since the time was not ripe. But as the war wore on, it became evident that Hess might become 'the centre of an intrigue' to conclude a compromise peace, one serving both the peace party in England and Hitler.[7] That, evidently, is the conclusion that Stalin came to. In Moscow in the summer of 1942, at a time of tense discussions over the second front, Stalin charged Churchill with 'keeping Hess in reserve'.

The enquiries over what exactly lay behind the 'Hess mission' continued. On 26 May 1941 Stalin received a copy of 'Preliminary data on the "Hess case"' transmitted by V.G. Dekanozov, the Soviet ambassador in Germany. The circumstances of Hess's flight remained unclear. Contradictory, conflicting views were expressed by observers. Nevertheless, some light was thrown on the actual situation in Germany, on tendencies within German foreign policy, also on 'the existence and exacerbation of "the crisis in the upper circles" of Germany'. Of that latter observation Stalin would take very particular note. Dekanozov divided his report into four parts. The first outlined the popular reaction to the Hess affair, press comments drawn from German and non-German news-papers, rumours and supposition. The second examined Hess's career, position and influence within the Nazi Party, with further press excerpts and commentary. In Berlin Hess was described as 'a romantic', convinced that Anglo-German conflict spelt disaster for the white races, and that he could avert this catastrophe through his own 'reckless act'.

According to an American correspondent, anti-Communist Hess opposed any *rapprochement* between Germany and the USSR, flying to England on his own initiative 'to advise the English on the senselessness of the struggle with Germany, on the overriding urgency to conserve Germany's strength which Germany would need in the east'. It was suggested to the Soviet assistant military attaché that the root of the matter lay in the differences of opinion over foreign policy between Hess, Ribbentrop and Himmler, Hess proposing ending the war with Britain, Ribbentrop and Himmler bent on continuing it. The third part of Dekanozov's report briefly analysed official statements, comparing them with other versions 'explaining' Hess's flight: first, Hess flew to England on the direct orders of Hitler to conclude peace with England; second, Hitler knew nothing of Hess's planned flight, which was prepared by Hess's assistants and in view of the danger strictly at his own risk; third, Hess fled to England to escape investigation.

According to Dekanozov, official German announcements

suggested the truth lay somewhere within the first and third versions. Citing Eisendorf's comments once again, Dekanozov reported that Hess had flown to England on a specific mission and with a proposal from the German government: 'You will soon see the persuasiveness and accuracy of my words.' In support of that last observation Dekanozov cited Ernest Bevin's comment on 15 May: 'I do not believe that Hitler knew nothing of Hess's flight to England.' American naval officers, discussing the Hess affair with the Soviet naval attaché M.A. Vorontsov in Berlin, dismissed the idea of a peace treaty with Britain. They viewed the flight as the consequence of disputes within the Nazi Party and government, leaving Hess 'fearing for his own skin'.

The fourth part of the report presented Dekanozov's 'preliminary results', with the proviso that it was presently impossible to state definitively what lay behind the Hess flight. Nevertheless, 'the German side' had temporised over Hess's talks and given it to be understood that Germany was ready for talks with England. The German press, particularly in the immediate aftermath of the flight, modified its tone towards England but continued its hard line towards Roosevelt. Latterly anti-Soviet propaganda had intensified and anti-Soviet publications proliferated. The German press had attempted to highlight the 'anti-English tendency' in Soviet policies, especially over the question of Iraq. Both Germany and England maintained complete silence on the contents of Hess's talks. Further clarification might produce more material on the 'Hess case', but at that juncture, reported Dekanozov, it was only possible to conclude that on the one hand the 'Hess case' disclosed divisions within the German government over the future course of foreign policy, and on the other hand demonstrated the strength of the tendency in Germany to come to an agreement with England to end the war.[8]

Late in May 1941 the plot thickened, complicated by British attempts to exploit the 'Hess case' and rumours that the British Secret Service had either enticed or lured Hess to Britain. The British silence over Hess, simultaneously inexplicable and disconcerting to the Russians, provided fertile grounds for a propaganda coup, though British efforts to capitalise on the Hess affair (or rather the failure) only excited Hitler's contempt for 'muffing their biggest political opportunity'.[9] Philby had already planted one potent insinuation, one upon which Stalin evidently brooded long and hard, that Hess was actually 'the trump card in waiting', to be played for negotiations leading to a separate peace at a critical point in the war. But more immediately 'the Hess card' would be used in an indirect attempt to influence Soviet policies.

Stafford Cripps, British ambassador in Moscow, proposed using the Hess affair and his 'revelations' as a means of stiffening Russian resolution in the face of German pressure by pointing out the dangers of 'being left alone to face the music' or encouraging them to join the orchestra, facing danger now and 'in company'. Propaganda, if it was that, was now transformed into disinformation, 'mendacious' exploitation designed to dissuade the Russians from concluding a suspected agreement with Berlin. The truth was that so far Hess had said 'nothing of note', obliging the British government to tread a dangerous tightrope – one step at a time, nothing rash.[10]

The formal directive to use 'covert channels' went to MI6 on 23 May 1941. In Moscow, Stafford Cripps was duly briefed and dissuaded from pursuing his own initiatives. The 'disinformation' conveyed the impression that Hess's flight signalled a split in German circles over Hitler's policy of collaboration with the Soviet Union. If Hitler persists, went the line, he will demand short-term benefits but, in the long run, he must abandon both his policy and promises given to the Soviet Union. The outlook for the Soviet Union is bleak; Moscow will end up the real loser. It will have lost 'potential friends'; concessions will only weaken it, in the end: left 'to face Germany single-handed'. Citing this material, Colonel Tsarev points out that this 'information' was at once confusing and conflicting, but could well be construed as a threat, particularly the reference to 'the loss of potential friends' (*poteryat potentsial'nykh druzei*) and, more ominously, to a Soviet Union 'left alone to face Germany single-handed' (*odin na odin s Gitlerom*).[11]

Given the murkiness of the entire Hess affair and the silence maintained by the British government, it was not surprising that Moscow inclined to the view that what this 'information' actually portended was some kind of Anglo-German deal, leaving Germany free to strike in the east. That interpretation could well have been reinforced by the publicity accorded by the British press to Anthony Eden's Foreign Office briefing on Hess, the gist of which was that Hess was the bearer of peace proposals and duly authorised by Hitler to present them. What further intensified Moscow's foreboding was the interview between Lord Simon, the Lord Chancellor, an avowed 'Munichite' in Soviet eyes, and Hess. If the idea was to keep the Russians guessing, then ironically the 'disinformation' played into Stalin's hands. When Eden deliberately 'misinformed' Ivan Maisky, the Soviet ambassador in London, that Hess had 'fled Germany' because of disputes with leading individuals, 'Ribbentrop, Himmler', this was music to Stalin's ears, reinforcing a key element of his 'war–avoidance strategy'.[12] Splits in the German leadership to deflect or postpone war were precisely what he increasingly counted on.

What did Hess know of German strategic plans, what did he tell (or not tell) of them to the British, and at whose prompting or by what arrangement did he allegedly 'flee Germany'? In what was obviously a tense conference in Berlin to discuss the 'Hess case' General Walter Schellenberg of the Sicherheitsdienst (SD) observed that Hess's 'fanatical devotion' would prevent him from disclosing 'details of our strategic planning . . . though he was certainly in a position to do so'.[13]

Given the scope of political and military activity connected with Operation Barbarossa and the involvement of multiple agencies, it is hard to believe that Hess was wholly oblivious to what was afoot. All senior Nazi Party officials, each in their respective bailiwicks, worked on the complicated plans drawn up for the coming invasion. That Hess was certainly acquainted with the forthcoming Operation Barbarossa was confirmed by his adjutant, Captain Karl-Heinz Pintsch, who was later dispatched to the Eastern Front in disgrace, taken prisoner by the Russians and interrogated by the NKVD. Soviet Military Intelligence had more immediate information from a highly placed agent, Richard Sorge, in Japan, reporting on disclosures in the German embassy in Tokyo to the effect that Hitler had ordered Hess to Britain in order to make peace before invading Russia.[14]

In *Double Deception* James Barros and Richard Gregor pointed to the significance of 'some indirect indication' of a German attack on Russia supplied by Hess on 10 June to Lord Simon, who was also a former Foreign Secretary. Oblique confirmation of this 'indirect indication' came later in November 1941 via the American military attaché in London, referring to material derived from a source evidently privy to highly sensitive information. Hess had flown to Scotland, to the Duke of Hamilton, to inform him that 'Germany was about to fight Russia'. Somewhat earlier Soviet Intelligence in London had also been made aware of what Hess had reportedly disclosed about an impending German attack in the east.[15]

Hess appeared to be remarkably confident about the existence of a powerful 'peace party' in Britain and knowledgeable about an active 'anti-Churchill' caucus. Enter Carl Burckhardt, vice-president of the Swiss Red Cross, and the Haushofers, father and son. Approaches had evidently been made to Burckhardt on the part of 'important English circles' with an eye to examining 'the possibilities of peace', with Burckhardt acting as a conduit between the British and the Germans in the summer of 1940. 'Leading conservative and city circles' had suggested British disinterest in Eastern and South-eastern Europe (except for Greece), restoration of the Western European state system, and restitution to Germany of its pre-1914 colonies. It was a logical step for Hess to employ the younger Haushofer in September 1940 in order to make the first approach to the British. Thus prompted, on 23 September 1940 Albrecht Haushofer wrote to the Duke of Hamilton enquiring of possible contacts which might lead to discussions to end the war. This letter ended up with MI5, which thereupon proceeded to engage upon a spurious correspondence with Albrecht, with the intention of luring Hess to Britain to discuss peace with this 'anti-Churchill faction'.[16]

David Irving notes that Hess claimed he had first come upon his 'mad and daring scheme' in 1939 when he was with Hitler in the course of Operation Yellow. He had held off from his proposed flight to Britain while British troops were conducting a successful offensive in Libya lest this denote German weakness, but German plans to expand the Luftwaffe and the submarine fleet changed his mind. He was now confident of ultimate German victory. That did not suggest any desire on Hitler's part to defeat Britain and its Empire or any quest for world domination. What was not acceptable, however, was Churchill as a negotiating partner.[17]

That Hess's flight was somehow 'prearranged', that Hess was, in fact, Hitler's emissary, captured Moscow's attention, Stalin's in particular. Khrushchev reports an exchange with Stalin on the 'Hess affair' in which he argued that Hess was undoubtedly on a 'secret mission from Hitler' to negotiate peace. Stalin responded curtly, without further elaboration: 'Yes, that's it. You understand correctly.'[18] It subsequently became a virtual article of faith that not only had Hess acted as Hitler's emissary proposing Anglo-German peace before the German attack on the Soviet Union but also that the British Secret Service had been deeply implicated in a plot to lure Hess to Britain.[19]

As late as 1991 the Soviet *Military History Journal* printed a lurid account of a British Secret Service 'entrapment' which invented a German–Scottish 'Scottish revolutionary movement', in turn supporting a 'Scottish independence movement', using names known to Berlin, and generating a fake correspondence using the Duke of Hamilton's name. The affair, conducted without Churchill's knowledge, involved the unlikely co-operation of the Gestapo and the British Secret Service. What wrecked the 'Scottish conspiracy' was Hess's own 'unexpected' arrival in Scotland.[20] Another version of British Intelligence's 'involvement' in the 'entrapment' of Hess gave as its origin British desire for revenge for the 'Venlo incident' (the kidnapping by the Germans of two British agents in November 1939); yet another suggested the British had taken a leaf out of Soviet Intelligence's book with the invention of an organisation, 'Trust', which, ostensibly anti-Soviet, was aimed at the entrapment of anti-Soviet groups.[21]

Evidence that was more immediate and more specific came via Colonel František Moravec. In March 1939 Moravec, the head of Czech Military Intelligence, fled Prague with his deputy and staff, an exit arranged by the local British Secret Service officer Harold Gibson. Colonel Moravec was duly enlisted within the SIS. He was a major asset, not least because of his association with Paul Thümmel, codenamed 'A-54', who volunteered to work for the Czech Secret Service as a double agent (known as Jochen Breitner, Dr Holm, Voral and 'Rene') and who enjoyed good German military and political contacts. Thümmel was finally arrested in 1942. Once in London Moravec was approached 'on a friendly basis' by Soviet Intelligence, a link approved by Moravec's British friends, though the relationship with the Russians declined until the German invasion of Russia.[22] Codenamed 'Accountant',

Moravec supplied information to the NKVD obtained from 'A-54' and his German sources and also from MI6.[23]

In October 1941 Soviet Intelligence's London *rezidentura* transmitted a report from a source 'close to the Prime Minister' confirming much of what Philby had already passed on to Moscow. A year later, on 24 October 1942, Beria submitted a report to Stalin and Molotov detailing the contents of Colonel Moravec's information supplied to the NKVD *rezidentura* in London. Reports to the effect that Hess arrived in England 'unexpectedly' were not true. Long before his flight Hess had corresponded with 'Lord Hamilton' on this matter, correspondence which covered all aspects of the flight. However, Hamilton took no part in this exchange. It was the 'Intelligence Service' which handled the correspondence, the replies to Hess made in Hamilton's name. Thus the English succeeded in luring (*zamanit'*) Hess to London. Colonel Moravec confirmed that he had seen the actual correspondence between Hess and Hamilton. According to Moravec, in the letters Hess had set out, with sufficient clarity, the German government's plans connected with an attack on the Soviet Union. The same letters set out arguments on the urgency of a truce between Germany and England. In conclusion Colonel Moravec asserted that the English had 'documentary proof' of the guilt of Hess and other Nazi hangmen in preparing the attack on the Soviet Union.[24]

In support of a British Secret Service plot or conspiracy and Hess's conviction that he had support from the 'Cliveden set', Colonel Tsarev quotes without reference an exchange between Hess and Ivone Kirkpatrick: 'I thought that here [in England] there is a strong desire to conclude peace and I was convinced that, if I returned to Germany and I said to the Führer that you are ready to abandon Churchill, he would agree to conclude peace on condition that England will refrain from the policy of "hands off Europe". I considered that through Hamilton I would find a way to a powerful party desirous of peace able to assist me to return to Germany in two-three days.' Ivone Kirkpatrick responded: 'It seems that you are suggesting that the Duke [of Hamilton] could somehow or other manage for England to make peace with Germany.' Hess replied: "Of course." He [Hamilton] could go to the King and tell him about our plans for war on Bolshevism, then the King could make peace with us.' Tsarev concludes that the fingerprints of the 'British special services' (*angliiskaya spetssluzhba*) were all over the 'Hess affair'. Hess was convinced that he could not only enlist the aid of the 'peace party' but also the crown. The spurious Hess–Hamilton correspondence was an entrapment device designed to lure Hess, Hitler's Deputy, to Britain.[25]

Tsarev goes to even further extremes. He argues that the 'Hess affair' should not be seen in isolation. He connects Hess's flight to Britain with previous plans in 1940 to 'extract' the Duke of Windsor from Portugal in an SD operation entrusted to Walter Schellenberg. The former King Edward VIII, now 'married to a twice-divorced American woman', had recently visited Germany and had been photographed with Hitler. Once 'extracted' to Germany and then returned to the British throne with Germany's help, the Duke would be a Nazi 'trump card'. In yet another unreferenced citation, Tsarev refers to Hitler's own plan for the Duke of Windsor. Germany's victory would coincide with Anglo-German reconciliation. The monarch would be a German protégé, and a treaty of perpetual peace would be concluded with him. Ribbentrop would be released from his duties, becoming general plenipotentiary and adviser to the English King and an English duke to boot. Germany had no intention of reducing England's status as a great power. On the contrary, England must become one of the cornerstones of Germany's new Europe. Presumably Tsarev intended to convey the idea of continuity in some of the ideas expressed by Hess, the preservation of Britain's status, Anglo-German reconciliation, Anglo-German partnership.

Tsarev does not adjudge the 'Hess affair' a total failure. On the contrary, the delay in opening a second front conformed exactly to Berlin's requirement not to interfere with Hitler's conduct of the 'eastern campaign' before it finally succeeded.

What cannot be excluded from consideration is that those within British Intelligence who prepared the fake Hamilton–Hess correspondence also sympathised with the advocates of peace with Germany. They had embarked on a dangerous game, leaving Russia to pursue the struggle with Hitler alone.[26]

What, then, did Stalin really know, as opposed to what he wished to think or was even induced to think? Having gained access to the files of Russian Intelligence, the FSB (successor to the KGB) and to ambassador Ivan Maisky's diary, Gabriel Gorodetsky is well placed to answer this question. Stalin gave perfunctory agreement to Khrushchev's rather banal, sycophantic comment on the Hess affair, but the issue was more than a routine one. At the time of the 'Hess affair' Stalin was in the midst of forming his fateful judgement on German intentions arising from a flood of Intelligence reports that detailed a continuous, menacing German military build-up in the east, a trickle which began in January 1941 and became virtual a flood by May. The 'Hess affair' had also coincided with the realisation within the Soviet General Staff, based on accurate Intelligence data, that the German army in the east was fully concentrated and on the verge of deployment.

The Soviet General Staff war plan predicted protracted frontier battles, affording time in which to mobilise and concentrate the Red Army before the main forces on both sides were engaged. But Soviet Military Intelligence now intimated that the Wehrmacht was already fully mobilised and deployed in the east. Attack appeared imminent. Soviet strategy was bankrupt, its predictions worthless, its provisions inappropriate. The Red Army could neither attack nor defend. General G. Zhukov, Chief of the Soviet General Staff, and Defence Commissar Marshal S. Timoshenko hastily cobbled together an emergency plan, dated 15 May 1941. Based largely on the strategic war-games of January 1941, it aimed to forestall a German attack, proposing a pre-emptive blow aimed at the German troop concentrations. Evidently submitted to Stalin, the plan was sensibly laid aside, but what it did demonstrate was that the Red Army could neither attack nor defend.[27] Against this background Stalin had to establish urgently the true significance of the 'Hess affair', specifically whether or not Hess was acting on behalf of Hitler. Rumours of an Anglo-German 'understanding', the precursor of an anti-Bolshevik crusade, made the German military concentration even more threatening than Soviet Military Intelligence reports of 105 to 107 German divisions already massed had conveyed. It hinted at the imminence of war. Yet the possibility of Hess, renegade or maverick, fleeing Party feuding, suggested divided German counsels. That might open the way to Soviet–German negotiation.

According to Gorodetsky it was the official British statement, expressing scepticism about Hess's role as an emissary or agent of

Hitler, which underwent NKGB examination. What attracted Moscow's particular attention was the intimation that there were 'differences of opinion within the National Socialist movement'. There was the coincidence of Hess's flight with reports of a possible Stalin–Hitler meeting. Avowedly anti-Communist, Hess would do anything to disrupt Soviet–German friendship, hence the move to talk first to the British. An Anglo-German 'understanding' would be a pre-emptive strike against a Soviet–German *rapprochement*.[28]

Russian sources emphasise the significance of the talk of 'meetings', or 'negotiations' or conceivably an ultimatum, much of it generated by a skilful German 'disinformation' campaign.[29] It was an undertaking in which one Orests Berlings, codenamed 'Litseist', a Gestapo double agent working for Soviet Intelligence in Berlin, though basically loyal to Germany, played a singular role.[30] 'Litseist' skilfully developed the theme of divisions within the German hierarchy and the prospect of negotiation. Here was Litseist's Hess, 'bitter opponent of the Soviet Union, enthusiastic supporter of England', lunatic to boot. Whispers of Hitler's part in the Hess flight persisted, but these carried diminishing credibility, while talk of dissension within the German government acquired greater credence, much to Stalin's relief. Given divided German counsels, war might yet be postponed. In London ambassador Maisky discovered an atmosphere of reticence over Hess, formidable enough to cause him to confine himself in an early dispatch to Moscow reporting Hess's hostility to the 1939 Nazi–Soviet pact, that the flight was Hess's own idea, and that German secrets were safe with Hess, hence no information on Hitler's plans for Russia.[31]

Probing the Hess affair whenever the opportunity presented itself, Maisky tackled R.A. Butler, who volunteered his personal opinion that Hess had come on his own account, further elaborating that this did not rule out the possibility that there was powerful backing for Hess's 'mission' within senior sections of the Nazi Party. Hess, however, would find no quislings in Britain. In something akin to a flight of his own fancy Butler later averred that Hess and Hitler had quarrelled, Hess decided on flight, hoping to find circles in England willing to consider peace. Butler's personal musings subsequently formed some of the stuff of British 'disinformation'. An increasingly bemused Maisky sought others' counsels, bent on seeking out the 'ground which might favour a separate peace with Germany'. What must have unnerved him was his private dinner with Lord Beaverbrook, the record of which Gorodetsky has retrieved from Maisky's diary. Beaverbrook categorically affirmed that Hess was indeed Hitler's emissary, a bearer of peace proposals duly reconfigured by Beaverbrook into an anti-Bolshevik crusade. As for a separate peace, present proposals were worthless; no one was about to 'dump Churchill'. On the other hand Churchill understood Hitler's genuine desire for peace. Then came the veiled threat. Given 'acceptable terms' the British government might well consider peace with Germany, though there was little prospect at this stage of such 'acceptable terms' being offered. Maisky sensibly concluded that what was critical in this situation was not Churchill the man, but rather what Germany might offer. Gorodetsky reports that on 10 June Maisky met Lloyd George in the House of Commons, the latter dispirited at the turn of events, and talking openly of a compromise peace. On what was for Maisky the all-important question of 'acceptable terms', Lloyd George suggested that Danzig, Silesia, Austria and Alsace-Lorraine be included in Germany's territory, a form of protectorate be started over 'some portions' of Europe and Poland and certain 'adjustments' made in Holland and Germany. He added: 'The proposals produced by Hess were absolutely unacceptable.' Hitler's insistence upon the proposals could only mean the continuation of war.[32]

An extraordinary myopia afflicted London and Moscow simultaneously, both mesmerised by the issue of negotiations reported, purported, pending, suspected, real or imagined. British Intelligence was not persuaded even at this late stage that Hitler intended all-out war on the Soviet Union, rather that the German military build-up was intended to exert pressure on Moscow to agree to wide-ranging concessions. At the worst the breakdown of these 'negotiations' would be followed by an ultimatum, at which point Stalin might conceivably succumb. Moscow feared that if London learnt of the existence of Soviet–German negotiations, the temptation to conclude a separate peace would be hard to resist. Accordingly, following instructions, on 5 June Maisky informed Eden that no negotiations were taking place between Germany and the Soviet Union, to which Eden replied that information was to hand which suggested that 'serious negotiations' bearing on matters of 'tremendous significance' were indeed afoot, reflecting Foreign Office suspicions of an imminent second Soviet–German pact, consummating 'Stalin's capitulation to Germany'.

Maisky had got the 'Hess affair' half right from his vantage point. Assuming that peace proposals were at issue, then 'acceptable terms' were critical. Disinformation planted by British Intelligence artfully diffused the notion of a counterfeit negotiation. It was not, however, the noise which had initially aroused some of Maisky's worst misgivings but rather the ominous, inexplicable silence of the British government. Hess had not talked, but assuredly he would. Had he? Did he? Coming after his early June exchange with Eden, information that none other than John Simon, 'arch-appeaser', was now responsible for dealing with Hess rocked Maisky back on his heels: was 'negotiation' high on the agenda? To rationalise what could not easily be rationalised, the behaviour of the British government, Maisky propounded his own 'theory of British politics', in which Churchill, Eden and all Labour ministers rejected the idea of negotiations, while 'men like Simon' among other ministers were not averse to sounding out Hitler on possible peace terms. To conclude the drama the 'Churchillites' won the day.[33] But this imaginative feat of reporting alone, even if it made for interesting reading in the Kremlin, did not and could not dispose of the spectre haunting the Kremlin of an Anglo-German separate peace.

Moscow never fully resolved its dilemma as to whether or not Hess's mission was undertaken with or without Hitler's authority and, more importantly, who was the source of the all-important if somewhat elusive 'peace proposals'. Stalin found the ambiguity over Hess useful, favouring his own interpretation of a divided German leadership which might lead to negotiation rather than war with Russia, at the same time reinforcing his own anti-British conspiracy theory, the attempts to inveigle the Soviet Union into war with Germany or to deflect the war in the direction of the Soviet Union.

The converse was reflected in Anthony Eden's approach, preventing a Soviet–German agreement while simultaneously not causing Moscow to suspect some manoeuvre designed to draw

Russia into war. In his anxiety to distract the Russians from an agreement with Germany, Eden managed to excite Stalin's suspicion of some last-ditch British attempt to entangle him in war. Eden had warned Maisky that Britain was more than capable of maintaining its position in the Middle East. Orders had, in fact, already gone to the Middle East command to prepare to invade Iraq, providing bases to bring the Soviet Baku oilfields within medium bomber range.[34] British concern over the threat to the Middle East from a supposed Soviet–German agreement must have bemused both Maisky and Stalin. What both really wanted to know was the view London took of Berlin's plans for Russia.

Pursuing this theme of protecting the Middle East against the consequences of Soviet–German compact or collusion, the recall of Stafford Cripps from Moscow caused much consternation at a time of British suspicion of Soviet–German negotiations and a mirror-image in Moscow of Anglo-German negotiations. Eden's rather nonchalant reassurance to Maisky about routine consultations ran counter to what had passed in Moscow. Cripps had indeed intimated to the Russians that he was leaving for consultations but in what was clearly a threat he hinted he might not be returning. His recall had also coincided with news of John Simon's contact with Hess, instantly reviving the whole 'Hess affair' and Moscow fears of some 'deal'.[35]

Leaving aside the question of Hess's 'peace proposals', Britain might simply intimate to Berlin that Britain would stand aside if Germany went to war on the Soviet Union, which the Soviet Union might see as tacit encouragement to do precisely that. German armies were now massed on Stalin's frontiers, concentrated, ready and waiting. But the immediate 'threat' as Stalin perceived it emanated not from the Wehrmacht but from the British, instigators of *provokatsiya* designed to ignite 'early war' between Germany and the Soviet Union. British warnings of an imminent German onslaught were construed in Moscow as yet one more attempt to involve Russia in war. Stalin's response was the infamous TASS communiqué of 14 June 1941, which denounced 'rumours of war' as baseless, stated that reports that Germany intended to 'launch an attack against the Soviet Union' were without foundation, and argued that recent German troop movements 'had nothing to do with Soviet–German relations'.

Though designed explicitly to elicit a response from the German government, Berlin remained silent. Stalin's tactic had failed. At home the TASS statement induced confusion within the Soviet military – who were aware of German troop concentrations in the east – bewilderment among civilians and contradictions in Party propaganda which tended to 'psychologically disarm' large sections of the populace.

The 'Hess affair' never died. The 'conspiracy theory' never subsided. For Moscow the German attack on 22 June 1941 confirmed an inextricable link between war and the circumstances of Hess's flight to Britain. Maisky did not doubt the existence of Hitler's desire to obtain British support for an anti-Bolshevik crusade nor the purpose of Hess's mission: to lay the groundwork for an Anglo-German alliance before or possibly in the early stages of war on Russia. Moscow was puzzled as to why Hess had not simply been shot out of hand. Was he being kept in reserve? At the International Military Tribunal in Nuremberg the Soviet judge, dissenting from life imprisonment, demanded the death penalty for Hess on the grounds of his facilitating aggression against the Soviet Union 'by temporarily restraining England from fighting'. Even though it was diplomatic use of language, it was extraordinarily devious, inverting what the Russians really believed, namely, 'by encouraging England not to fight'. The question of the punishment of war criminals had aggravated the Russians as early as 1942. In January 1942 representatives of the Allied nations proposed judicial procedures to deal with war criminals. In October Moscow produced a unilateral declaration to the effect that war criminals in Allied hands should be tried immediately by International Tribunal. Eden rejected the idea of starting with Hess. Moscow wheeled out the 'Hess weapon' in an article in *Pravda* on 19 October 1942, hinting that London might well become a bolthole for Nazi gangsters. The argument that Hess was not liable for trial until the war had ended was tantamount to ignoring his crimes and conferring on him immunity as Hitler's emissary. In the event this row died down. If Stalin feared that the British might send Hess back to Germany, such fears were evidently assuaged, culminating in him making friendlier noises and finally remarking that Hess 'was not worth all this trouble'.[36] Though lacking (as did everyone else) definite proof of Hitler's part in the affair, Moscow never abandoned its belief that Hess came to Britain on Hitler's orders, that his 'peace proposals' were directly related to the launch of Operation Barbarossa, but the Germans misjudged what the British response would be.

The suspicions never abated, many of them generated not by conspiracy but by initial British clumsiness, aggravated by an ill-conceived disinformation campaign. For the Russians the 'Hess affair' provided something of an all-purpose alibi, an opportunity to be uncooperative or overweening, as was their wont. Whatever its true origins, the 'Hess mission' was never likely to succeed. For all their paranoia the Russians were aware of this, even as they played on the incident. The 'conspiracy theory', assiduously cultivated in Moscow, served multiple purposes but it is arguable that the virulent suspicions surrounding British attitudes and policies had more to do with long-standing ideological hostility and ingrained animosity than with the immediacy of the 'Hess mission'.

Hess's death in Spandau in 1987 offered one more occasion for the Soviet press to trot out the old arguments. Reporting the death on 19 August 1987, *Izvestiya* could not resist reminding its readers of Hess's criminality, his role as Hitler's right-hand man, and above all of his flight to England fulfilling the mission entrusted to him by Hitler, the conclusion of an Anglo-German armistice, in order to free Germany's hands in the east.

Notes and References

1 For a recent survey of Soviet/Russian publications on Hess, see Peter Schupljak, 'Wahrnehmungen und Legenden: Das Bild von Rudolf Hess in sowjetsichen Publikationen', in Kurt Pätzold and Manfred Weissbecker, *Rudolf Hess. Der Mann an Hitlers Seite* (Leipzig, 1999), pp. 393–409. I am indebted to Professor Lothar Kettenacker, Deputy Director of the German Historical Institute, for drawing my attention to this source.

2 Published in the series *Rossiya XX vek.Dokumenty* (Moscow, 1998).

3 In the 1930s Cliveden, the country estate of the Astors, attracted into its aristocratic circle leading intellectuals of the day, among them politicians, academics, financialists and writers. They became know as the 'Cliveden set' and in the late 1930s were viewed in certain quarters

as self-interested appeasers with pro-German sentiments, trying to manipulate British foreign policy to sue for peace with Hitler. See Norman Rose's recent study *The Cliveden Set: Portrait of an Exclusive Fraternity* (London, 2000), demonstrating that there was no organised body, no conspiracy, not even 'a set'.

4   Colonel O. Tsarev, 'Poslednii polet "Chernoi Berty" ', in *Ocherki istorii rossiiskoi vneshnei razvedkii* (Moscow, 1997), 3, pp. 434–5, also Tsarev's earlier presentation under the same title in *Trud* (Moscow, 13 May 1990); also J. Costello, *Ten Days That Saved the West* (London, 1991); also P. Padfield, *Rudolf Hess: The Führer's Disciple* (London, 1993) (recently translated into Russian).

5   *1941 god. Dokumenty*, vol. 2, see document no. 467, SVR Archive: 'Spravka vneshnei razvedki NKGB SSSR' (no. 376, dated 14 May 1941): pp. 200–1.

6   Tsarev, 'Poslednii polet', pp. 435–7.

7   See Document no. 485 in *1941 god. Dokumenty*, vol. 2, pp.248–9. NKGB Intelligence report dated 22 May 1941, added note 'Po [*soobsheniyu] ot 18 maya 1941 g., No. 338'.

8   Document no. 494, *1941 god. Dokumenty*, vol. 2, pp. 261–6. Senior Assistant to the Commissar for 'Foreign Affairs S. Kozyrev, No. 64/M 26 May 1941. At Molotov's suggestion, transmission to Stalin of V.G. Dekanozov's report 'Preliminary Findings on the "Hess case" 21 May'.

9   David Irving, *Hitler's War* (London, 1977), Hitler to Goebbels, September 1943, footnote to p. 247. Lord James Douglas-Hamilton observed that Goebbels 'dreaded the British drugging Hess and making him broadcast, with appalling consequences to the morale of German soldiers': Hess Workshop, University of Edinburgh, 15 May 2000.

10 Sir Llewellyn Woodward, *British Foreign Policy in the Second World War* (London, 1970), vol. 1, pp. 614–15 on Cripps' suggestion of 13 May that Hess's disclosures might be used to stiffen Russian resistance. He was informed that he appeared to be 'jumping to conclusions' about Hess, 'hints about a compromise peace would be too dangerous'. The Foreign Office would let him know 'if and when' Hess produced any material suitable for the purpose Cripps had in mind. Also Gabriel Gorodetsky, *Stafford Cripps' Mission to Moscow 1940–1942* (Cambridge, 1984), pp. 134–5. The most judicious analysis of this deception exercise and the entire 'Hess affair', one based on the most recent access to former Soviet archives and British archives, is Gabriel Gorodetsky, *Grand Delusion: Stalin and the German Invasion of Russia* (London and New Haven, 1999): see 'Running the Bolshevik Hare', pp. 262–7.

11 Tsarev, 'Poslednii polet', p. 436. The Foreign Office retained the right to use secret propaganda, though what Tsarev recorded compared with

Cadogan's comment about the irresponsibility of 'whispers' which can be 'conflicting and confusing'.

12 Gorodetsky, *Grand Delusion*, Eden to Maisky, p. 266.

13 Walter Schellenberg, *The Schellenberg Memoirs. A Record of the Nazi Secret Service,* trans. Louis Hagen, intro. Alan Bullock (London, 1956), pp. 201. Emphasis mine. Schellenberg also dismissed the theory of Hess's 'derangement'. 'Nor was his intellect so deranged that he would be incapable of giving a clear account of our [German] plans.'

14 Barton Whaley, *Codeword BARBAROSSA* (Cambridge, Mass., 1973), pp. 79–82.Whaley argues that the notion that Hess knew nothing of Barbarossa, or at least 'did not know of its imminence', was the result of Churchill and Eden 'uncritically' accepting Kirkpatrick's judgement. Whaley cites Sefton Delmer, *Black Boomerang* (London, 1962), pp.52–60, to the effect that nothing of Intelligence value was obtained from Hess due to 'unprecedentedly incompetent interrogations'. Gorodetsky, *Grand Delusion*, pp.255–6 cites the Kirkpatrick interview with Hess 12 May (FO 1093). Hess dismissed rumours of an impending German attack on Russia. Gorodetsky adduces Hess's reaction on news of the German attack – 'so they have attacked after all' – as an indication of his astonishment. But that can be read another way; what Hess knew was planned was now accomplished.

15 James Barros and Richard Gregor, *Double Deception. Stalin, Hitler, and the Invasion of Russia* (DeKalb, 1995), pp.122–4. The reference here to what Soviet Intelligence learnt of Hess's 'disclosures' is taken from Costello, *Ten Days That Saved the West*, pp. 447–9.

16 On the 'Haushofer–Hamilton correspondence', Barros and Gregor, *Double Deception*, pp. 130–1. The most extensive discussion and the closest to an 'insider' account is Lord James Douglas–Hamilton, *The Truth about Hess* (London, 1993).

17 Irving, *Hitler's War*, footnote to p.249. Hess stated that he had come unarmed and asked for release on parole.

18 *Khrushchev Remembers*, trans. Strobe Talbot, (London 1971), p. 116.

19 Christopher Andrew and Vasili Mitrokhin, *The Mitrokhin Archive. The KGB in Europe and the West* (London, 1999), p.157, noting Stalin's conviction that Hess was part of a British conspiracy to abandon alliance with the Soviet Union and conclude a separate peace with Germany. 'As late as the early 1990s' the KGB propounded the same conspiracy theory, Hess brought Hitler's peace proposals with him and 'a plan for the invasion of the Soviet Union'. Some within the SVR, the post-Soviet successor to the KGB, apparently still give credence to this myth. On conspiracies, Christopher Andrew, *Timewatch*, BBC 2, 17 January 1990: 'Hess: An Edge of Conspiracy'.

20 For this version of a conspiracy within conspiracies, what might be called the 'Matrioshka doll theory', see 'Neozhidannyi zakhvat Gessa v lovushku, postroenniyu angliiskoi "Sikret Servis"', *Voenno-istoricheskii Zhurnal* (1991) pp. 37–42. Bizarre in the extreme, this version at least has the virtue of real novelty. Hess came neither as a refugee from Nazi Germany nor as Hitler's peace emissary but – 'we can now say' – as Hitler's faithful servant aiming to begin a broad-based revolution and offer German military assistance to Scotland.

21 For these suggestions, Barros and Gregor, *Double Deception*, p.131.

22 On Colonel Moravec, his early association with SIS, contacts with the NKVD, Nigel West, *Venona: The Greatest Secret of the Cold War* (London, 1999), pp. 66–7.

23 Further details on Moravec and Czech Intelligence, Barros and Gregor, *Double Deception*, pp. 30–6. For a recent study of Paul Thümmel see 'Dvì Tváøe Agenta A-54' ('The Two Faces of A-54'), *ATM Armádní Magazín*, Prague, 11 (2000), pp. 34–6.

24 *1941 god. Dokumenty*, vol. 2, pp. 249–50: NKVD SSSR to GKO [State Defence Committee] SSSR – addressees I.V. Stalin and V.M. Molotov. 24 October 1942. Signed by L. Beria. Also note to this document, vol. 2, p. 296: the Hess flight was 'one of the events' which alerted Stalin to the possibility of an Anglo–German agreement. Whatever Hess's true intentions, 'disputed to this day', Moscow construed the flight as an attempt at agreement. Though the German invasion pushed this into the background, Stalin did not lose sight of it.

25 Tsarev, 'Poslednii polet', vol. 3, pp. 438–9 for text.

26 Ibid., pp. 439–40.

27 The Soviet General Staff 15 May 1941 plan remains a highly controversial subject. Colonel-General Yu. Gor'kov published the text of this document in *Kreml', Stavka, Genshtab* (Moscow, 1995), ch. 4, 'Strategicheskoe planirovanie voiny', pp. 54–69 and Appendix 2, pp. 303–9; also on Soviet war planning P.N. Bobylev, 'K kakoi voine gotovilsya General'nyi shtab RKKA v 1941 godu?', *Otechestvennaya istoriya* 5 (1995), pp. 3–20. Also on Soviet operational planning see Colonel N.M. Ramanichev, 'Plan "otvetnogo udara"' in *Velikaya Otechestvennaya voina 1941–1945* (Moscow, 1998), Kn.1, pp. 103–12.

28 Gorodetsky, *Grand Delusion*, p. 268, citing the FSB archives, 'press summaries with departmental markings 13 May 1941'.

29 See *Sekrety Gitlera na stole y Stalina. Razvedka i kontrrazvedka o podgotovke germanskoi agressii protiv SSSR. Mart-iyun' 1941* (Moscow, 1995), pp. 14–15, also docs nos 4 and 51, pp. 31–2 and 124–7.

30 See 'Portret Litseista', *Ocherki istorii rossiiskoi vneshnei razvedki*, vol. 3, pp. 441–50. Also Gorodetsky, *Grand Delusion*, 'Soviet Intelligence and

the German Threat', pp. 52–3; Barros and Gregor, *Double Deception*, 'Berlin Embassy: The Order of Battle', pp. 133–43.

31 Gorodetsky, *Grand Delusion*, pp. 270–1, based on ambassador Maisky, Foreign Policy Archive (AVP RF).

32 Ibid., pp. 273–4 from handwritten entry, Maisky diary, AVP RF.

33 See Gabriel Gorodetsky, *Stafford Cripps' Mission to Moscow 1941–42*, on 'victory' in 'the fictitious struggle', pp. 122–3; see also Barros and Gregor, *Double Deception*, 'Hess's Flight: Moscow's Perceptions', pp. 122–33, 126 on rumours in Washington, DC.

34 See V.I. Chukreev, 'Zagadka 22 iuniya 1941', *Voenno-istoricheskii Zhurnal*, 6 (1989) pp. 36–8; on Allied plans to attack the Soviet oil industry, see a recent study by Patrick R. Osborn, *Operation Pike: Britain Versus the Soviet Union, 1939–1941* (London, 2000).

35 Gorodetsky, *Grand Delusion*, p. 289, points out that the strained circumstances of Cripps's recall coincided with the departure for Washington of the US ambassador Gilbert Winant in London and 'rumours circulating' of American pressure on Churchill to entertain the German peace feelers and abandon Russia. See also Barros and Gregor, *Double Deception*, on the role of former President Hoover. The reason for Winant's recall was Conservative pressure on Churchill to consider Hess's 'proposals'. Churchill urged Winant's return to Washington to obtain President Roosevelt's permission for the British government to consider Hess's 'proposals', pp. 126–8.

36 See Woodward, *British Foreign Policy in the Second World War*, vol. II, on the 19 October *Pravda* article and its repercussions, pp. 276–80.

WARREN F. KIMBALL

The Hess Distraction:
A Footnote from America[1]

In May 1943, the British Prime Minister Winston Churchill, accompanied by General George C. Marshall, the US Army Chief of Staff, left Washington after meetings with President Franklin D. Roosevelt, and flew to Algiers for talks with American General Dwight Eisenhower, commander of Allied forces in North Africa and of the impending invasion of Sicily. The issue was, in Roosevelt's words, 'Where do we go from Sicily?'[2] Churchill's preference was emphatically clear. The long promised cross-Channel invasion would not come until mid-1944, so move on to the Italian mainland and seize whatever opportunities that invasion provided – campaigns in Yugoslavia, Greece, the Aegean and the Levant? But for the Americans, the Mediterranean was, in the words of the Secretary of War Henry Stimson, 'pinprick warfare'.[3]

General Marshall, all too familiar with Churchill's tactic of non-stop arguments, searched for ways to distract the Prime Minister from turning the trip into an endless harangue about the importance of Mediterranean operations. During one conversation, Marshall disingenuously posed a question about Warren Hastings, the eighteenth-century British Governor-General in India who was impeached for corruption. That worked for a while, but Churchill 'suddenly ran out of soap after about twenty minutes of this'. Caught up by the Englishman's grand tour of Anglo-Indian history, Marshall had to scramble for his next diversion and came up with Rudolf Hess's 'famous parachute jump'. That worked for about fifteen minutes, whereupon Marshall brought up Edward VIII and the abdication crisis. 'It was a marvelous lecture, just marvelous,' recalled the general. 'Then the steward, thank God, announced supper.'[4]

For Americans, leaders and public alike, that is all the Hess mission turned out to be – a brief distraction.

Americans learnt of Rudolf Hess's startling arrival by plane and parachute in Great Britain when they read their morning newspapers on Tuesday 13 May 1941. But, as in Britain, the news media in the United States were, in Walter Lippmann's words, 'dependent on what British authorities find it wise to publish'. 'HESS TAKEN BY SCOTTISH FARMER WITH PITCHFORK', lampooned *The New York Times*. A full-page headline in the *Washington Post* screamed 'HESS FLEES TO SCOTLAND', but then could only parrot the short official British statement and reflect the excited speculation in London's newspapers, information all carefully managed by the Churchill government. The *New York Herald Tribune* and *The New York Times* both repeated speculation that Hess had come carrying peace terms. The British ambassador in the United States, Lord Halifax, took an optimistic tack by suggesting that Hess had seen 'the writing on the wall', although that intimation of impending victory was hardly how the War Office privately viewed things, and fell between the two stools of confident British statements versus British need for the American air support and (by implication) all-out intervention. Equally Pollyannaish was the notion that Hess had 'fled a revolt's consequences' and that Hitler's regime was under attack from within Germany. With hard news at a premium, the inside pages of the *Washington Post* contained file stories and photographs of Hess, usually standing next to Adolf Hitler. The German government, unwittingly perhaps, touched on the truth when it blamed 'hallucinations' on the part of Hess, a conclusion echoed in a *Herald Tribune* editorial that compared the Hess flight to the 'whimsical' book, *The Flying Visit* by Peter Fleming, about a fictitious, hasty trip to Britain by Hitler.[5] There was a significant comment, one that the British government must have been pleased to see: 'so far as was known, the duke [of Hamilton, on to whose estate Hess parachuted] had not been connected in any way with any peace movements'. Peace, in that context, meant compromise and appeasement, a conflation Winston Churchill intended.[6]

Hess and his bizarre 'mission' were the main story – at least for that day.

By the next day, 14 May, lack of new information about the Hess mission began to squeeze newspaper coverage. The *Washington Post* gave over a half-page headline to Hess being 'quizzed' by Churchill himself (not true), along with the news that Hitler had personally taken over Hess's job. But US naval measures to keep open the supply lines through the Red Sea received equal billing. Churchill, trying to use the Hess flight to suggest that the Nazi regime was decaying, was quoted saying that 'the maggot is in the apple', but another quote (from the London *Daily Herald*), warned cautiously that there was no reason to conclude that the Hess mission indicated 'widespread revolt' against Hitler. Editorial writers interpreted the episode as a British propaganda victory, and there were some anodyne comments from two members of the British Home Guard who briefly had had custody of Hess. But the lack of substantive news forced the *Washington Post* to print background information and even a silly squib about a Canadian prognosticator who had foretold in November 1940 that 'a great man would leave Germany and go to Britain thus greatly speeding the British victory.'

On 15 May, *The New York Times*, echoing British reports, trumpeted a three-column headline that 'HESS SOUGHT TO BRING PEACE', but that short five-paragraph story ended on the front page. Otherwise, Hess began to move to the inside pages. One *Washington Post* columnist, apparently prompted by stories in the British press, implicitly connected the Hess flight with 'signs' of another Nazi–Soviet deal, a possibility the British themselves greatly feared.[7] Other reports suggested opposition within Germany to Hitler's policy towards the USSR, including a story from the 'official organ' of the Swedish Communist Party depicting Hess as opposed to Hitler's programme of co-operation with the Russians. Most interesting of all, the *New York Herald Tribune* summarised reports of increased German threats against Moscow coupled with demands for concessions in the Ukraine, leading to a 'forecast of a possible German-Soviet clash this summer'. Various newspapers, relying on British news stories, passed on rumours that Hess had brought peace plans from Hitler.

More ominously for Churchill and his government, references cropped up to the Buchmanite (Oxford/MRA) peace movement that had spread in England before the war.[8] But within a few days, the Hess story had starved for lack of information, and all but disappeared from major American newspapers. A fluff background piece, buried on page nine of the *Washington Post* of 18 May, excitedly proclaimed 'WORLD AWAITS CHURCHILL'S WORD ON WAR'S GREATEST RIDDLE'. That definitive word never came.

Five days later, at one of Roosevelt's press conferences, reporters tried to dig a bit, but to no avail. Asked if he had received any reports on the 'Hess affair', FDR answered 'No'. His facial expression must have indicated finality, for no one asked a follow-up question. On 3 June, after the American ambassador to Great Britain, Gilbert Winant, arrived in Washington and met with the President, FDR was asked if he had any more information on 'this Hess affair'. Roosevelt replied sharply that he had just told reporters that Winant had not finished his report. The last try by the news media came in mid-July, by which time the matter had degenerated into burlesque:

Q: . . . one of the largest papers in the country carried a rather circumstantial story that the Hess proposal was that the British Empire and the British fleet should be retained intact. There hasn't been anything of that kind has there . . .?

A: I must say the circumstantial story that you discuss in the great influential paper is unknown even to Mr Churchill.

Q: You mean the paper is? [laughter][9]

The 'circumstantial story' was, apparently, a variation on a theme that the 'isolationists' had been trumpeting ever since Hess dropped down out of the sky. The various anti-interventionist groups (all invariably and disparagingly lumped together and discredited by Roosevelt as 'isolationists' – those in America opposed to being militarily involved in the war) were as uncertain about the meaning of the Hess mission as the newspapers. They proffered images of the Nazi official as a 'bewildered and naïve idealist', as 'in an abnormal mental condition', as 'a rat leaving a sinking ship', and as a decoy bringing false information to the British – all mirroring widespread press speculations. Former President Herbert Hoover publicly alleged that Hess had brought 'specific and concrete German peace proposals and an offer of an Anglo-German alliance against the Soviet Union', striking a responsive chord among those who were already deeply suspicious of New Deal 'socialism'. As one anti-interventionist leader later put it, Britain's failure to capitalise on that opportunity for negotiations helped explain why Hitler attacked the Soviet Union just six weeks after Hess landed in Scotland.[10]

Herbert Hoover's claims worried a British government that expressed more anguish about American public opinion than did the White House. In Washington on the morning of 22 June, some twelve to fourteen hours after German forces attacked Soviet positions along a vast front from the Baltic to the Black Sea, ambassador Halifax telephoned the Under-Secretary of State Sumner Welles and asked for a meeting. Whether or not the subject of the war in Russia came up is speculation – the ambassador wanted to complain about Hoover's campaign. The former President had claimed that Churchill, under pressure from Conservative Party leaders, asked ambassador Winant to return to Washington and persuade FDR to agree to having the British government consider the peace proposals supposedly brought over by Hess. Moreover, insisted Hoover, Hess was the 'seventh peace emissary' sent to Britain, with the other six having come over from Ireland. And Mr Hoover had evidence! His information came from former diplomat and Hoover favourite Hugh Gibson, who was then in London and who got the information from that old standby 'reliable inside sources'. Halifax assured Welles that the American government 'was aware of the general nature' of what Hess had said.[11]

'Aware of the general nature' of what Hess had said! In such circumlocutions and diplomatic caution lie visions of conspiracy. Just what did Franklin Roosevelt know about the Hess mission? More to the point, what did the British government *tell* him about the affair? The President told Welles in mid-June that Halifax's complaint merited 'a communication to Mr Hoover', but was that because the White House really knew by then what Hess had said?[12]

In 1950, Churchill published *The Grand Alliance*, the third volume of his wartime memoir, *The Second World War*. In it he revealed that, on 17 May 1941, he had sent FDR an extensive summary of three interviews British officials had conducted with Hess.[13] The Prime Minister did not point out that his message was prompted by a request from Roosevelt on 14 May to pass on anything the German was saying about Hitler's plans for the United States or the Western Hemisphere. The President had repeated a suggestion made by James Rowe, an administrative assistant, that the American public would 'begin to wake up' if the British allowed Hess 'to tell the world what Hitler has said about the United States . . .' FDR hoped that Hess was saying things that would help convince the American public and Congress that Germany was a threat, and that Hess could 'be persuaded to tell . . . what Germany's plans really are in relation to the United States or to other parts of the Western Hemisphere, including commerce, infiltration, military domination, encirclement of the United States, etc.' As Rowe put it: 'Recollection of the unpleasant Zinovieff [sic] letter indicates the possibilities.' In a memo to Roosevelt's personal secretary, Rowe warned that the career professionals in the State Department or the British Foreign Office would bury the proposal, so 'it is a telephone job between the President and Churchill, both of whom have the imagination to see the advantage to both countries . . .'[14]

The report Churchill sent Roosevelt about the Hess interrogations was reasonably full, even mentioning the precondition that 'Hitler would not negotiate with present [Churchill] government in England', information not revealed in the British official statement. The Nazi Reichsführer surveyed, from a predictable perspective, Anglo-German relations over thirty years; 'emphasised certainty of German victory'; made 'disparaging remarks' about how little the United States could help Britain; and 'expected to contact members of a "peace movement" in England. . . .' According to Churchill's telegram, Hess denied reports of plans for a German attack on Russia. The message 'is for your own information', warned Churchill, who changed the original draft which recommended not letting the press 'romanticise' the Hess mission, scrawling instead: 'Here we think it best to let the Press have a good run for a bit and keep the Germans guessing.'[15]

Roosevelt and Churchill exchanged no more correspondence about Rudolf Hess until October 1942, when the Soviet Union raised the issue of the Hess mission and its suspicions that the British had been inclined at the time to negotiate with Hitler. If, in mid-1941, 'the thirst for news [about Hess] was phenomenal', then how was Roosevelt's thirst sated?[16]

With the Hess interrogations continuing, on 14 June Churchill proposed sending Roosevelt the transcripts of the interviews, commenting to the Foreign Secretary Anthony Eden that 'they are like a conversation with a mentally defective child who has been guilty of murder or arson'. The Prime Minister suggested sending them by hand, claiming they were 'not worth cabling'. But Churchill's advisers obviously believed the transcripts were worth keeping to themselves, and two days later Alexander Cadogan, the Permanent Under-Secretary in the Foreign Office and a frequent conduit for Churchill's information from British Intelligence (SIS/MI6), minuted that the Prime Minister had agreed at cabinet not to send the transcripts.[17]

Why not? By June 1941, Churchill was already in the habit of routinely sending messages to Roosevelt. Since New Year's Day of that year, the Prime Minister had sent thirty-seven such messages, many of which were as long or longer than the telegram about Hess – and less significant.[18] Was there a reason (just a week before the German attack on the Soviet Union) why the British did not want the Americans to have the details about what Hess had said – at least not right away? Nothing in the documents explains the decision, but if British Intelligence had mounted a disinformation campaign aimed at discouraging the Russians from making another accommodation with Hitler, as argued by one historian, then perhaps Cadogan and MI6 were following standard procedures by limiting strictly the number of those in the know.[19]

Churchill did offer Harry Hopkins, Roosevelt's closest adviser, a chance to talk to Hess with a 'free hand', but that was in July 1941, when Hopkins visited London (he would go from there to Moscow for talks with Stalin). Although Hopkins declined, lest word leak out and generate rumours of some sort of arrangement with the Nazis, the offer suggests that Churchill was not concerned about what Hess would say. That lends credence to the assumption that the British passed on information about Hess beyond what is found in the files, at least after the outbreak of the Soviet–German war.[20]

Did Churchill ever give Roosevelt the details of British reactions to the Hess mission beyond what was included in their correspondence? Did the Americans receive information about British Intelligence efforts to pressure Stalin into co-operating against Hitler by manipulating Soviet fears that Hess's visit foreshadowed an Anglo-German *rapprochement*? During the Atlantic Conference in August 1941, the first of the many wartime meetings between Churchill and Roosevelt, Alexander Cadogan recorded in his diary: 'Talked to S.W. [Sumner Welles] Gave him some dope about Hess, which I think interested him.'[21] But Welles seems not to have made a record of what Cadogan told him, and there is no mention of the conversation outside of that cryptic diary entry. Yet it is almost certain that Welles relayed what he heard to FDR. Whether or not that included the details of British Intelligence attempts to use the Hess mission in a futile attempt to pressure the Soviets is sheer speculation. What is not speculation is that Roosevelt seems to have lost interest in the Hess story with surprising speed.[22]

Roosevelt's private secretary and confidante, Missy LeHand, commented that, while FDR spent much of mid-May in bed suffering from 'one of the most persistent colds he had ever had', the reality was what 'he's suffering from most of all is a case of sheer exasperation' presumably because of the pressures from the 'isolationists' on one side and the 'extreme interventionists' on the other. White House speech writer Robert Sherwood recalls a dinner in late May, some ten days after Hess had dropped into Scotland, with Roosevelt, Hopkins and Welles during which FDR suddenly prompted Welles: 'Sumner, you must have met Hess when you were in Europe last year.' After Welles provided his unfavourable impression of Hess, the President paused, then commented: 'I wonder what is *really* behind this story?' No one could answer. '*Everybody* was mystified', wrote Sherwood, even Stalin.[23]

Sherwood's memoir-history provides, as is so often the case, a sense of the atmosphere, of the context, within which FDR viewed the Hess affair. Two weeks after it began, the huge German battleship *Bismarck*, escorted by a cruiser, made a run for the open seas. After a brief engagement with British warships, the Germans escaped, heading in the direction of the convoy routes across the North Atlantic. After receiving the news, Roosevelt sat in the Oval Office with his jacket off and mused in what Sherwood described as a 'detached, even casual manner' about what he should do. 'Suppose she [*Bismarck*] does show up in the Caribbean? We have some submarines down there. Suppose we order them to attack . . .? Do you think the people would demand to have me impeached?' Those present assured FDR that the call for impeachment would come only if 'the Navy had fired and missed', but Roosevelt had made a powerful point.[24] In mid-1941, what he disingenuously called 'isolationism' set the stage upon which the Hess matter played out.

That explains Roosevelt's initial concerns about the Hess mission – he feared there was some substance to rumours of it being a serious peace mission, and worried that it would provide a rallying point for American anti-interventionists. But why, if the President and his advisers were so very worried about appeals to a British peace movement, did FDR settle for just a single message from Churchill about what Hess was saying?[25]

In reality, Congress seemed unconcerned,[26] even disinterested in the Hess mission, while the anti-interventionists mentioned it only in passing as another example of either British or Rooseveltian chicanery. The America First Committee (AFC), the major and most effective nationwide anti-interventionist organisation, used various appeals for a negotiated peace in its publicity, including the claim by Senator Burton K. Wheeler (Democrat, Montana) that Hess had flown to Great Britain for the purpose of offering peace proposals. The same notion cropped up in some internal AFC correspondence, but Hess never became a staple of AFC publicity.[27]

There is one tantalising hint that the British provided Roosevelt with the details of the Hess interrogations. Robert Sherwood, in a passage he chronologically situated in the autumn of 1941, quotes from what he calls 'Hess's interminable monologue' aimed at convincing Britain to negotiate with Germany. In the context of a discussion about FDR's ongoing concern about pressure in and on Britain for a negotiated peace, Sherwood quotes Hess. It is the usual rant – fear of the Bolsheviks, Germany will win, American intervention would not happen. But it would seem to be post-June

1941 information since Hess is quoted as saying 'I am convinced that in any event – whether an Eastern Front persists or not – Germany and her allies are in a position to carry on the war until England collapses from lack of tonnage . . .' After saying Germany would occupy 'only the most important airfields' if it had to conquer Britain, Hess (according to Sherwood) went on: 'I am conscious that in the above I have partly given away military secrets. But I believe I can answer to my conscience and to my people, for I believe that frankness makes possible the ending of a senseless war.'[28]

Assuming the quote is accurate, when did Hess make those statements? How did Sherwood get them? (I should add that I have yet to find any of Sherwood's direct quotations in error, although in this case neither I nor the staff at the Roosevelt Library have found the material quoted by Sherwood.) The likely answer is that FDR and Hopkins received transcripts of the various interrogations that continued throughout 1941. What Sherwood quoted may have come from the report prepared for the Nuremberg War Crimes Tribunal by Hess's primary interrogator, Ivone Kirkpatrick, but more probably it came from Max Beaverbrook via Averell Harriman. Beaverbrook had interviewed Hess in September 1941, and kept notes of those conversations. He worked closely with Harriman, and the two were together in Moscow in October 1941 when Stalin asked Beaverbrook to give his explanation of the Hess affair.[29] Whatever the source, such detailed information, received after the Churchill to Roosevelt telegram of 17 May 1941, suggests why Roosevelt did not maintain a sustained interest in Hess and repeat his request for information.

The historical context and the evidence together indicate that Franklin Roosevelt did receive extensive reports about what Rudolf Hess had told British interviewers, but, except for Churchill's message of 17 May, that information was provided after the German attack on the Soviet Union.

In late autumn 1942, after the Soviet Union had called for a public trial of Hess, the British provided Roosevelt with a report on the Hess interrogations that largely summarised what Churchill had told FDR in May 1941, adding only that there had been subsequent interviews by Lord Simon on 9 June and Lord Beaverbrook on 9 September, neither of which gleaned any new information. The report went on to point out that Hess's 'mental state appeared peculiar'. A few months later, Halifax sent a fuller report on Hess's health. The only response from FDR was a brief acknowledgement: 'Many thanks for that most interesting report of the physical condition of your national guest in England.' Nothing more. Then, on 21 September, ambassador Halifax told Roosevelt that despite recent public statements about the Hess case, no mention would be made of his mental state lest it 'be used publicly by the Germans to expose our original propaganda that Hess was sane and bear out their own original contention that he was mentally deranged when he flew to the United Kingdom'. So we are left with a British admission of a propaganda effort, but no clear explanation of just what that entailed.[30]

There is an amusing postscript. On 23 April 1942, the other Hoover weighed in. J. Edgar Hoover, head of the US Federal Bureau of Investigation, reported to Roosevelt that the Duke of Windsor (then 'exiled' as Governor-General of the Bahamas) was 'very much worried' that he would be kidnapped by the Germans and traded for the release of Rudolph Hess. Hoover noted that there were 200 Canadian soldiers in the Bahamas protecting the Duke. Somehow, one has the image of King George VI and most of Britain saying, ever so softly, 'Let the Germans keep the silly fool.'[31]

Finally, in April 1945, Churchill instructed that the Duke of Hamilton, whom Hess ostensibly had come to see in 1941, should not go to the United States for a meeting (unconnected to the Hess affair) where, British authorities feared, he would be grilled by reporters:

> The Russians are very suspicious of the Hess episode and I have had a lengthy argument with Marshal Stalin about it at Moscow, he steadfastly maintaining that Hess had been invited over by our Secret Service. It is not in the public interest that the whole of this affair should be stirred at the present moment. I desire therefore that the Duke [of Hamilton] should not, repeat not undertake this task.[32]

Why? Did Britain still have something to hide? Was Churchill worried about a Soviet reaction to the full story? Or was he simply eager to get beyond unfounded and/or by then irrelevant Soviet suspicions and work, with Roosevelt, to create a harmonious relationship with Stalin? Fittingly, the bizarre mission of Rudolf Hess remains a bit mysterious.

Notes and References

1 My thanks to David Stafford and his colleagues at the Centre for Second World War Studies at the University of Edinburgh, as well as the other participants in the May 2000 symposium on the Hess mission, for their constructive comments on this piece. I appreciate the help of Allen Packwood of the Churchill Archive (Cambridge, England), Ray Teichman and Bob Parks of the Franklin D. Roosevelt Library, Milt Gustafson of the National Archives, and Dr William Slany for their assistance. Karen Mitchell helped with the newspaper research, for which I am grateful, as I am to Gabriel Gorodetsky for providing copies of some British Foreign Office documents and for responding to my questions.

2 Winston S. Churchill, *History of the Second World War*, vol. 4, *The Hinge of Fate* (Boston, 1950), p. 793. For a summary of that Washington (TRIDENT) conference, see Warren F. Kimball, *Forged in War: Roosevelt, Churchill, and the Second World War* (New York and London, 1997), pp. 214–16.

3 Stimson as quoted in Mark A. Stoler, *Allies and Adversaries: The Joint Chiefs of Staff, the Grand Alliance, and US Strategy in World War II* (Chapel Hill, NC, 2000), p. 120.

4 *George C. Marshall: Interviews and Reminiscences for Forrest C. Pogue*, Larry I. Bland (ed.) (Lexington, VA, George C. Marshall Research Foundation, 1991), p. 553.

5 This and the following summary of newspaper coverage of the Hess mission is from the *Washington Post, The New York Times, New York Herald Tribune*, 13–17 May 1941. A reading of those papers quickly shows that they were recycling each other's stories. Lippmann's comment was in the *Washington Post*, 15 May 1941. British government management of public information about the Hess story is the theme of other essays in this collection; the American military attaché, Brigadier General Raymond Lee, reported that there were no statements issued about Hess 'and that everything he had said was being held as a great state secret over here'; Raymond E. Lee, *The London Journal of General Raymond E. Lee, 1940–1941* [*Lee Journal*], James Leutze, (ed.) (Boston

and Toronto, 1971), pp. 287–8 (24 May 1941). See also Gabriel
Gorodetsky, *Grand Delusion: Stalin and the German Invasion of Russia*
(New Haven and London, 1999), ch. 12; and Gorodetsky, 'The Hess
Affair and Anglo-Soviet Relations on the Eve of "Barbarossa" ', *English
Historical Review* 101, April 1986, p. 399, pp. 405–20.

6 Roosevelt and Secretary of State Cordell Hull similarly and just as
disingenuously lumped their foreign policy opponents under the label
'isolationist'.

7 That is the theme of the treatment of the Hess episode in Gorodetsky,
Grand Illusion, ch. 12.

8 The columnist quoted was Barnet Nover in the *Washington Post*, 15 May
1941. The speculation about a German–Soviet clash was carried on 14
May 1941. That same day, *The New York Times* reported German
denials of an imminent meeting between Stalin and Hitler. The Oxford
(Buchmanite) Group was led by an American evangelical, Frank N.D.
Buchman, who asserted that a reaffirmation of spiritual and moral
values could prevent war. The movement held a series of well-attended
conferences in Britain, Western Europe, South Africa and the United
States during the mid-1930s, and changed its name to MRA (Moral Re-
Armament) in 1938.

9 *Complete Press Conferences of Franklin D. Roosevelt* (New York, 1972),
17, p. 347 (23 May 1941); 17, pp. 371–2 (3 June 1941); 18, p. 33 (15 July
1941).

10 Justus D. Doenecke, *Storm on the Horizon: The Challenge to American
Intervention, 1939–1941* (Lanham, MD, and Oxford, 2000), pp. 186,
217. The description of Hoover's claims is in a memorandum by
Sumner Welles of a conversation with ambassador Halifax, 22 June
1941, PSF:Welles (FDR papers, Franklin D. Roosevelt Library, Hyde
Park, NY [hereafter FDRL]). The papers/diaries of two close Roosevelt
advisers, Adolf Berle and Henry Morgenthau, Jr, yielded no mention of
the Hess case.

11 Ibid. Gibson later wrote a book with Hoover titled *Problems of a Lasting
Peace* (Garden City, NY, 1942).

12 FDR to Welles, 25 June 1941, PSF:Welles (FDRL).

13 Sometimes mistakes in the memoirs of great leaders occur for no
apparent reason other than a bad memory and poor fact checking
(whatever the suspicions of historians). Churchill has Hess's landing in
Scotland being reported to him on the evening of 10 May, while the
Prime Minister was, fittingly, watching a Marx Brothers film. That
dating error is repeated by Robert E. Sherwood, *Roosevelt and Hopkins*
(rev. edn.; New York 1950) p. 293. Hess flew out of Germany on that
date, but his capture was not reported to British Air Intelligence until

1 a.m., 11 May. Hess did not reveal his identity to Hamilton until 10 a.m. that same day. Churchill's biographer silently corrected the error. Winston S. Churchill, *History of the Second World War*, vol. 3, *The Grand Alliance* (Boston 1951), p. 48; the message to Roosevelt is on pp. 51–3; Martin Gilbert, *Finest Hour: Winston Churchill, 1939–1941* (Boston 1983), p. 1087. Gorodetsky, *Grand Illusion*, pp. 246–62, has the fullest and best documented discussion of the Churchill government's initial handling of the Hess affair.

14 Memos from James Rowe, Jr, to FDR, and to Missy [Marguerite] LeHand, 14 May 1941, Map Room files (FDRL), box 1; Warren F. Kimball (ed.), *Churchill and Roosevelt: The Complete Correspondence* (3 vols, Princeton, 1984), I, R–40x (14 May 1941). The Zinoviev (Zinovyev) letter, purportedly written in the mid-1920s by a Soviet government official, called for British Communists to resort to violent subversive activities in order to advance the cause of socialist revolution. The letter contributed to the collapse of the first British Labour government (Ramsay MacDonald). The letter may well have been a British forgery, but in 1941 American officials assumed the letter was genuine; see Gill Bennett, ' "A most extraordinary and mysterious business": The Zinoviev Letter of 1924', *Foreign & Commonwealth Office History Notes*, no. 14 (February 1999). British ambassador Halifax also sent a request to London from Washington for information about the Hess affair; Gorodetsky, *Grand Illusion*, p. 258.

15 Churchill, *The Grand Alliance*, pp. 51–3; Kimball, *Churchill and Roosevelt*, I, C–87x (17 May 1941). The final paragraph of the message to FDR was added to the draft in Churchill's handwriting; United Kingdom, Foreign Office files [FO], Public Record Office (Kew, England), 1093/11, pp. 111–14. Hess's precondition is quoted from the diary of John Colville by Gilbert, *Finest Hour*, pp. 1087. Gorodetsky, *Grand Illusion*, p. 259.

16 The phrase is that of Gorodetsky, *Grand Illusion*, p. 258.

17 Churchill to Eden, 14 June 1941, FO 1093/10, p. 81, with marginalia written by Eden and Cadogan. Presumably, the interviews Churchill had in mind were those conducted on 9 June by Lord Simon. See also James Barros and Richard Gregor, *Double Deception: Stalin, Hitler, and the Invasion of Russia* (DeKalb, 1995), p. 122.

18 In 1947–8, when Robert Sherwood, a speech writer in the Roosevelt White House, wrote his insightful part-history, part-memoir, *Roosevelt and Hopkins*, he downplayed the extensive pre-Pearl Harbor correspondence between Churchill and Roosevelt. Churchill, proud of his efforts to create an Anglo-American alliance, revealed in 1948 the existence of 'perhaps a thousand communications' between himself and

Roosevelt. Even though the 1946 Pearl Harbor Congressional Hearings in the United States, with their undercurrent of the Pacific War as a 'back door' to the war in Europe, had exposed the existence of Churchill–Roosevelt exchanges prior to US entry into the war, Sherwood apparently wanted to avoid giving any appearance of substance to accusations that FDR had allowed Churchill and the British to drag the United States into the conflict. Sherwood referred to Roosevelt initiating the 'historic correspondence' as the war began, and occasionally quoted specific exchanges, although Churchill and his publishers did not always grant permission to quote in full. But for the most part, during the pre-Pearl Harbor years, the Churchill–Roosevelt correspondence is only a faint shadow hovering in the background. Sherwood, *Roosevelt and Hopkins* (first published in 1948), e.g., pp. 126, 350, 949n. from p. 223. Winston S. Churchill, *History of the Second World War*, vol. 1, *The Gathering Storm* (Boston, 1948), p. 441.

19　This is the well-documented thesis of Gorodetsky, *Grand Delusion*, pp. 254–74.

20　*Lee Journal*, p. 344 (21 July 1941). John Costello incorrectly puts Harry Hopkins at Ditchley (the impressive Georgian home of Ronald and Nancy Tree, located some miles north of Oxford) on the evening of 11 May where Churchill was dining when he received a telephone call from the Duke of Hamilton regarding Hess's capture. Hopkins did visit Ditchley in January 1941, and returned to London in July, but was not in England in May of 1941. John Costello, *Ten Days to Destiny: The Secret Story of the Hess Peace Initiative and British Efforts to Strike a Deal with Hitler* (New York, 1991), pp. 417–18; Sherwood, *Roosevelt and Hopkins*, pp. 240–2.

21　*The Diaries of Sir Alexander Cadogan*, David Dilks (ed.) (New York, 1972), p. 398. (10 August 1941). The handwritten diaries at the Churchill Archive (Cambridge, England) show the same entry, nothing more.

22　Theodore Wilson, who has written the most extensively researched and thoughtful study of the Atlantic Conference, has not seen any evidence that Roosevelt and Churchill discussed the Hess affair during that meeting; *The First Summit* (rev. edn.; Lawrence, Ks, 1991). Wilson finds it quite plausible that Welles passed on to FDR what Cadogan said about Hess, but found no evidence to prove the point. (Wilson to Kimball, 4 Feb. 2001.)

23　Sherwood, *Roosevelt and Hopkins*, p.294 (Sherwood's emphasis).

24　Ibid. pp. 294–5. Kimball, *Churchill and Roosevelt*, I, C–90x (23 May 1941), R–42x (27 May 1941). The brief naval engagement, which took place between Iceland and Greenland, resulted in light damage to the

British battleship, *Prince of Wales*, and loss of the battle cruiser HMS *Hood*. Roosevelt received regular summaries from Halifax of British military actions. Those reports are found frequently in PSF: GB and, for 1942 and after, in the Map Room papers (FDRL). They do not discuss Hess. In the weeks after Hess landed, the pursuit of the *Bismarck* dominated those reports, which seemed generally balanced. For example, the deterioration of the British position in Crete was reported, but overall the reports struck a gently optimistic note. They were certainly carefully crafted, and the pitch was clear – the British had to strike a careful balance between their *need* for help and the American fear that aid would be wasted since Britain could not survive.

25 Sherwood, *Roosevelt and Hopkins*, p. 374, writes that FDR and Hopkins 'knew well' that 'sentiment for appeasement . . . was still alive in a small but potentially powerful minority' in Britain, and that Hess's continued calls for an end to 'a senseless war' could support the arguments of that minority. Some twenty years after the Hess affair, when the then British Foreign Secretary Anthony Eden wrote his memoirs, he still resented rumours in the American press ' "that our silence about Hess connotes peace talks through him". So little was our temper understood even by our best friends.' Anthony Eden, *The Reckoning* (Boston, 1965), p.301. The internal quote is from a telegram from Halifax to Eden.

26 There are but three entries in the *Congressional Record* [*CR*]. On 20 May, a Congressman inserted, without comment, an editorial about the Hess mission from the London *Daily Express* (Beaverbrook) that had been reprinted in the *Nashville Tennessean* – an editorial that opened and closed with a recommendation: 'Bail him back!' On 28 June, Rep. Lee Geyer of California inserted an article about Hess as a 'Buchmanite' (i.e. a peace advocate). Thereafter, there is nothing in the *CR* until 20 October 1942 when another Representative stated briefly that, while he understood how the Russians felt about Hess, it was Britain's 'own affair'. *Congressional Record (CR)*, 87:12, A2399 (20 May 1941); *CR*, 87:12, A3140–41 (28 June 1941); *CR*, 88:7, p. 8487 (20 October 1942).

27 *In Danger Undaunted: The Anti-Interventionist Movement of 1940–1941 as Revealed in the Papers of the America First Committee*, Justus D. Doenecke (ed.) (Stanford, 1990), pp. 61, 70 n., 250, 261.

28 Sherwood, *Roosevelt and Hopkins*, p 374. Sherwood provides no citation. The phrase 'an Eastern Front' as opposed to 'the Eastern Front' is ambiguous (as is so much of this) since it could refer to a future situation.

29 Beaverbrook, one of the Fleet Street 'press lords', was a favourite of Churchill's and was, for a time, in the cabinet. The Beaverbrook–Stalin exchange is described in W. Averell Harriman and Elie Abel, *Special*

Envoy to Churchill and Stalin, 1941–1946 (New York, 1975), p.91.

30 The initial report mentioning Hess's health was mistakenly noted as received November 1942 but later referred to as a message of 8 December 1942 from Halifax to Roosevelt; see Halifax to Roosevelt, 9 March 1943, and FDR to Halifax, 12 March 1943. On 30 June 1943, Halifax told the President of Red Cross interest in Hess's condition. The comment on earlier British propaganda is in R.J. Campbell (British embassy) to Roosevelt, 21 September 1943; all in PSF:GB, box 36 (FDRL). On Soviet statements in 1942 about Hess, see Churchill, *The Hinge of Fate* p. 581, and the brief comment in a Churchill to Roosevelt message of 24 October 1942 in Kimball, *Churchill and Roosevelt*, I, C-172, pp. 637–8. According to the American embassy in Moscow, Stalin 'was still suspicious that the British might use Hess to make some kind of deal with Germany at Russia's expense'. Henderson to the Secretary, 26 November 1942, US Dept. of State, *Foreign Relations of the United States* (Washington: USGPO, 1862–), 1942, vol. I, p. 65.

31 J Edgar Hoover to E.M. Watson (Secretary to the President), 23 April 1942, Official File 10b, item 2110 (FDRL). The Duke had allowed himself to become associated with the British peace movement, and there were persistent stories of his being pro-Nazi. Churchill defended the Duke's loyalty, but was inclined to follow the advice 'that HRH had to be treated like a petulant baby'. See Gilbert, *Finest Hour*, pp. 698–709, quotation on p. 703.

32 As quoted from PREM 3/219/7, p. 167, in Peter Padfield, *Hess: Flight for the Führer* (London, 1991), p. 350.

JAMES DOUGLAS-HAMILTON

Hess and the Haushofers

Just as some people appear to be sexy for no apparent reason, so some stories attract far more interest that their real importance would merit. Such a story is Hess's flight to Britain. Seen from one angle, it is about a brave but not very intelligent Nazi leader undertaking a hare-brained project involving a dangerous flight to see someone he did not know in order to persuade him to do something completely beyond his powers, to which in any case he was opposed. The whole sorry exercise was based on a total misunderstanding by Hess both of the Intelligence briefings he had received and of the real political situation in Britain. The end result made no impact whatever on the course of the war, and surprisingly little even on the morale of the people in Britain and Germany.

And yet every couple of years a new book appears brandishing some fantastic theory – for instance, that Hess was not Hess, or that he was lured to Britain as a result of a brilliant plot by British Intelligence – and these always seem to attract public interest and attention. In fact there are fascinating and tragic aspects to the story, but they are personal rather than political, and concern in particular a character who tends to receive hardly any attention in most coverage of the subject, but who actually albeit unintentionally caused the whole episode to happen. This man was Dr Albrecht Haushofer, a senior adviser to the German Foreign Office and to Rudolf Hess personally.

The story begins in the immediate aftermath of the First World War with Albrecht's father, Karl. Karl Haushofer had served as artillery commander during the battle of the Somme and, like for so many others, the German defeat and the Treaty of Versailles came as a terrible shock. In 1919 Haushofer established the new academic discipline of geopolitics, in fact the study of political geography seen from a German perspective. It was a form of geographical imperialism, and in his own words, 'geopolitics wants to and must become the geographical conscience of the state'.[1]

It was to the frustrated nationalism of a defeated country that Karl Haushofer was appealing in learned academic language. As Professor of Geopolitics at Munich University many students came to hear him after the war, embittered that the fighting had all been in vain. One of them was Rudolf Hess, a fanatical young man and an intimate friend of Hitler. Hess became the professor's personal assistant at the German Academy, and while Haushofer thought that Hess's 'heart and idealism were greater than his intellect', he also regarded Hess as 'my favourite pupil'.[2]

After the failure of Hitler's Munich *Putsch* in 1923 it was with Karl Haushofer's help that Hess escaped to Austria, a favour which Hess would never forget. When Hess returned, he was given a lenient sentence and joined Hitler in Landsberg prison where the Nazi leader served a nine-month sentence. Here Hess became Hitler's principal secretary and typed out Hitler's political programme, *Mein Kampf.*

Karl Haushofer paid a few visits to his former pupil Hess at Landsberg, bringing him reading material. He also had the occasional conversation with Hitler, and as a result certain geopolitical ideas were transmitted to Hitler, either directly or through Hess.[3] But Haushofer never joined the Nazi Party: his wife was half-Jewish, therefore, according to the Nazi ideology, she and their children were in line to be persecuted.

After coming to power Hitler appointed Hess in April 1933 'my deputy with the power to take decisions in all questions relating to the conduct of the Party'.[4] Haushofer assisted Hess with the Auslandsorganisationen, which were set up within Germany and elsewhere to foster contacts and comradeship between Germans in the Reich and German minorities outside. On 12 February 1934 Hess appointed Haushofer the president of the new council for those of German origin who were living in countries outside the Reich.

Throughout this period Hess and Karl Haushofer remained

close and Hess came to know Karl's son Albrecht, a young man of exceptional ability, a scholar, geographer, poet, musician and playwright. When Hess brought in anti-Semitic legislation, he issued protective letters, sent to the Ministry of Propaganda, declaring the two sons of Karl Haushofer to be 'Honorary Aryans'. By 1934 Albrecht Haushofer had become Hess's personal adviser, and acted as Hess's representative on a number of occasions.[5] He was appointed a special adviser to the Dienststelle Ribbentrop, a bureau under the immediate control of the German Foreign Secretary, Joachim von Ribbentrop, but subject to the supervision of Hess. Albrecht was employed late in 1936 by Hitler both as a special adviser and as a secret envoy to visit President Beneš of Czechoslovakia.[6] He came back with a report of 'attainable' objectives, but Hitler put a red line through Haushofer's final suggestion for a non-aggression pact, the obvious reason being that Hitler had already decided to destroy Czechoslovakia by force.[7]

But he was most influential through his work as a special adviser on Britain to Hess, Ribbentrop and Hitler. Albrecht Haushofer spoke English like an Englishman, had a great admiration for the British Empire, and wanted Germany to have peaceful relations with Britain. In August 1936 Albrecht Haushofer met a group of British MPs at the Berlin Olympic Games, one of whom was the Marquis of Clydesdale, who became Duke of Hamilton in 1940. Clydesdale was of interest to the Germans, because he had been the first man in the world to fly over Mount Everest. Aviators in those days were regarded in much the same way as the early astronauts, and aviation was looked upon as a top priority by the leaders of the Third Reich.

Clydesdale kept in contact with Albrecht Haushofer and, after a skiing holiday in Austria, visited him and his father at Hartschimmelhof in January 1937. Clydesdale later sent his book *The Pilot's Book of Everest* to Karl Haushofer, who replied saying he would review it in the *Zeitschrift für Geopolitik*.[8] What Clydesdale did not know was that four days after his visit to the Hartschimmelhof, Hess would arrive. He would be told about Clydesdale's visit, and be shown *The Pilot's Book of Everest*, which interested him greatly.

In June 1938, Albrecht Haushofer met Clydesdale in London, and subsequently wrote the most important report that he ever submitted to Ribbentrop and Hitler, dated 26 June 1938.

The belief in the possibility of an understanding between Britain and Germany is dwindling fast. A new imperialism is suspected behind the Pan-German programme of National Socialism . . . Here the Czech question assumes the significance of a decisive test case. A German attempt to solve the Bohemian–Moravian question by a military attack would under present circumstances present for Britain (and in British opinion also for France) a *casus belli*.

In such a war the British government would have the whole nation behind it. It would be conducted as a crusade for the liberation of Europe from German militarism. London is convinced that such a war would be won with the help of the USA (whose full participation, within days, not weeks, is anticipated) at the cost, of course, of an incalculable expense of Bolshevism outside the Anglo-Saxon world.[9]

Ribbentrop dismissed the report by contemptuously adding the marginal note 'secret service propaganda' before passing it to Hitler.[10] Albrecht Haushofer had fallen into the 'deepest disfavour because of his warnings',[11] and his drive for an Anglo-German understanding.

On 16 July 1939 he sent a letter to Clydesdale, while cruising the coast of western Norway. It was a remarkable letter from a former special adviser to Hitler to an officer of another country, with whom Germany might soon be at war. His writing could not have been more frank as to when war would break out:

To the best of my knowledge there is not yet a definite timetable for the actual explosion, but any date after the middle of August may prove to be the fatal one. So far they want to avoid the 'big war'. But the one man on whom everything depends is still hoping that he may be able to get away with an isolated 'local war': he still thinks in terms of British bluff . . .

I am very much convinced that Germany cannot win a short war and that she cannot stand a long one – but I am thoroughly afraid that the terrific forms of modern war will make any reasonable peace impossible if they are allowed to go on for even a few weeks.[12]

The letter ended with the request that it be destroyed after having been shown to Lord Halifax or Mr Butler, Secretary of State and Under-Secretary of State for Foreign Affairs, respectively. Clydesdale showed it to Churchill, Halifax and the Prime Minister, Chamberlain, and then he locked it up.

After the outbreak of war Albrecht started to work with men who were associated with the opposition to Hitler, namely Johannes Popitz, Carl Langbehn, and Ulrich von Hassell, the former German ambassador in Italy. Through Popitz, Albrecht became acquainted with the Wednesday Society, which later on would become a centre for the German resistance to Hitler.[13]

In 1940 he also prepared a peace plan which was transferred from the German embassy in Spain to the British embassy there, but without results.[14] It appears that Albrecht was a troubled German patriot relying on his wits. He had one foot firmly planted in the German resistance to Hitler, and the other in the Nazi camp as assistant of Ribbentrop and personal adviser to Hess. But it was not until 8 September 1940 that Albrecht would become deeply involved in discussions with Hess on the possibilities of a German–English peace.

In the meantime, after the fall of Poland and France, Hitler had made abortive peace offers to the British. On 31 August Hess had a lengthy discussion with Karl Haushofer lasting up to nine hours. Hitler was making preparations for launching an invasion against Britain, but Hess was hoping for a peaceful way out and was wondering whether a peace feeler could be made through a British intermediary in a neutral country. Karl Haushofer wrote to Albrecht on 3 September:

As you know everything is so prepared for a very hard and severe attack on the island in question that the highest ranking person only has to press a button to set it off. But before this decision, which is perhaps inevitable, the thought once more occurs as to whether there is really no way of stopping something which would have such infinitely momentous consequences. There is a line of reasoning in connection with this which I absolutely must pass on to you, because it was obviously communicated to me with this intention. Do you, too, see no way in which such possibilities could be discussed at a third place with a middle man, possibly the old Ian Hamilton or the other Hamilton?[15]

Both Hamiltons were known to Karl Haushofer. General Sir Ian Hamilton, the veteran of the Gallipoli campaign in the First World War, had once had lunch with Hitler and Hess,[16] and Karl Haushofer had met the Duke of Hamilton at Hartschimmelhof in 1937. In due course Albrecht Haushofer was summoned by Hess to Bad Godesberg for a lengthy talk on 8 September. After the meeting Albrecht drew up a memorandum, marked 'top security', dated 18 September 1940.

ARE THERE STILL POSSIBILITIES OF A GERMAN–ENGLISH PEACE?

On 8 September, I was summoned to Bad G [Godesberg] to report to the Deputy of the Führer on the subject discussed in this memorandum. The conversation which the two of us had alone lasted two hours. I had the opportunity to speak in all frankness.

I was immediately asked about the possibilities of making known to persons of importance in England Hitler's serious desire for peace . . . The Führer had not wanted to see the Empire destroyed and did not want it even today. Was there not somebody in England who was ready for peace?

First I asked for permission to discuss fundamental things. It was necessary to realise that not only Jews and Freemasons, but practically all Englishmen who mattered, regarded a treaty signed by the Führer as a worthless scrap of paper. To the question as to why this was so, I referred to the ten-year term of our Polish Treaty, to the Non–Aggression Pact with Denmark signed only a year ago, to the 'final' frontier demarcation of Munich. What guarantee did England have that a new treaty would not be broken again at once if it suited us? It must be realised that, even in the Anglo-Saxon world, the Führer was regarded as Satan's representative on earth and had to be fought.

After this blunt assertion, a long discussion took place. Towards the end Hess asked Haushofer to name those who might be reached as possible contacts. Albrecht replied:

As the final possibility I then mentioned that of a personal meeting on neutral soil with the closest of my English friends: the young

Duke of Hamilton who has access at all times to all important persons in London, even to Churchill and the King. I stressed in this case the inevitable difficulty of making contact and again repeated my conviction of the improbability of us succeeding – whatever approach we took.

The upshot of the conversation was Hess's statement that he would consider the whole matter thoroughly once more and send me work in case I was to take steps. For this extremely ticklish case, and in the event that I might possibly have to make a trip alone – I asked for very precise directions from the highest authority.

From the whole conversation I had the strong impression that it was not conducted without the prior knowledge of the Führer, and that I probably would not hear any more about the matter unless a new understanding had been reached between him and his Deputy.

On the personal side of the conversation I must say that – despite the fact that I felt bound to say unusually hard things – it ended in great friendliness, even cordiality.[17]

Working for the still embryonic German resistance to Hitler as well as for the Foreign Office and Hess, Albrecht was walking a tightrope. As a patriotic German Albrecht believed that any peace with Britain was better than no peace, and it appeared that Hess was the only Nazi leader who could be of assistance to him. Trying to open up a channel to Britain on Hess's behalf with, as he believed, Hitler's knowledge, he had put forward Hamilton's name as a desperate man clutches at a straw. Albrecht knew that the British were in no mood for Nazi peace feelers. He had told Hess that his friend the Duke of Hamilton had access at all times to all important persons in London, although Hamilton had in fact been called up before the outbreak of war and was serving full-time with the RAF in the east of Scotland. Nevertheless, once the idea had been put into the mind of Rudolf Hess nothing in the world would get it out.

Although there has been some doubt among historians as to whether Hitler knew that Hess was trying to make contact with the British through Albrecht Haushofer, it appears from several sources that Hitler did know about Hess's plans. Hewel, Ribbentrop's liaison man with Hitler, told Fritz Hesse that Hitler was using Albrecht Haushofer to make contact with the British, and that Haushofer had connections with the British through the Swiss professor, Carl Burckhardt.[18] Frau Hess was more definite: she wrote that her husband tried to get in touch with prominent circles in Britain through Albrecht Haushofer via Spain or Switzerland, with Hitler's knowledge.[19] As for Albrecht Haushofer himself, he had written in his memorandum on the possibilities of a German–English peace that Hess had given him the impression that their conversation had been conducted with Hitler's prior knowledge.[20] According to Otto Dietrich, Hess did indeed have a conversation with Hitler. He asked him whether his policy towards Britain remained unchanged and Hitler told Hess that he still desired an Anglo-German understanding.[21] The most that can be assumed from these sources is that Hitler gave a measure of approval to Hess to make enquiries through Albrecht Haushofer. It may well be that Hitler did not wish anyone else to know that such enquiries were being made with his approval. Be that as it may, Hess in due course took action and contacted the Haushofers.

Hess knew that, notwithstanding Karl Haushofer's refusal to join the Nazi Party, his teachings on geopolitics had provided Hitler's expansionist policies with a cloak of intellectual respectability. On 27 August 1939 Hitler had written to Karl on the German Chancellor's headed paper.

> Esteemed Professor, may I convey my sincerest congratulations upon the occasion of your 70th birthday. At the same time I confer upon you the Order of the Eagle of the German Reich, with the dedication 'To the important German Geopolitician' in recognition of your achievements in the field of geopolitics. With best wishes for your continued work and wellbeing I remain with German greeting,
>
> Yours, A. Hitler.[22]

On 10 September 1940 Hess wrote to Karl Haushofer referring to the professor's letter to his son of 3 September. Obviously Hess had been toying with the mechanics of opening peace feelers.

> The prerequisite naturally is that the enquiry in question and the reply would not go through official channels, for you would not in any case want to cause your friends over there any trouble.

It would be best to have the letter to the old lady, with whom you are acquainted, delivered through a confidential agent of the AO to the address that is known to you. For this purpose Albrecht would have to speak either with Boble or my brother. At the same time the lady would have to be given the address of this agent in L. or if the latter does not live there permanently, of another agent in the AO who does live there permanently, to which the reply can in turn be delivered.

As for the neutral I have in mind, I would like to speak to you orally about it some time. There is no hurry about that since, in any case, there would first have to be a reply received here from over there.

Meanwhile let's both keep our fingers crossed. Should success be the fate of the enterprise, the oracle given to you with regard to the month of August would yet be fulfilled, since the name of the young friend and the old lady friend of your family occurred to you during our quiet walk on the last day of that month.

With best regards to you and to Martha.

Yours, as ever
R. Hess[23]

It was obvious from the tone of his letter that Hess was determined to make a peace overture. On 18 September Albrecht wrote to his parents, pointing out that it was not as easy as Hess imagined to make contact with a person such as Hamilton in a country with which Germany was at war. He also did not wish to endanger their friend Mrs Roberts who would have to see that a message was conveyed from Portugal.[24] On the next day, 19 September, Albrecht wrote to Hess mentioning that he had seen the latter's letter to his father.

TOP SECRET

My dear Herr Hess

I have been thinking of the technical route by which a message from me must travel before it can reach the Duke of H. With your

(*Above left*) In his element: Hess speaks at the laying of the foundation stone of the Adolf Hitler Canal, May 1934. (*Above right*) A frank tête-à-tête between Hitler and Hess at the 1937 Nuremberg Party Congress. (*Below*) In descending order, outlined against Speer's breathtaking 'cathedral of light' at the 1938 Nuremberg Conference: Hitler, Goering and Hess.

Hess and Hitler on a forest ramble.

Hitler and Hess take a picnic.
Next to Hitler sits the film director
Leni Riefenstahl.

Hitler inspects one of
Hess's early aeroplanes.

A youthful Rudolf Hess seen here with Professor Karl Haushofer, his intellectual mentor.

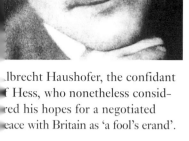

lbrecht Haushofer, the confidant f Hess, who nonetheless considred his hopes for a negotiated eace with Britain as 'a fool's erand'.

The Duke of Hamilton, the unwitting target of Hess's mission. He is shown here, as the Marquis of Clydesdale, leaving for the Mount Everest Flight Expedition in 1933.

(*Above*) A pensive-looking Hess captured on camera with Hitler and Goebbels just weeks before his flight. Seen here at the Sportpalast Berlin, on the 8th anniversary of the Nazi seizure of power.

(*Right*) The shock to the Nazi faithful by Hess's flight can readily be imagined from this enthusiastic scene in Vienna just three years earlier following the *Anschluss*.

(*Below*) Hess the aviator prepares for a flight in his Messerschmitt 110.

The front page of the *Daily Record* breaks the news of Hess's dramatic flight to its readers on 13 May 1941.

Nazi Leader Flies To Scotland

Daily Record

RUDOLF HESS IN GLASGOW -OFFICIAL

HERR HESS, HITLER'S RIGHT-HAND MAN, HAS RUN AWAY FROM GERMANY AND IS IN GLASGOW SUFFERING FROM A BROKEN ANKLE. HE BROUGHT PHOTOGRAPHS TO ESTABLISH HIS IDENTITY.

AN OFFICIAL STATEMENT ISSUED FROM 10 DOWNING STREET AT 11.20 LAST NIGHT SAID—

"Rudolf Hess, Deputy Führer of Germany and Party Leader of the Nationalist Socialist Party, has landed in Scotland under the following circumstances:

"On the night of Saturday, the 10th, a Messerschmitt 110 was reported by our patrols to have crossed the coast of Scotland and be flying in the direction of Glasgow. Since a Messerschmitt 110 would not have the fuel to return to Germany this report was at first disbelieved.

THIS WAS HIS 'PLANE

Two pictures of the wreckage of Hess's Messerschmitt 110.

Benghazi Shelled

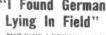

Rudolf Hess

"I Found German Lying In Field"

DAVID McLEAN, A PLOUGHMAN, WAS THE MAN WHO FOUND RUDOLF HESS. HERE IS McLEAN'S OWN STORY AS TOLD TO THE DAILY RECORD, FIRST NEWSPAPER ON THE SCENE—

"I was in the house and everyone else was in bed late at night when I heard the 'plane roaring overhead. As I ran out to the back of the farm, I heard a crash, and saw the 'plane burst into flames in a field about 300 yards away.

"I was amazed and a bit frightened when I saw a parachute dropping slowly earthwards through the gathering darkness. Peering upwards, I could see a man swinging from the harness.

Continued on Back Page, Col. 1

He was taken to a hospital in Glasgow where he at first gave no name as Herr, but later as he declared he was Rudolf Hess.

"He brought with him various photographs of himself at different ages, apparently in order to establish his identity. These photographs were shown to be photographs of Hess by several people who knew him personally.

HOW GERMANY BUILT UP THE HESS AFFAIR. See Back Page.

Good Morning! Another Day Nearer Victory!

The local soldiery poses next to the wreckage of Hess's Messerschmitt in a Scottish field.

"HE MUST HAVE BEEN MAD"

The famous wartime cartoonist David Low captures a widespread view of Hess's flight at the time.

Taken in 1933, this photograph shows three of the principal British actors in the Hess drama. On the left and right, respectively, Sir Alexander Cadogan and Sir Anthony Eden, whose efforts to exploit the affair inadvertently fuelled theories of a British conspiracy. Sir John Simon interviewed Hess for the War Cabinet in June 1941, and his report convinced Churchill that Hess's statements resembled 'the outpourings of a disordered mind'.

(*Above left*) Sir Anthony Eden with the Soviet ambassador to Britain, Ivan Maisky, who took a suspicious view of Hess's flight. (*Above right*) Kim Philby, the SIS officer working for Moscow, whose reports on the Hess affair helped distort the story. He is shown here in 1955 falsely maintaining his innocence of betrayal to the British press. (*Below*) Seen here at the 1945 Yalta Conference, Churchill, Roosevelt and Stalin each had his particular 'spin' on the Hess affair. Behind each leader stands his Foreign Minister – Eden, Stettinius and Molotov; behind the last two stands a hatless Sir Alexander Cadogan.

(*Above*) Hess's return to Nuremberg – this time in the dock. Arms folded, he listens to proceedings without benefit of earphone translation. To his right sits Goering.
(*Below*) Hess frequently bewildered his interrogators at Nuremberg and claimed amnesia. Ten days after the trial began, Hess declared his memory had returned.

help, delivery to Lisbon can of course be assured without difficulty. About the rest of the route we do not know. Foreign control must be taken into account; the letter must therefore in no case be composed in such a way that it will simply be seized and destroyed or that it will directly endanger the woman transmitting it or the ultimate recipient.

In view of my close personal relations and intimate acquaintance with DH I can write a few lines to him (which should be enclosed with the letter to Mrs R without any indication of place and without a full name – so A would suffice for signature) in such a way that he alone will recognise that behind my wish to see him in Lisbon there is something more serious than a personal whim . . .

Let us suppose that the case were reversed: an old lady in Germany receives a letter from an unknown source abroad, with a request to forward a message whose recipient is asked to disclose to an unknown foreigner where he will be staying for a certain period – and this recipient were a high officer in the Air Force (of course I do not know exactly what position H holds at the moment; judging from his past I can conceive of only three things; he is an active Air Force general or he directs the air defence on an important part of Scotland, or he has a responsible position in the Air Ministry).

I do not think that you need much imagination to picture to yourself the faces that Canaris or Heydrich would make and the smirk with which they would consider any offer of 'security' or 'confidence' in such a letter if a subordinate should submit such a case to them. They would not merely make faces, you may be certain! The measures would come quite automatically – and neither the old lady nor the Air Force officer would have an easy time of it. In England it is no different . . .

If it should be decided that I was to comply with the wish for a meeting with my friend, I would then be most anxious to get my instructions if not from the Führer himself, at least from a person who receives them directly and at the same time has the gift of transmitting the finest and lightest nuances – an art which has been mastered by yourself but not by all Reich Ministers . . .

It is no different with H. He cannot fly to Lisbon – any more that I can! – unless he is given leave, that is unless at least Air

Minister Sinclair and Foreign Minister Halifax know about it . . .

My proposal is therefore as follows:

Through the old friend I will write a letter to H – in a form that will incriminate no one but will be understandable to the recipient – with the proposal for a meeting in Lisbon. If nothing comes of that, it will be possible (if the military situation leaves enough time for it), assuming that a suitable intermediary is available, to make a second attempt through a neutral going to England, who might be given a personal message to take along. With respect to this possibility, I must add, however that H is extremely reserved – as many Englishmen are towards anyone they do not know personally. Since the entire Anglo–German problem after all springs from a most profound crisis in mutual confidence, this would not be immaterial . . .

I already tried to explain to you not long ago that, for the reasons I gave, the possibilities of successful efforts at a settlement between the Führer and the British upper class seem to me – to my extreme regret – infinitesimally small.

Nevertheless I should not want to close this letter without pointing out once more that I still think there would be a somewhat greater chance of success in going through ambassador Lothian in Washington or Sir Samuel Hoare in Madrid rather than through my friend H. To be sure, they are – practically speaking – more inaccessible.

Would you send me a line or give me a telephone call with final instructions? . . .

With cordial greeting and best wishes for your health.

Yours etc

AH[25]

On the same day Albrecht drafted a letter to Hamilton and wrote to his parents: 'The whole thing is a fool's errand'.[26] He wrote to Hess on 23 September 1940, reporting that the letter to Hamilton had been dispatched via Alfred Hess, brother of the Deputy Führer:

In accordance with your last telephone call I got in touch with your brother immediately. Everything went off well, and I can now report that the mission has been accomplished to the extent that

the letter you desired was written and dispatched this morning. It
is to be hoped that it will be more efficacious than sober judgement
would indicate.[27]

Albrecht wrote to his father on the same day enclosing a copy of
the letter to Hamilton, mentioning his gravest misgivings about
this overture and the situation in general:

I am convinced, as before, that there is not the slightest prospect
of peace; and so I don't have the least faith in the possibility about
which you know. However, I also believe that I could not have
refused my services any longer. You know that for myself I do not
see any possibility of any satisfying activity in the future.

If the 'total victory' from Glasgow to Capetown were to be
achieved for our savages, then the drunk sergeant and the corrupt
exploiters will call the tune anyhow; experts with quiet manners
will not be needed then. If it is not achieved, if the English succeed
in delivering the first blow with American help and in creating a
long protracted war equilibrium with the aid of the Bolshevist
insecurity factor, then, however, there will sooner or later be a
demand for the likes of us – but in conditions in which little
enough will be left to salvage any . . .[28]

The letter to Hamilton[29] suggested a meeting on the outskirts of
Europe, in Portugal. It was never answered.[30]

On 10 May 1941 Hess departed from Augsburg in an Me 110
fitted with extra fuel tanks, aiming to parachute over Dungavel
House, the home of the Duke of Hamilton. He was being following
by an RAF Defiant and baled out over Eaglesham, where he gave a
false name, Hauptmann Horn, and asked to see the Duke of
Hamilton. At the same time in London the House of Commons
was hit by incendiary bombs.

On Sunday 11 May Wing Commander Hamilton arrived at
Maryhill Barracks and examined the personal effects of the
prisoner, which included the visiting cards of General Professor
Karl Haushofer and his son Dr Albrecht Haushofer. After his
meeting with Hess, Hamilton made arrangements to see Churchill,
typed out his report and, before flying south in a Hurricane,
collected the letter which Albrecht Haushofer had written to him

in July 1939. The first paragraph of Hamilton's report to Churchill revealed the key influence on Hess of Albrecht Haushofer:

> He said, 'I do not know if you recognise me, but I am Rudolf Hess.'
> He went on to say that he was on a mission of humanity and that
> the Führer did not want to defeat England and wished to stop
> fighting. His friend Albrecht Haushofer told him that I was an
> Englishman whom he thought would understand his (Hess's)
> point of view. He had consequently tried to arrange a meeting with
> me in Lisbon. (See Haushofer's letter to me dated 23 September
> 1940.)[31]

In his history of the Second World War, Churchill recorded:

> On Sunday 11 May, I was spending the weekend at Ditchley –
> presently a secretary told me that somebody wanted to speak to me
> on the telephone on behalf of the Duke of Hamilton. The Duke
> was a personal friend of mine, and was commanding a fighter
> section in the east of Scotland, but I could not think of any
> business he might have with me which could not wait till morning.
> However, the caller pressed to speak with me, saying the matter
> was one of urgent cabinet importance. I therefore sent for him.[32]

When he heard the news of Hess's flight Albrecht Haushofer was beside himself with anxiety. Rainer Hildebrandt wrote after seeing him on 11 May 1941.

> I found Haushofer, whom I had always known as being
> completely collected, in utter despair and helplessness. He said,
> 'The motorised Parsifal wants to bring peace to Hitler, and he
> imagines that he could get round the Churchill government and
> could sit down at the negotiating table with the King.'
> Haushofer had calculated all possibilities. The most improbable
> and unusual developments were included in his reckoning, but
> here something had happened which brought his whole edifice of
> thought crashing down. Haushofer walked about like a wounded
> animal not knowing what to do with himself.[33]

Ever since 1933 it was as though Albrecht had been standing with a noose around his neck on account of his Jewish ancestry, and the chair upon which he had been standing was Rudolf Hess. He had now learnt that this chair had been swept from under his feet. A few hours later he was arrested by the Gestapo. Hitler wanted an account of his recent activities at the Obersalzberg, Berchtesgaden.[34]

After the news of Hess's flight was broken to him by Hess's adjutant Pintsch, Hitler was seething.[35] Whatever his knowledge of Hess's plans, Hitler had never imagined that his Deputy would fly into enemy territory without authorisation. Reading Hess's letter handed to him by Pintsch, Hitler was 'overcome by a tremendous agitation'.[36] He was extremely concerned about Hess's flight on three counts: first, he believed that once the German people learnt that his Deputy had flown to Britain on a peace mission, the German soldiers at the front would fight less hard; secondly, he feared that Hess's action might lead to the disintegration of the Anti-Comintern Pact between Germany, Italy and Japan and that Mussolini, not to be outdone, would hasten to make his own peace terms with Britain; and lastly and probably most important, Hitler was afraid Hess would reveal the Nazi plans to attack Russia.[37]

According to Albert Speer, Hitler 'put the blame for Hess's flight on the corrupting influence of Professor Karl Haushofer'.[38] Goebbels wrote in his diaries that he believed that Hess had gone 'soft', that Professor Karl Haushofer had been an 'evil genius' in this affair, while Hitler's view was that 'one can be prepared for anything except the aberrations of a lunatic'.[39] On 1 July Goebbels recorded that General Professor Karl Haushofer and Albrecht Haushofer had been drummed out of public life. He blamed both of them for the Hess affair and alleged that they had peddled 'mystic rubbish' to Hess.[40]

When Albrecht arrived at Berchtesgaden on 12 May he knew that his life was in danger. He was not admitted to Hitler's presence, but was ordered to make a report for Hitler in writing. This he did and entitled it 'English Connections and the Possibility of Utilising Them'. What he wrote, however, did not represent his real belief, which was that Britain would never consider peace talks of any description with Nazi Germany. Instead he was trying to convince Hitler that in any possible future negotiations with Britain he would be indispensable on account of his numerous English connections.[41] As there is no doubt that this report went straight to Hitler, who must have given it his closest attention, it is reproduced here in full:

> The circle of English individuals whom I have known very well for years, and whose utilisation on behalf of a German–English understanding in the years from 1934 to 1938 was the core of my activity in England, comprises the following groups and persons.
>
> A leading group of younger Conservatives (many of them Scotsmen). Among them the Duke of Hamilton – up to the date of his father's death, Lord Clydesdale – Conservative Member of Parliament; the Parliamentary Private Secretary of Neville Chamberlain, Lord Dunglass; the present Under-Secretary of State in the Air Ministry, Balfour; the present Under-Secretary in the Ministry of Education, Lindsay (National Labour); the present Under-Secretary of State in the Ministry for Scotland, Wedderburn.
>
> Close ties link this circle with the court. The younger brother of the Duke of Hamilton is closely related to the present Queen through his wife; the mother-in-law of the Duke of Hamilton, the Duchess of Northumberland, is the Mistress of the Robes; her brother-in-law Lord Eustace Percy, was several times a member of the cabinet and is still today an influential member of the Conservative Party (especially close to former Prime Minister Baldwin). There are close connections between this circle and important groups of the older Conservatives, as, for example, the Stanley family (Lord Derby, Oliver Stanley) and Astor (the last is owner of *The Times*). The young Astor, likewise a Member of Parliament, was Parliamentary Private Secretary to the former Foreign and Interior Minister, Sir Samuel Hoare, at present English ambassador in Madrid.
>
> I have known almost all of the persons mentioned for years from close personal contact.
>
> The present Under-Secretary of State of the Foreign Office, Butler, also belongs here; in spite of many of his public utterances he is not a follower of Churchill or Eden. Numerous connections lead from most of these named to Lord Halifax, to whom I likewise had personal access.
>
> The so-called 'Round Table' circle of younger imperialists (particularly colonial and Empire politicians), whose most

important personage was Lord Lothian.

A group of the Ministerialdirektoren in the Foreign Office. The most important of these were Strang, the chief of the Central European Department, and O'Malley, the chief of the South-Eastern Department and afterwards Minister in Budapest.

There was hardly one of those named who was not at least occasionally in favour of a German-English understanding.

Although most of them in 1939 considered that war was inevitable, it was nevertheless reasonable to think of these persons if one thought the moment had come for investigating the possibility of an inclination to make peace. Therefore when the Deputy of the Führer, Reichsminister Hess, asked me in the autumn of 1940 about possibilities for establishing contacts, it seemed to me that the following could be considered for this:

Personal contact with Lothian, Hoare or O'Malley, all three of whom were accessible in neutral countries.

Contact by letter with one of my friends in England. For this purpose the Duke of Hamilton was considered in the first place, since my connection with him was so firm and personal that I could suppose he would understand a letter addressed to him even if it were formulated in very veiled language.

Reichsminister Hess decided in favour of the second possibility. I wrote a letter to the Duke of Hamilton at the end of September 1940 and its dispatch to Lisbon was arranged by the Deputy Führer. I did not learn whether the letter reached the addressee. The possibilities of its being lost en route from Lisbon to England are not small, after all.

Then in April 1941 I received greeting from Switzerland from Carl Burckhardt, the former League of Nations Commissioner in Danzig and now vice-president of the International Red Cross, whom I had also known well for years. He sent the message that he had greetings to pass on to me from someone in my old circle of English friends. I should please visit him some time in Geneva. Since the possibility existed that these greetings were in connection with my letter of last autumn, I thought I should again submit the matter to the Deputy of the Führer, though with the reservation (as already last autumn) that the chances of a serious peace feeler seemed to me to be extremely slight. Reichsminister Hess decided that I should go to Geneva.

In Geneva I had a long conversation with Burckhardt on 28 April. I found him in something of a quandary between his desire to support the possibilities of a European peace and the greatest concern lest his name might somehow be involved with publicity; he expressly asked that what went on be kept strictly secret. In consideration of the discretion enjoined upon him he could only tell me the following.

A few weeks ago a person well known and respected in London, who was close to the leading Conservative and City circles, had called on him in Geneva. This person, whose name he could not give, though he could vouch for his earnestness, had in a rather long conversation expressed the wish of important English circles for an examination of the possibilities for peace; in search for possible channels my name had been mentioned.

I for my part informed Professor Burckhardt that I had to expect the same discretion with regard to my name. Should his informant in London be willing to come to Switzerland once more and should he further be willing to have his name communicated to me in Berlin through confidential channels, so that the earnestness of both person and mission could be investigated in Germany, then I thought that I, too, could agree to taking another trip to Geneva. Professor Burckhardt stated that he was willing to act as go-between in this manner; it would simply be communicated to England through an entirely safe channel that there was a prospect for a trusted representative from London, after he himself had given his name, to meet in Geneva a German also well known in England, who was in a position to bring such communications as there might be to the attention of the competent German authorities.

My own conversation with Professor Burckhardt furnished a number of important points regarding the substantive part of possible peace talks. (Burckhardt has not only been in England during the war – for example, he had a long and detailed conversation with Halifax – but he also has frequent contact with the English observer in Geneva, Consul General Livingston, who likewise is one of those Englishmen whom the war does not please.) Burckhardt's general impression of the opinions of the more moderate groups in England can be summarised as follows:

The substantive English interest in the areas of Eastern and South-eastern Europe (with the exception of Greece) is nominal.

No English government that is still capable of action will be able to renounce [the aim of] a restoration of the Western European system of states.

The colonial question will not present any overwhelming difficulties if the German demand is limited to the old German possessions and if the Italian appetite can be curbed.

All of this, however – and this fact could not be stressed seriously enough – under the assumption, which overshadowed everything else, that a basis of personal confidence could be found between Berlin and London; and this would be as difficult to find as during the Crusades or in the Thirty Years' War.

As matters stood, the contest with 'Hitlerism' was being considered by the masses of the English people, too, to be a religious war with all the fanatical psychological consequences of such an attitude. If anyone in London was inclined towards peace, then it was the indigenous portion of the plutocracy, which was able to calculate when it, along with the indigenous British tradition, would be destroyed, whereas the indigenous, mainly Jewish element, had already in large part completed the jump to America and the overseas dominions. It was Burckhardt's own and deepest concern that if the war continued for a considerable length of time every possibility that the reasonable forces in England would force Churchill to make peace would disappear, since by that time the whole power of decision regarding the overseas assets of the Empire would be taken over by the Americans. Once the remainder of the indigenous English upper class had been eliminated, however, it would be impossible to talk sense to Roosevelt and his circle.[42]

Hitler read Albrecht's report when he was still uncertain as to how Hess was being received in Britain, and he had no means of checking its truthfulness or accuracy. He gave orders that Haushofer was to be sent to the Prince Albrecht Strasse Gestapo prison in Berlin, so that he could be interrogated by SS Gruppenführer Mueller, chief of the Gestapo.

In the prison Albrecht was relatively well treated. His father, who had been arrested and then released after a short time, was allowed to visit him. The most unpleasant aspect of his imprisonment were the interrogations by Mueller, a coarse, ruthless and brutal man. Mueller continually accused him of sending Hess to Britain, but in no way was he able to incriminate Albrecht, although he regarded him with loathing and suspicion.[43]

There were other Nazi leaders interested in Albrecht and on 15 May 1941 Heydrich sent the following telegram to Himmler, after discussions with Albrecht's old enemy, Gauleiter Bohle of the Nazi Auslandsorganisation:

> 1. After today's conversation with Gauleiter Bohle, the result of which I am transmitting to you today by courier within the next few hours, I have the profound impression that Rudolf Hess was in a particular measure under the influence of both Haushofer senior and Haushofer junior. Gauleiter Bohle thinks that Haushofer junior in particular influenced Rudolf Hess in his evaluation of British neutrality. He [Bohle] is also convinced that Haushofer junior is well able to supply possibly valuable information. I share this view and I would ask your permission to have Haushofer junior thoroughly interrogated about his knowledge of the matter. In the meantime, I shall have his flat and office watched, so that, according to the result of the interrogation, any material found there can be seized. I shall of course once again ask for your views.
>
> The postal and telephone surveillance ordered a few days ago will be carried out . . .
>
> As regard the Item 1 I shall be glad of any early decision.[44]

It appears that Himmler gave Heydrich permission to interrogate Albrecht. One day Heydrich appeared in Albrecht's cell without warning and asked many questions, which resulted in Albrecht giving a long talk on the incompetence, inability and stupidity of Ribbentrop. He may well have convinced Heydrich that Ribbentrop was a disastrous Foreign Minister. However, Heydrich also believed that Albrecht was a potential traitor. Ribbentrop, who had been described in such disparaging terms to Hess and Heydrich by Albrecht, was smouldering with hostility. He sacked Albrecht from his position in the Foreign Office on 28

May and tried to get him suspended from his professorship, but without success, as Himmler refused to let him be removed. And Himmler had his reasons.

Himmler was enthusiastic about the planned war against Russia, but he had a clear sense of self-preservation. He wished to make peace with Britain, as he did not want to fight a war on two fronts. He therefore wanted to keep alive anyone who might help him to conduct such negotiations behind Hitler's back.[45] So when Lorenz of the SS recommended to Himmler that it was the right moment to finish off all the Haushofers, Himmler replied that he did not think it would be necessary yet.[46]

Nobody understood this situation better than Albrecht, who wrote to his parents from the Gestapo prison on 7 July 1941: 'I know exactly that at present I am a small beetle which has been turned on its back by an unexpected and unforeseeable gust of wind, and which realises that it cannot rise to its feet by its own strength.'[47] After Hess's flight Albrecht knew that he owed his survival to the fact that Hitler and Himmler had no wish for the time being to destroy an expert who might be able to formulate peace plans with Britain.[48] Consequently, Albrecht wrote 'Thoughts on a Peace Plan' for Hitler's consumption in November 1941, which was submitted to his friend Weizsaecker, the Secretary of State of the Ministry for Foreign Affairs. It can safely be assumed that Weizsaecker ensured that the document reached Hitler without it being seen or blocked by Foreign Minister Ribbentrop, who had become Albrecht's dedicated enemy.[49] His very lengthy document had no effect on practical politics but it did help to keep him alive for a considerable period, as Hitler took a decided interest.

Himmler had taken up the idea of making peace overtures precisely where Hess had left off. He knew a good deal about the German resistance to Hitler, but had good reason for wanting to keep Albrecht Haushofer alive, although he was having him watched after his release from prison. If the resistance were to eliminate Hitler and thereby destroy an obvious obstacle to peace negotiations, resisters like Albrecht Haushofer and Dohnanyi, the senior Abwehr official, who were believed to have connections in Britain and the USA, could be utilised as middlemen in a bid for peace with Britain.[50]

When the bomb planted by Stauffenberg exploded at Rastenburg on 24 July 1944, Albrecht knew that he was in imminent danger of arrest and went into hiding. On 7 December the Gestapo finally caught up with him and he was taken to Berlin.[51]

During the following days and months he was interrogated constantly. His connections with the resistance were established beyond doubt, and whatever Albrecht might say there was no adequate excuse to be given for his flight from Berlin after the July plot.[52]

The theologian Eberhard Bethge, also in Moabit prison, noticed that Albrecht enjoyed certain privileges, such as books, newspapers, pencils and writing paper: 'Haushofer . . . mentioned some very friendly interrogation when he was requested to write down things for Himmler. We believed that it was the intention to make use of Haushofer at a later date.'[53] What Albrecht wrote to his captors we do not know, but we do know that Albrecht was using his time and energies in writing his last work, *The Sonnets of Moabit*, which later made him famous throughout Germany. They were desperate poems set down by a man who keenly felt the destruction of his country, and knew that his days were almost certainly numbered.

By March 1945 Himmler's interest in Albrecht Haushofer was beginning to slacken because he had found a more suitable intermediary to take messages to the Western Allies. In February he met Count Folke Bernadotte of the Swedish Red Cross and in April he dispatched the Swedish Count with an offer to capitulate to the Western Allies (but not to the Russians). By this time Himmler no longer cared whether the last remnants of the resistance in Moabit prison lived or died and he was content to leave Albrecht Haushofer and his companions to the care of the head of the Gestapo.[54] At a meeting at the Reich Security Main Office on 21 April to discuss the future of the last prisoners in Moabit, Gestapo chief Mueller ordered Haushofer's execution.[55]

On 12 May Albrecht's body was found where he had been shot. Clutched in the dead man's hand were scraps of the manuscript of *The Sonnets of Moabit*. The thirty-eighth sonnet was called 'Guilt':

I lightly carry what the judge calls my guilt
Guilt in planning and caring
I would feel guilty had I not from inner duty
Planned for the people's future
But I am guilty other than you think:
I should have sooner seen my duty
I should have sharper condemned evil
I have too long delayed my judgement.
I now accuse myself
I have long betrayed my conscience
I have lied to myself and to others.
I soon foresaw the evil's frightful path;
I have warned,
But my warnings were too feeble,
I know today wherein lies my guilt.[56]

Albrecht's parents were still alive. In the aftermath of the July plot Karl Haushofer had been imprisoned in Dachau concentration camp for a short period, but even that experience had not shaken his loyalty to the German state. After the unconditional surrender Karl Haushofer was a broken man. He realised that all his teachings had been in vain, and he now said in explanation that his teachings had been misused by the Nazis, and that for the last seven years – especially since Hess had left for England – he had lived under the fear that his half-Jewish wife would be taken to Theresienstadt or Auschwitz.[57] In his 'Last Defence of German Geopolitics' he wrote that he had interceded with Hitler on 8 November 1938 because he had hoped that Hitler would be satisfied with the solution reached at Munich. He called the period from 1938 onwards 'The Way of Sorrow for German Geopolitics'.[58]

Karl Haushofer was not put on trial at Nuremberg because the American prosecuting team regarded his role as being academic and advisory.[59] He was taken to Nuremberg merely to see Hess who was alleged to be suffering from amnesia and who refused to recognise him. On his way to his lodgings, Karl Haushofer said that Hess was completely sincere in his fanatical support of Hitler, that his flight to Britain was characteristic of him, and that at no other time had Hess concealed his plans from him. While being driven back from Nuremberg he could see the ruins and devastation of the bombed city and he was dismayed.[60]

Throughout his life Karl Haushofer had been an admirer of the ancient Stoics and on 11 March 1946 he carried his admiration to its logical conclusion. On that Monday Karl and Martha Haushofer set out for their last walk through the woods. They stopped about half a mile from their house in a hollow by the stream under the willow tree where they took poison. They were found the next day by their son Heinz.[61]

At Nuremberg the court found Hess guilty of making preparations for war and conspiring against the peace; he was sentenced to life imprisonment and transferred to Spandau prison in Berlin.[62] Years later he spoke about his request to see the Duke of Hamilton in 1941, implying that he had been much influenced by the Haushofers. When cross-examined by Colonel Bird, he explained:

> It was the Haushofers who knew the Duke of Hamilton. Contrary to what books say since I flew, I had never met the man. Maybe I saw him across a room at a reception in Berlin and I certainly knew about him and his flying exploits. When I flew I took Haushofer's visiting card with me to present to him.[63]

It was the Haushofers who provided Hess with the knowledge and information required as to how to open up a channel of communication, although they never imagined that he would fly into British hands. Hess and the Haushofers wanted peace with Britain, at a time when Hitler's megalomania was thrusting him irrevocably in the direction of the dreaded war on two fronts. Of the three men Hess was the fanatical Nazi who hero-worshipped Hitler, but believed a war on two fronts could be disastrous for Germany; General Professor Karl Haushofer was the former artillery commander who wanted to avoid a protracted war with the British Empire; and his son Albrecht, an Anglophile, was the far-sighted special adviser who could see all too clearly the catastrophe which was about to overwhelm Europe and the civilised world.

It was the war which Hitler himself had warned against in *Mein Kampf* and the war which would lead to untold suffering, sorrow and sacrifice. It was also the war which would end with Hitler's suicide, the destruction of the German armed forces and cities, and the total annihilation of Hitler's dreams for a '1,000–year empire'.

Notes and References

The following publications and papers have provided documentary evidence for this chapter. The sources are given in detail in *Motive for a Mission: The Story Behind Hess's Flight to Britain*, by James Douglas-Hamilton, published by Macmillan in 1971. The second edition, which contained additional information, was published in 1979 by Mainstream and by Corgi in 1981 and it again published the sources fully.

The Truth about Rudolf Hess, published by Mainstream in 1993, had yet more information, and it gave the newer sources at the end of each chapter, the previous sources being well documented and well known.

The British Official papers including those of the Prime Minister Winston Churchill are held currently at the Public Record Office at Kew. The Haushofer Papers are in the German Federal Archives in Koblenz, with copies in the National Archives in Washington, DC, and other papers in the Manuscript Division of the Library of Congress, Washington, DC.

The Haushofer family papers are kept at Hartschimmelhof by Paehl, Bavaria, and the papers of the 14th Duke of Hamilton are accessible to scholars, having been catalogued by the Scottish Record Office.

1 Karl-Heinz Harbeck, *Die Zeitschrift für Geopolitik 1924–44* (Kiel University, 1963).
2 Edmund Walsh, *Total Power* (New York, 1948), p. 26.
3 Ibid., pp. 14–15; Konrad Heiden, *Der Fuehrer* (London, 1967), pp. 225, 254–5.
4 Fritz Thyssen, *I paid Hitler* (London, 1941), p. 129; Otto Dietrich, *The Hitler I Knew* (London, 1957), pp. 172–3; Heiden, *Der Fuehrer*, p. 127; *Trial of German Major War Criminals at Nuremberg Proceedings*, part VI, p. 148.
5 Hans Adolf Jacobsen, *Nationalsozialistische Außenpolitik 1933–38* (Metzner, 1968), pp. 587–8, 593, 790.
6 Federal Archives in Koblenz, HC833. Albrecht Haushofer's Memorandum for Hess, 'The Operation of Germany's Foreign Policy'; Weinberg, G.L; Secret Hitler/Beneš Negotiations in 1936–7; *Journal of Central European Affairs* (January, 1960), pp. 367–71.
7 *Journal of Central European Affairs* (January, 1960), pp. 368–71.
8 Hamilton Papers catalogued by the Scottish Record Office.
9 Walter Stubbe, 'In Memoriam Albrecht Haushofer', *Vierteljahreshefte für Zeitgeschichte* (July, 1960), pp. 239–42.
10 Ibid. p. 242

11 Fritz Hesse, *Das Spiel um Deutschland* (Munich, 1953); *Hitler and the English* (London, 1954), p. 155.

12 Hamilton Papers catalogued by the Scottish Record Office.

13 Rainer Hildebrandt, *Wir sind die Letzten* (Berlin, 1950), pp. 58, 99, 100, and chapter entitled 'No. 50 Brentano Strasse'.

14 Dr Ursula Michel, *Albrecht Haushofer and National Socialism*, Thesis (Kiel University, 1964), p. 262; Viscount Templewood (formerly Sir Samuel Hoare), *Ambassador on a Special Mission* (London, 1946), p. 275.

15 Documents on German Foreign Policy, 1918–45, Series D, vol. XI, pp. 15, 16 ff.

16 I.B.M. Hamilton, *General Sir Ian Hamilton* (London, 1966), pp. 448–9.

17 Documents on German Foreign Policy, 1918–45, Series D, vol. XI, pp. 78–81.

18 Hesse, *Hitler and the English*, p. 93.

19 Ilse Hess, *Prisoner of Peace* (London, 1954), p. 15.

20 Documents on German Foreign Policy, 1918–45 Series D, vol. XI, p. 81.

21 Dietrich, *The Hitler I Knew*, pp. 62–3.

22 Hartschimmelhof Papers, c/o Hartschimmelhof, by Paehl, Bavaria.

23 Documents on German Foreign Policy, 1918–45, Series D, vol. XI, pp. 60–1.

24 Federal Archives in Koblenz, HC832 (C.002.195).

25 Documents on German Foreign Policy, 1918–45, Series D, vol. XI, pp. 129–30.

26 Federal Archives in Koblenz, HC832 (C.002.197–202).

27 Ibid. (C.002.203).

28 Ibid. (C.002.204–5).

29 Hamilton Papers catalogued by the Scottish Record Office. A photocopy of the original letter is at the Public Record Office in FO 1093/12, folios 92–4.

30 Hamilton Papers catalogued by the Scottish Record Office.

31 Ibid.

32 Sir Winston Churchill, *History of the Second World War*, vol. 3, *The Grand Alliance* (London, 1950), p.43 ff.

33 Hildebrandt, *Wir sind die Letzten*, pp. 112–13.

34 Ibid. pp. 112–13.

35 Albert Speer, *Erinnerungen* (Berlin, 1969), p. 189; Dietrich, *The Hitler I Knew*, pp. 62–3; Dr Paul Schmidt, *Hitler's Interpreter* (New York, 1951), p. 233.

36 Speer, *Erinnerungen*, p. 189; Schmidt, *Hitler's Interpreter*, p. 233.

37 William Shirer, *The Rise and Fall of the Third Reich* (London, 1964) p. 998; Speer, *Erinnerungen* pp. 189–91. See also Albert Speer, *Inside the*

Third Reich (London, 1970), pp. 174–6, and Articles in *Weltbild*, second, third, fourth and fifth issues in 1951 under the title 'And This Fool Flies to England'.

38 Speer, *Erinnerungen*, p. 190.

39 *The Goebbels Diaries: 1939–41* (London, 1982), pp. 363–75, 424, 440; Curt Reiss, *Joseph Goebbels* (London, 1949), p. 205; Rudolf Semmler, *Goebbels, The Man Next to Hitler* (London, 1947) p. 32.

40 *The Goebbels Diaries, 1939–41*, pp. 363–75, 424, 440.

41 Stubbe, 'In Memoriam Albrecht Haushofer', pp. 253–4.

42 Documents on German Foreign Policy, 1918–45, Series D, vol. XII, pp. 783–7.

43 Hildebrandt, *Wir sind die Letzten*, pp. 114–15.

44 National Archives of the USA, Washington, DC, Record Group No. 242, T175 Roll 128.

45 Gerald Reitlinger, *The SS Alibi of a Nation* (London, 1956) pp. 160–6.

46 Michel, *Albrecht Haushofer and National Socialism*, p. 269.

47 Hartschimmelhof Papers, c/o Hartschimmelhof, by Paehl, Bavaria.

48 Reitlinger, *The SS Alibi of a Nation*, pp. 160–6; Michel, *Albrecht Haushofer and National Socialism*, p. 269; Rainer Hildebrandt also touches on the same theme in *Wir sind die Letzten*.

49 Ernst von Weizsaecker, *Memoirs* (London, 1951), p. 182.

50 Reitlinger, *The SS Alibi of a Nation*, pp. 289–313.

51 Hildebrandt, *Wir sind die Letzten*, p. 186.

52 Ibid., pp. 192, 196.

53 The Reverend Eberhard Bethge, *Dietrich Bonhoeffer. A Biography* (London, 1970), pp. 807–8; Bethge, letter to the author dated 4 January 1969.

54 Count Folke Bernadotte, *The Fall of the Curtain* (London, 1945); Hildebrandt, *Wir sind die Letzten*, p. 203.

55 Ibid., p. 204; Peter Paret, 'An Aftermath of the Plot against Hitler: The Lehrterstrasse Prison in Berlin 1944–5', *Bulletin of the Institute of Historical Research*, vol. 32, no. 85 (1959), pp. 88–93, 98.

56 Albrecht Haushofer, *The Sonnets of Moabit* (Berlin, 1948), no. 38.

57 Walsh, *Total Power*, p. 16.

58 Ibid., p. 351.

59 Ibid., p. 12.

60 Ibid., pp. 25–6.

61 Hildebrandt, *Wir sind die Letzten*, p. 129.

62 Walsh, *Total Power*, pp. 32–4.

63 *Trial of German Major War Criminals at Nuremberg Proceedings*, part XXII, pp. 487–9, 540–1; Eugene K. Bird, *The Loneliest Man in the World* (London, 1974), pp. 216–17, 250.

PETER LONGERICH

Hitler's Deputy: The Role of Rudolf Hess in the Nazi Regime

Those interested in the role of Rudolf Hess within the NSDAP and within the Nazi regime have for a number of years had at their disposal a substantial and, in this form at least, most probably unique collection of documents: the microfiche edition of Akten der Partei-Kanzlei der NSDAP (Documents of the Party Chancellery of the German National Socialist Party), which was published in two parts, in 1982 and 1992, by the Institut für Zeitgeschichte (Institute for Contemporary History) in Berlin. The aim of this project was to reconstruct the documents of one of the most important organisations of the Third Reich, which had largely been lost. For almost two decades, members of the Institute searched through the most important documentary archives of both party and state departments that contained indications about the activity of the Partei-Kanzlei (Party Chancellery) or of the Stab des Stellvertreters des Führers (Staff of the Deputy of the Führer), as this department was known before Hess's flight to Scotland in May 1941. This collection of more than 20,000 documents made possible exhaustive answers to the question of what role was played by Rudolf Hess, the Führer's Deputy, within the Third Reich.[1]

To understand the question, we have initially to go back to the early 1920s. At this period Hess was at university in Munich. He had been born in Alexandria in 1894, the son of a businessman, and after four years of military service as a lieutenant had been discharged from the army. In Munich two individuals came to exercise a decisive influence over him: he was a pupil of Professor Karl Haushofer and became a supporter of his geopolitical teachings; at the same time he was an enthusiastic disciple of the political newcomer and Party leader, Adolf Hitler. In November 1923 Hess was actively engaged in the so-called Beer Hall *Putsch*. After the *Putsch* failed he had the privilege – which is doubtless how he saw it – of spending seven months in Landsberg prison with his adored mentor Hitler. During this period in particular, he assisted Hitler with compiling the manuscript of *Mein Kampf*. In Landsberg Hess became an unconditional follower and admirer of Hitler.[2]

What followed was an eight-year assignment as Hitler's secretary. In a letter to his parents Hess justified his decision to devote himself full-time to politics in part by saying that he felt suited to act as 'a connecting link between the mass movement and the educated classes'.[3] Fragments of the correspondence from this period have survived and they provide us with some insight into the work of Hess as Hitler's private secretary. This private secretariat gave Hitler the means of circumventing the growing Party bureaucracy and of getting into direct contact with Party functionaries in the field. It also served as a kind of filter to keep Hitler out of conflicts and intrigues among rival factions of the Party. In his role as private secretary Hess acted mostly independently – answering letters in Hitler's name, for example.[4]

It is obvious that the basis for this close symbiosis between Hitler and Hess was Hess's deep loyalty towards Hitler (or to the 'tribune' as he called him in his private correspondence), and, in return, Hitler's trust in Hess's loyalty. This strict loyalty and obedience was decisive in Hitler's decision to give Hess a key position in the Party in December 1932, at a time when it found itself in perhaps its most severe crisis. In this situation Hitler appointed Hess the head of a new body, the Politische Zentralkommission der NSDAP (Party Central Commission), which was in effect responsible for all the sensitive areas of Nazi policy in this difficult phase of transition between the late Weimar Republic and the Nazi 'seizure of power' in 1933.[5]

After this crisis was finally overcome, in April 1933 Hitler appointed Hess his Deputy in Party affairs and gave him *carte blanche* to make decisions in his name in all matters concerning the Party leadership.[6] Hess succeeded in getting a new title, but in fact this appointment was a form of continuation and expansion of his earlier role as a private secretary.

During the next two years Hess managed to expand and secure this position, and built up a substantial office with several hundred employees. Naturally he could not have done this without the support of an energetic Party functionary, Martin Bormann, whom he appointed his chief of staff in July 1933.[7]

One of the things that contributed to the consolidation of Hess's power was his absolute loyalty to Hitler during the so-called 'Röhm Crisis' of 1934. When the conflict between the political organisation of the Party and the SA, the paramilitary corps of the NSDAP, flared up again in the first half of 1934, Hess played a significant role in the Party leadership's policy of disciplining the discontented 'Brown Shirts'. This conflict mainly concerned the demands of the SA – which numbered several million members – for greater influence on the exercise of power. In this context the SA used the slogan – 'continuing the National Socialist Revolution', after Hitler had officially declared in summer 1933 that the revolution of National Socialism was over. The background to the conflict was the growing general dissatisfaction of the population.[8]

The Party leadership's campaign against the demands of the SA for the continuation of the revolution reached its height on 25 June 1934 when Hess made a speech in Cologne that was broadcast by all German radio stations. In this speech Hess established that the person of the Führer was above all criticism: 'He has always been right, and he will always be right. In uncritical loyalty, in devotion to the Führer that does not ask about the whys and wherefores of individual cases, in the silent execution of his orders – that is where the National Socialism of us all lies anchored.'[9] After this oath of loyalty, Hess delivered a clear warning to the SA leadership in unambiguous terms:

> Woe to those who break their allegiance in the belief that they are able to serve the revolution by means of a revolt. They are poor in spirit who believe themselves chosen to serve the Führer in revolutionary fashion by agitating from below.

Hess's speech plainly shows the important public role of the Führer's Deputy. It was not the Führer himself, in a position beyond all internal rivalries, but his Deputy who urged the people to absolute loyalty and delivered a final warning to the opposition within their own ranks. Five days later, on 30 June 1934, Hitler was to dismiss the leadership of the SA around Ernst Röhm and have many of them murdered, along with various critics of the regime from the conservative camps.

In order to understand Hess's position in the Third Reich, closer attention must be paid to the role and the mission of his office, the Stab des Stellvertreters des Führers. In essence, this office had two different tasks: directing the Party in Hitler's name, and controlling the state apparatus.

As deputy of the Führer Hess's role was not only to execute Hitler's orders. Hess operated on the 'philosophical' assumption that a particular sphere of power existed in the Third Reich, the power of the Führer, the will of the Führer, an absolute power, which – in principle – could not be challenged and could not be limited. Hess held the conviction that he and his office were the essential expression and instrument of this particular sphere of power. His position had been created by Hitler alone and therefore its very existence meant that he acted in Hitler's name. Hitler's unlimited power was the legitimation of Hess's own actions.[10] Because Hitler's power was unlimited, Hess and Bormann consistently refused to define the competences of their office in any detail. They even refused to hand over to other institutions charts that would indicate the internal organisation of their office.[11]

If we take into account the particular position that Hess held, his extreme loyalty to Hitler and his dependence on him were not merely incidental aspects of his personality; they were necessary tools for securing and expanding his position as Hitler's Deputy for Party affairs.

In order to lead and direct the Party in Hitler's name, the Office of the Deputy of the Führer first of all pursued the strategy of strengthening the hierarchical structure of the Party. In particular, it tried to bring the conglomerate of heterogeneous organisations that made up the Nazi movement under the control of the regional and local chiefs of the political organisation of the Party, i.e. the Gauleiter, the Kreisleiter and the Ortsgruppenleiter.[12]

The Office of the Führer's Deputy managed to gain control over large areas of personnel policy within the Party. For example, the Office was successful in appointing a number of new Gauleiter, which could be described as a new generation of Party managers, who had been selected from the Party cadre by the Stab des Stellvertreters des Führers and who had worked in that Office.[13]

To some extent Hess's Office also managed to control and unify the stream of decrees issued by different Offices within the Party, and it therefore established a kind of Party legislation. Bormann, who became a member of Hitler's entourage, also managed to monopolise access to Hitler. He was extremely successful in preventing other high-ranking officials from finding out from personal conversations with Hitler whether the actions of Hess and the Office always reflected the will of the Führer.[14]

On the other hand the attempts of the Office of the Führer's Deputy to bring the Party under full control had clear limits: in the end, it was only able to act in Hitler's name. As the documents compiled in the project Akten der Partei-Kanzlei show, the Office was forced in many instances to expend much time and energy in proving that its work was backed by the Führer. In order to strengthen the hierarchical structure of the Party, it fostered the increasing bureaucratisation of the Party machinery, and thereby paradoxically strengthened the position of Hess's opponents and limited its own power.

In addition, the Staff of the Führer's Deputy attempted to monopolise certain internal Party functions by appointing a number of 'special representatives' and 'experts', and by establishing other commissions and offices that were mostly only related to the Staff proper in a fairly loose way.[15] Some of these 'special representatives' created extensive offices, but often it was merely a question of consolidating the relationship of the heads of existing offices with the Staff proper by giving them an additional title. Some of these 'special representatives' and 'experts' functioned as executive organs of the Staff; others, however, used their appointment to the Staff only as a means of securing their position within the Party. The growth in the authority of the Staff of the Führer's Deputy is therefore to be regarded as ambivalent in many respects.

Thus the future Foreign Minister Ribbentrop, who received

special commissions from Hitler from 1934 and in this capacity operated under the Foreign Ministry, was at the same time given 'special responsibility for foreign affairs' by Hess. In this capacity Ribbentrop maintained his own office, and this made him independent of the Foreign Ministry. In addition, Hess made the Secretary of State in the Treasury, Fritz Reinhardt (a National Socialist of long standing), his 'expert on all questions of finance and tax policy'. As such, for example, Reinhardt represented the Führer's Deputy in discussions about the drafting of tax and finance law. In 1937, to give one further example, Albert Speer, Hitler's Generalbauinspektor (Inspector-General of Building for the Reich Capital) was simultaneously given 'special responsibility for construction' in Hess's Staff. But Hess also maintained a 'Department for Matters of Special Technical Importance', which dealt among other things with inventions presented to Hitler.[16] In total there were nearly forty 'special representatives', 'experts' and other Special Offices of the Staff, all of which together made up an impenetrable and heterogeneous conglomerate of responsibilities. This nomination policy stood in stark contrast to the other attempts of the Staff of the Führer's Deputy to reinforce the hierarchical structure of the Party.

The second main area of Hess's Office was the attempt at controlling the state apparatus. In order to achieve this, Hess's Office had to make sure that it was the sole, or at least the highest representative of the Party *vis-à-vis* the state. In principle this was acknowledged in 1933 when Hess was appointed to the cabinet as a minister. But in fact it turned out that the basic precondition for an effective control of the state by the Party – a clear separation of state and Party functions – was never achieved. In fact the Party took over state functions at all levels and managed to escape the control of a central institution like Hess's Office. What Hess's Office did achieve was a form of veto position in the process of legislation. The appointment and promotion of higher civil servants were also dependent on the approval of Hess's Office, and it also claimed the right to intervene in any matter of fundamental political significance.

The impact of these attempts at state control was mixed. Hess's Office could certainly delay, modify or even block many of the measures planned by the state bureaucracy, but it never succeeded in controlling the state machinery effectively. It could clearly hold up the career of civil servants, but it failed to infiltrate the bureaucracy with a new elite of devoted National Socialists. In fact the Office found itself engaged in endless infighting with the state apparatus, in which the main tactic of the bureaucrats – delaying matters – proved most effective.[17]

The Second World War had ambivalent effects on Hess's position within the dictatorship. Hess was not involved directly in the military or diplomatic preparations for war, or in the economic preparations for rearmament, but at the start of the war his position was conspicuously enhanced: on 1 September Hitler declared that Goering would be his successor if anything were to happen to him, and that Hess was to take over the leadership if Goering should also be lost.[18] Furthermore, Hess became a member of the Ministerial Council for the Defence of the Reich, an inner cabinet that was formed mainly in order to be able to pass laws rapidly but which was not intended to perform the function of a war cabinet.

The enhanced rank that Hess enjoyed at the start of the war brought to the fore the greater importance that the Party had during the war. The NSDAP became the keystone for holding together the home front. It was given responsibility for many war-related tasks, such as the care of evacuees, the distribution of ration coupons, the collection of materials important to the war effort, and above all small-scale propaganda intended to raise the 'mood' on the home front – while the Gauleiter were given increasingly important responsibilities for the co-ordination of regional state administration. The Party also succeeded in assuming a greater role in the administration of the areas annexed since 1938 than elsewhere in the Reich. From this emerged a plethora of new tasks for the Führer's Deputy. Above all Hess was to interest himself personally in the supply situation of the population and the improvement of the 'mood', and that also involved the task of adapting the public face of Party functionaries to the conditions obtaining in time of war.[19]

Despite this important role on the home front, Hess was not involved in the actual conduct of the war or in decision-making on political and strategic questions. He will thus have been informed in a general sense about the planned attack on the Soviet Union, but will not have been aware of planning details or about the precise timing of the attack. It is unfortunately not possible to be more precise than this, because of the lack of documentation.

Although Hess's activities tended to increase after the start of the war, and despite his formal elevation in rank, the longer the war lasted, the more removed he became from the inner circle of power. Overcoming this distance (and thereby re-establishing his absolute loyalty to Hitler) via an extraordinary independent initiative may have been part of the psychological motivation for Hess's decision to undertake his solitary 'mission' in May 1941

As the Führer's Deputy, Hess never spent much time in his office but left the daily routine to Bormann. He was clearly not an efficient bureaucrat, nor was he very much interested in many of the routine details of the work of state and Party bureaucracy. But it would be completely false to assume that Hess neglected his duties as the Deputy of the Führer, or that he had no further political ambitions after the establishment of the National Socialist dictatorship. Hess, who was not fond of paperwork, kept himself constantly informed of the work being done by his Staff via verbal presentations. He left most matters to be dealt with by Bormann and his staff, but continually took up himself things that particularly interested him, including both fundamental issues and matters of detail.[20] These were above all topics that were among the central ideological objectives of National Socialism, and these will be discussed in detail below. Hess was particularly concerned about preserving his areas of authority, and made sure that at public functions he was treated as the second-in-command within the Nazi hierarchy.[21]

It would also be completely wrong to assess Hess's role in the Third Reich primarily according to the efficiency or the commitment with which he led his Staff. As the Führer's Deputy, Hess had above all a public function. He served as a kind of medium between the Führer and the *Volk*, principally in two different but complementary roles: as high priest of the cult of the Führer, and as keeper of the Holy Grail – as he saw it – of the Nazi Party's true values. This double role was described by one of the Nazi papers in a tribute for his forty-fifth birthday in 1939 as that of *Künder und Mahner* (herald and prophet). According to this piece, Hess was the man who 'more than any of the movement's other mouthpieces, was the herald of the National Socialist idea and thus the servant of Adolf Hitler's mission'. On the other hand the people also saw in him 'the wakeful prophet, ensuring that National Socialism remains pure and undistorted, that everything that happens in the name of National Socialism is truly National Socialist'.[22]

As far as his role as 'herald' was concerned, it is fair to say that, after Goebbels, Hess was clearly the main architect of the myth of the Führer. Hess voiced what was evidently a deeply felt veneration of Adolf Hitler in countless speeches in which, whenever he came to speak of the person of the Führer, he always assumed a solemn and respectful declamatory style. As an example taken from this vast source of rhetorical deference may stand the speech that Hess made in Kiel on 14 August 1939, after Hitler's assumption of the office of Reichspräsident, in which he attributed 'supernatural powers' to the Führer sent by 'Providence':

> However great is the need of our people, so great is the man who was to come and overcome this need. Providence gave him the gifts and powers to take the favourable and unfavourable circumstances that he found and which were developing with time, and to employ them for the attainment of his goal: the salvation of Germany! Providence works through him in a mysterious way, but one that is at the same time evident to all those who have the good fortune to be able to observe him in his doings from close proximity. How often he said to me, 'I know that this decision of mine or this action of mine is right; I cannot say at the moment why, but I feel that it is right, and the course of events will prove its rightness.' With unfailing regularity this mysterious feeling proved to have led the Führer along the right path.[23]

This unconditional admiration for, and absolute devotion to, Hitler was not simply a facet of his own personal mentality or psychology but must be seen as an element necessary for the smooth functioning of the charismatic dictatorship of the Third Reich – and for Hess's own position within this system. It was Hess's role as Hitler's Deputy, as the Party mouthpiece, continually to stress Hitler's supposedly extraordinary and super-natural capacities and thus to legitimise his position of unshackled power – and in the shadow of this unshackled power to establish his own position of authority.

In his role as 'prophet' Hess was principally concerned with maintaining discipline within the Party. Mention has already been made of the public role he played in removing the opposition from within the Party in 1934 when he delivered a final warning to the Party leadership in June of that year. In the years to come, as National Socialist power was consolidated, this 'prophet' role took on a more kindly and considerate aspect; Hess became a sort of ombudsman for the Party. In the Party's propaganda he was portrayed as the 'wailing wall', or its moral conscience. He was presented as 'the good Nazi', a modest man, a man of integrity, someone with no lust for personal power and representation, a fellow Party member concerned about the ordinary day-to-day problems of the population, and somebody who felt the need to raise his voice from time to time to intervene on behalf of common people. Hess contributed to this image with his modest manner, his ascetic mode of living and his general rejection of all forms of pomp.

Hess's role as 'prophet' was important in two respects. On the one hand he embodied the opposite of the 'peacocks', a group not well liked among the populace, career functionaries of the NSDAP, whose extravagant lifestyle and tyrannical or arbitrary exercise of power were among the most common targets of popular criticism. On the other hand, his Staff generated a constant stream of directives that called to order Party functionaries who had exceeded their competences.[24] These efforts were consolidated by Hess's public appearances.

In particular, he used his annual speech to the Party functionaries at the Nuremberg Party Rally to warn them about their public behaviour. His patronising attitude to the Party functionaries became obvious when he used the Party Rally to express his concerns about the health of the Party Functionary Corps. Repeatedly he asked them not to smoke too much, to abstain from the abuse of alcohol, to do some sport – but not too much, so as not to threaten their health – and to work harder, but not too hard.[25]

These appearances might have contributed to his image as an unworldly outsider in Party circles, where after the establishment of the regime it was customary to give oneself up completely to the enjoyment of power. He became more and more isolated and found himself largely excluded from the political process. Skiing and flying were among his favourite activities. He was an introvert, and his behaviour is described in contemporary sources as reserved.[26]

During the 1930s Hess, who was plagued by a variety of illnesses, developed a growing interest in alternative medicine and diets. He was profoundly interested in astrology, anthroposophy, the occult and related areas. He expressed his interests in more practical ways. In 1937 he took on the patronage of the Twelfth International Homeopaths' Congress in Berlin and succeeded in founding a 'Rudolf Hess Academy for Modern German Medicine', which was based in Dresden alongside a hospital likewise named after him.[27]

Many of the people who met him simply found his behaviour increasingly curious. Shortly after the beginning of the war, when he was presiding over a meeting of high-ranking state and Party officials to discuss the food situation within the Reich, he obviously saw a chance to use this unique opportunity of improving the German people's diet. He was particularly interested in the question of whether food could be broken down better if taken at the same time as liquid, a suggestion rejected by the Secretary of State of the Ministry for Agriculture as absurd. Hess then turned to the Reichsärzteführer (head of the organisation of Nazi doctors) and tried to persuade him that infants should not drink unboiled milk because of the danger of tuberculosis. At the end of the meeting he announced a propaganda campaign for wholemeal bread.[28]

Hess also left a decidedly odd impression on the American Under-Secretary of State, Sumner Welles, when they met for a discussion in the context of Welles's peace mission in March 1940: 'the effect he made upon me at the time was that of a man who had only the lowest order of intelligence'. During the meeting Hess is said to have stared fixedly at the papers prepared for him so that Welles received the impression that Hess was merely reporting the position taken by the Foreign Ministry and was not capable of making any contribution of his own. The American diplomat's conclusions were thus: 'Hess was patently of abnormal mentality. His was a personality subject to domination by a stronger character.'[29]

Of course it would be very easy and tempting for a biographer of Hess to portray him as a loner, an eccentric or a lunatic, who was increasingly excluded from the inner circle of power and who tried – desperately – to win back the love of his tribune by the outstanding, courageous operation that came to its conclusion in Scotland in May 1941. It might also be persuasive to try to present him as someone who wanted to distance himself from Nazi policy and took refuge in illness and hocus-pocus. I would argue that such attempts to caricature Hess are misguided. In addition to his role as a medium, as a 'herald' and 'prophet', it is important to stress that Hess was still a politician who vigorously pursued essential parts of the Nazi Party programme. The files of Hess's Office show that he was a politician who had a strong interest in many of the central matters dealt with by his Office. In these areas he would express his opinion in lengthy memoranda and in detailed instructions to his Staff. Thus, Hess displayed particular interest in the whole field of National Socialist family and population policy, especially in questions of marital and family law. He interceded to have existing regulations altered when this seemed favourable to more active policies on behalf of the family.

Shortly after the beginning of the war, when Hess was asked for help by a young woman who was expecting a child by her fiancé, a soldier who had been killed in the war against Poland, he replied with a detailed letter that was circulated to the press during the Christmas period as a 'Letter to an Unmarried Mother'. Hess first declared that he was prepared to stand as the child's godfather. As to their care, he suggested that mother and child should be treated as if the marriage had already taken place. Hess announced that this individual case was the stimulus for creating general regulations for the treatment of pregnant women in the same circumstances.

> Thus if racially pure young men who are sent into the field leave behind children to pass on their blood for future generations, children by mothers of a similar age and of equal genetic health, with whom an immediate marriage is for whatever reason not possible, then the maintenance of this valuable national asset will be assured.

While he conceded that the family was 'the necessary

fundamental unit of the state', he also insisted that in time of war a people should not neglect 'the furtherance and maintenance of its racially healthy inheritance to the greatest possible extent'. Hess was therefore giving expression to his firm conviction that the 'entire German people' would in future stand by those mothers 'who, beyond the boundaries of what is otherwise perhaps sound bourgeois convention and custom, help to compensate for the losses suffered during the war'.[30] Hess saw to it that the Minister for the Interior brought about the appropriate legal process, and when the consultation on the draft was not proceeding quickly enough, prompted it once more – albeit in vain.[31]

In the spring of 1940 Hess took issue with the draft of a directive that planned to punish adultery committed with the wives of members of the armed forces. This idea he said was a 'defamation of German womanhood'.[32] In April 1941, going into some detail, Hess expressed reservations about the draft of another directive aimed at preventing marriage in cases where the man was more than twenty years older or more than ten years younger than his future wife. Although he believed in principle in the 'ban on marriage on grounds of difference in age', he thought that so rigid a proscription was 'not fair to the multiplicity of life'. He felt that the proposed regulation would in certain circumstances prevent marriages that might produce children, and his view was that a brief period of child-raising by the parents together was preferable to the woman's not having children at all. A more flexible regulation should therefore be made.[33]

A second area in which Hess displayed great interest was the regime's anti-Jewish policies. The Staff of the Führer's Deputy pursued the policy of unceasing restriction of the lives of Jews by constantly exerting its influence over Party and state.[34] This stance corresponded completely to the anti-Semitic convictions of Hess, who never concealed his attitude. His first political essay, which probably dates from 1921, was a defamatory anti-Semitic pamphlet,[35] and he would maintain this stance consistently throughout his political career. Thus, for example, he openly declared his anti-Jewish views in a speech he made on 14 May 1935 to the German-Swedish Society in Stockholm: he was not, he said, naturally hostile to Jews, but felt more inclined to protect Jews against unjust attacks; he had nonetheless found the 'facts of 1918 and afterwards . . . to be so blatant' that he was 'obliged to acknowledge his anti-Semitism', however much he felt reluctant within himself 'to correct his previous conviction of the innocence of persecuted Jewry'. National Socialist law had 'intervened to correct their domination', he said, but Judaism in Germany had by no means been 'ruthlessly exterminated'.[36]

Just over a year later, during his annual speech at the Reichsparteitag (Party Conference), Hess struck a significantly more radical tone. The concept of an 'extermination' no longer looked to be completely unthinkable: 'It is my firm conviction that we still face hard battles; but this notwithstanding, I am just as firmly convinced that Judaism has already lost its battle.' After talking about atrocities allegedly perpetrated by Jews in the Spanish Civil War, which had just begun, he went on to say: 'And the columns of fire over the most magnificent cultural monuments will one day perhaps be described as torches on the Jewish people's road to destruction. . . . We are aware of the brutal force that Jews will sooner or later perhaps attempt to employ in order to crush their great opponents and take revenge.'[37] In his Party Conference speech of 1937 Hess abused the Soviet Foreign Minister, calling him a 'disgusting Jew'.[38] After the pogrom of 9 November he spoke about criticism received from abroad when 'a few Jews had their windows broken' in Germany.[39]

A few days after the beginning of the Second World War, Hess called up 'anti-Jewish material' from the main archive of the NSDAP in order to use it in 'propaganda in England and France'. The 'striking power' of the material was to be 'Germany's battle against plutocrats, against the wealth in the hands of the Jews'. A similar request for material was directed to the 'chief ideologist' of the NSDAP, Alfred Rosenberg.[40] In the next few months Hess was to draw heavily on the copious material that he received from both these sources. Thus in a speech on 2 May 1940 he explained to workers of the Krupp factory in Essen – in a degree of detail that he was so fond of – the allegedly extensive international connections of the Hambros, the Jewish 'family of plutocrats'.[41]

No less obvious was the great personal interest of the Führer's Deputy in National Socialist ecclesiastical politics. Hess set great store by suppressing ecclesiastical influence in public life. This stance was perfectly consonant with the policies of his department which used its leading role within the Party and its capacity for control over the state apparatus as a means of pushing the churches further and further away from public prominence. Hess reinforced this fundamental attitude with a series of personal decisions. In May 1940, for example, he demanded resistance to the practice of sending confessional literature to the troops, because it had a deleterious effect on their morale. And an edict from January 1941 forbidding Catholic parish libraries from lending non-religious literature was made at his particular request.[42]

On the other hand, Hess was perfectly willing to be influenced by carefully considered tactical considerations when it was a question of weighing up against each other the possibly ambivalent effects of anti-ecclesiastical measures. Thus in a six-page statement written in April 1940, Hess made a detailed response to the Minister for Education's intention to subject the religious instruction organised by the church to stronger state supervision. Despite welcoming this plan in principle, Hess advised against taking decisive steps in this direction, at least during the war.[43]

To conclude, I would argue that the surviving files from Hess's Office show him not as an unworldly outsider but as a politician whose interest was confined to a relatively small number of political areas that were related to the central elements of Nazi ideology. He invested much time and energy, and deployed a strong grasp of detail, in implementing these political aims. If we consider in addition his two roles as one of the most important proponents of the cult of the Führer and as the 'conscience of the Party', then Hess emerges as one of the most important pillars of the National Socialist regime.

Notes and References

1 *Akten der Partei-Kanzlei der NSDAP. Rekonstruktion eines verlorengegangenen Bestandes. Sammlung der in anderen Provenienzen überlieferten Korrespondenzen, Niederschriften von Besprechungen usw. Mit dem Stellvertreter des Führers und seinem Stab bzw. der Partei-Kanzlei, ihren Ämtern, Referaten und Unterabteilungen sowie mit Hess und Bormann persönlich*, ed. by the Institut für Zeitgeschichte, pt I , 3 vols, compiled by Helmut Heiber et al. (Munich, 1983); pt II, 3 vols, compiled by Peter

Longerich (Munich, 1992). The introduction to part II of this project, a history of the Staff of the Deputy of the Führer and of the Party Chancellery, was printed as a separate volume: Peter Longerich, *Hitlers Stellvertreter. Führung der Partei und Kontrolle des Staatsapparates durch den Stab Hess und die Partei-Kanzlei Bormanns* (Munich, 1992). Since then a comprehensive biography has been published: Kurt Pätzold and Manfred Weissbecker, *Rudolf Hess. Der Mann an Hitlers Seite* (Leipzig, 1999).

2 Pätzold and Weissbecker, *Rudolf Hess*, pp. 54 ff.

3 Letter of 24 April 1925, printed in *Rudolf Hess. Briefe 1908–1933*, Wolf Rüdiger Hess (ed.) (Munich and Vienna, 1987), p. 366 ff.

4 Longerich, *Hitlers Stellvertreter*, p. 8 f.; Pätzold and Weissbecker, *Rudolf Hess*, p. 58 ff.

5 Longerich, *Hitlers Stellvertreter*, p. 9 f.

6 Order of Hitler's of 27 April 1933, printed in *Völkischer Beobachter*, 28 April 1933; cf. Longerich, *Hitlers Stellvertreter*, p. 8 ff.

7 Longerich, *Hitlers Stellvertreter*, pp. 10 ff. and 146 ff.

8 For the background, see Peter Longerich, *Die braunen Bataillone. Geschichte der SA* (Munich, 1989), p. 206 ff.

9 Rudolf Hess, *Reden* (Munich, 1938), p. 15.

10 Longerich, *Hitlers Stellvertreter*, p. 91 ff.

11 *Akten der Partei-Kanzlei*, pt I: Mf 117 04010–04015, Bormann to Ley, 31 August 1939.

12 Longerich, *Hitlers Stellvertreter*, p. 12.

13 Ibid., p. 99 ff.

14 Ibid., p. 93 ff.

15 Ibid., p. 24 ff.

16 Ibid., p. 16. The existence of this office explains for instance why in March 1941 Hitler ordered a plan he had been given for large stretches of the English Channel to be covered by a smoke screen to be passed on to Hess. Cf. *Der Dienstkalender Heinrich Himmlers 1941/42*, compiled by Peter Witte et al. (Hamburg, 1999), 7 and 15 March 1941.

17 Longerich, *Hitlers Stellvertreter*, p. 40 ff.

18 *Völkischer Beobachter*, 2 September 1939.

19 Longerich, *Hitlers Stellvertreter*, p. 184; Pätzold and Weissbecker, *Rudolf Hess*, p. 207 ff.

20 Ibid., p. 114 ff; ibid., p. 94 ff.

21 Ibid., p. 90 ff; ibid., p. 92.

22 *NS-Rheinfront*, 26 May 1939. (Editor's Note: There is no exact translation in English for the word *Mahner*. One meaning is 'admonisher', and it also carries the connotation of 'enforcer' or 'mentor'. The use of the word 'prophet' here should be read with that in mind.)

23 Hess, *Reden*, p. 52 ff.

24 Josef Henke (ed.), *Parteikanzlei der NSDAP. Bestand NS 6, Teil 2: Parteiverlautbarungen* (Koblenz, 1991).

25 Bundesarchiv (BA), NS 26/183, contains a collection of his speeches at the Nuremberg Party Rally.

26 Longerich, *Hitlers Stellvertreter*, p. 113.

27 Hess, *Reden*, p. 260 ff.; *Akten der Partei-Kanzlei*, pt II, Mf 10381 f., 10394.

28 *Akten der Partei-Kanzlei*, pt II, 70474 ff., 15 November 1939.

29 Sumner Welles, *The Time of Decision* (New York, 1944), p. 110 f.

30 *Akten der Partei-Kanzlei*, pt I, Mf 101 22562–22578.

31 Longerich, *Hitlers Stellvertreter*, p. 110 ff.

32 *Akten der Partei-Kanzlei*, pt I, Mf 101 08666–08704.

33 Ibid., Mf 101 27578–27580.

34 Longerich, *Hitlers Stellvertreter*, p. 210 ff.

35 'Der Nationalsozialismus in München', mentioned in Pätzold and Weissbecker, *Rudolf Hess*, p. 219.

36 Hess, *Reden*, p. 104.

37 BA, NS26/1183.

38 Quoted from Pätzold and Weissbecker, p. 217.

39 *Völkischer Beobachter*, 2 December 1938.

40 BA 26/1413; Longerich, *Hitlers Stellvertreter*, p. 116.

41 BA, NS 23/1183.

42 *Akten der Partei-Kanzlei*, pt I, Mf 103 01673–01675, 103 04364 f.

43 The statement (18 April 1940) is quoted in John S. Conway, *Die nationalsozialistische Kirchenpolitik 1933–1945. Ihre Ziele, Widersprüche und Fehlschläge* (Munich, 1969) pp. 372 ff.

LEN DEIGHTON

Hess the Aviator

. . . it now seems likely that two separate aircraft were involved. Circumstantial evidence suggests that Hess may have been shot down by the Luftwaffe while leaving German airspace . . . the absence of certain known distinguishing marks on the body of the last prisoner of Spandau have led medical authorities to conclude that it was not Hess.'[1]

This entry is to be found in the second edition of the *Macmillan Dictionary of the Second World War*, published in 1995. The two authors were scholars at Cambridge and Oxford. It is evident that controversial theories about Hess are not confined to cranks on the internet.

Some conclusions do not withstand scrutiny. Albert Speer, who spent twenty years in Spandau prison with Hess, dismissed the suggestion he was anyone other than the man he had known before 1941. The theory of a substitute aircraft is also difficult to sustain. The Messerschmitt BF 110 at Augsburg had been painted with the letters VJ+OQ , which correspond with the large section of fuselage that was dumped in Castlehill coal depot at Carluke, Glasgow, by the No. 63 Maintenance Unit of the RAF. It is currently on display at the Imperial War Museum in London. The flying overalls that Hess borrowed from Helmut Kaden for the flight were still in the possession of Hess in Spandau on the day he died.

Most conspiracy theories centre upon the flight that Hess made. Could this man, who was variously described as being anything from unintelligent to psychotic,[2] have planned, prepared and made this 900-mile flight at night in wartime and landed by parachute with such remarkable accuracy? This is the question I will try to answer.

When the First World War began in July 1914 Hess was twenty years old. He volunteered for the Bavarian army and by the end of that year had been accepted into an elite infantry regiment: the 1st Bavarian Foot. As the war carried on he was continually engaged in combat. He won the Iron Cross second class and suffered several serious wounds, including a punctured lung. After officer training he was, in the normal German army method, sent to serve a probationary period as a senior NCO (*Vizefeldwebel*). At about the same time as his commission was approved, so was his application for pilot training. After the aviation physical in Munich he wrote home on 3 January 1918 to say 'nerves, lungs, heart all perfect' and added that his eyesight was above average. The medical board seemed rather less convinced. They said he could become a flyer only because he was unfit for the infantry! His mother, while regretting the additional hazards, told him that she felt he was well suited for the flying corps because of his strength, presence of mind and sang-froid.[3] Someone seemed to share her view because the army sent him to fly their Fokker D-VII, which was one of the finest aircraft of that war. Hess flew with Jagdstaffel 35 and engaged in air battles over the Western Front but within a week of his arrival the war had ended.

Few German military aviators ever flew again after the war, but Hess was one of the rare exceptions. In Munich in 1920, when he first met Ilse Pröhl, the woman he married, Hess was wearing his army uniform with an arm badge of Freikorps Epp. He had been flying with the air component of Epp's anti–Marxist 'army' which had returned from suppressing a Communist seizure of power in the Ruhr. That was probably the way he explained it to Ilse, although more exact accounts[4] say that on 29 March 1920 he was employed by the Reichswehr Fliegerhorst Schleissheim to ferry aircraft to a Bavarian unit in the Ruhr. Whatever his actual employment, it did not last long. On the last day of April he resigned and went back to his studies.

Hess was a man of obsessions. He did not mind who knew this; he thought it desirable that men should be so. He was obsessed with aviation, he was obsessed with politics and most of all he was obsessed with Adolf Hitler. Hess was one of half a dozen men – others included Alfred Rosenberg and Dietrich Eckart – who directly influenced Hitler's thinking. In 1924 Hess spent months in Landsberg prison in free association with Adolf Hitler. Joachim Fest[5] – said by Albert Speer to be a particularly reliable biographer – says 'The notion of living space seems to have been a borrowing from Rudolf Hess.' The notion of *Lebensraum* as motive for colonial expansion had been a German obsession for many years before Hitler's birth, as Ian Kershaw's recent work points out.[6] But the overseas colonial geopolitics of Karl Haushofer (a close friend of Hess) evolved into a plan to wage war upon Eastern Europe's 'sub-humans' and if necessary eliminate them. This was the demented theory that was taking shape in Hitler's mind when he emerged from prison and began to reorganise his Nazi Party.

Hess's formal education enabled him to provide a structure upon which Hitler's disparate, disorganised, facile and emotional ideas could be arranged. The Nazi Party programme always remained a vague ragbag of ideas but this contrived structure was to stand Hitler in good stead when Otto Strasser, using uncomplicated socialist theories, tried to take over the Nazi Party. And it was Hess's business training, and the background provided by his father's prosperous trading agency, that made Hess an effective emissary when Hitler sought donations from tycoons such as Fritz Thyssen. The resulting large injection of cash transformed the Nazi Party and was a decisive factor in the final push for seats in the Reichstag.

The new affluent face of the Nazi Party was to be seen on 10 August 1930 when Hess was flying a sports plane painted to advertise the name of the Nazi Party newspaper. Having obtained a Class A private pilot's licence in 1929, Hess purchased a Messerschmitt M 23b. In 1930 two more M 23 monoplanes were registered in his name. These sports monoplanes were two-seaters and could be used as training aircraft or taxis. Anyone who suspected that Hess was given Nazi Party money to buy them – they cost 13,000 RM each – would have had even fewer doubts when on 10 August 1930 Hess flew low over a mass meeting of socialist war veterans and circled for three hours to drown out the speeches with engine noise.

When the Nazi Party formed a government in 1933 he was made a cabinet minister. Hess set up a number of offices and departments, and appointed a junior official named Martin Bormann as his chief of staff. One of the offices was devoted to technical questions. As its chief he appointed Theo Croneiss, a wartime pilot and by now senior director and test pilot for BFW Bayerische Flugzeugwerke AG. This company (later to be renamed Messerschmitt GmbH Regensburg) was coming to terms with the unpleasant fact that the government would control both commercial and military aviation (although the existence of the Luftwaffe would not be announced until March 1935). Reich Commissioner for Aviation Hermann Goering left most decisions to his deputy, Erhard Milch. Milch was a cruel and vindictive man who would ultimately hound Professor Hugo Junkers to death. He hated Willy Messerschmitt. When the big aircraft-building programme started, in January 1934, Milch gave orders that BFW be permitted to build aircraft only to other companies' designs. To complete Messerschmitt's humiliation, Ernst Heinkel – another enemy of Messerschmitt – arranged that Willy Messerschmitt, a designer noted for his devotion to monoplanes, would build Heinkel He 45c biplanes. In this hostile atmosphere Messerschmitt and Croneiss appreciated the hand of friendship that Hess offered them. They would owe him a favour.

Hess did not indulge in the relentless vendettas that characterised the Nazi leadership, nor did he use this time to extend his power. He was self-effacing – 'colourless' remarked those who met him – and believed that efficiency, hard work and a dog-like devotion to Hitler would be enough to secure his position at the top. This proved to be a grievous miscalculation. Cold-hearted clowns such as Goering, ruthless schemers such as Himmler and obsequious sycophants such as Bormann expertly elbowed Hess aside. This does not mean that Hess bears less responsibility for German crimes. He was always ready to persecute Jews, Poles or anyone else to please Hitler. And, like his master, Hess was ready to believe that the Anglo-Saxons were not irredeemably sub-human.

Bavaria remained the spiritual home of the Nazi Party. Hess had a residence and offices in Berlin but found that his work for the Nazi Party could be conveniently done in Munich. His home in the green and pleasant Munich-Harlaching district was only a short drive from the Messerschmitt factory at Augsburg-Haunstetten. Aviation remained an important interest. In 1934 he won the prestigious *Zugspitze* air race flying a Messerschmitt M 35. And when Hess flew Messerschmitt's delightful four-seater BF 108 he ignored the factory restrictions and demonstrated his skill at aerobatics. Such episodes suited the propaganda services and it also suited Willy Messerschmitt, who was fighting for contracts from the Reich Air Ministry.

By 1937, Deputy Führer Hess had been sidelined. The man who had once been Hitler's constant companion was lost in the crowd. Had this resulted in disillusion and disaffection all might have been well for him, but Hess was devastated by this rejection. Hitler was a man for whom he felt a loyalty so profound that it is more accurately called love. It was clear that only extraordinary achievement could restore Hess to his former close relationship with the man he called 'the Tribune'.

When war began in 1939, Hess, and his Party responsibilities, sank lower on the scale of priorities. He asked permission to join the Luftwaffe but Hitler refused him, forbidding him from flying as long as the war lasted. Hess persuaded Hitler to reduce this grounding to one year only.

The summer of 1940 brought consternation to the leaders of the Third Reich. Poland fell, followed by Denmark and Norway. The Germans occupied Holland, Luxembourg, Belgium and France but Hitler was exasperated by the British refusal to seek peace terms. What do I have to do? asked Hitler. Do I have to go over there myself and talk to them?

As soon as Hess's year of grounding ended he went to Generalluftzeugmeister Ernst Udet, an easy-going First World War fighter ace who had once owned Messerschmitt's factory at Augsburg. Hess asked if he could use one of the planes from the airport pool at Berlin-Tempelhof. The director of the Luftwaffe's Technical Department, Udet certainly had the authority and might have been easy to persuade. He was enjoying a steady diet of pep pills and alcohol at the time and Hess found him in a negative mood. What would happen to me if you crashed? asked Udet. A few days afterwards Udet himself had an accident while flying a Fiesler Stork, a light communications aircraft. He received a sarcastic note from Hess. But the answer was still no. Before the year was out, Udet had been found dead, beside him two empty cognac bottles and a revolver. Goering announced that he had died testing a new weapon. Milch took over Udet's department in addition to his own.

Meanwhile Hess went to Willi Stör, Messerschmitt's chief of production flight testing, and asked for use of a Messerschmitt BF 109E, the Luftwaffe's standard single-seat fighter. Stör said no and Willy Messerschmitt backed him up. Hess went to all the factories that were building the BF 109 (for now the tide had turned and Arado and Fiesler factories were assigned to manufacturing Messerschmitt's designs). They all said no. In October 1940 Hess came back to Messerschmitt with a new request. Could he fly the Messerschmitt BF 110? This was a twin-engined machine large enough to carry bombs and fitted with a second seat. It could be used for training. Theo Croneiss and Messerschmitt owed Hess many favours and Hess decided to call them in. After a few flights with Willi Stör[7] Hess was permitted to fly solo. Satisfied with Hess's flying skills the factory gave him a brand new aircraft, flight-tested but otherwise straight off the production line. The aircraft was a BF 110E 1/N, a bomber variant equipped with enlarged fuel tanks, a K 4ü autopilot and additional wing pylons for two 50-kg bombs. Its works number was 3869 and its fuselage bore the letters VJ+OQ. These were factory delivery markings that remained on a plane only until it was delivered to a squadron where it acquired the squadron's codes. Hess claimed VJ+OQ for his own use.

Hess had always been interested in machines and equipment. His visits to the Augsburg factory airfield were followed by suggestions for improvements and requests for a series of modifications. He made no secret of the fact that he was interested in long-distance flights. A memo of 7 January 1941 requested an improved heater valve. A works memo dated 2 May and signed by Messerschmitt asked for his plane to be modified so that the oxygen bottles for the rear seat were fed into the pilot's facemask. Many years later Hess recalled: 'I had lived those months in a whirl of instruments, cylinder head pressures, jettison fuel containers, auxiliary oil pumps, coolant temperatures, radio beam widths – which didn't even work when the time came – the heights of Scottish mountains and God knows what else.'

All this time Hess, avoiding his office in Berlin, asked Hildegard Fath, his secretary in Munich, to obtain copies of the (secret) weather reports for the North Sea and British Isles.

While Hess was planning his flight he heard about the new 900-litre drop tanks that the Junkers company was now manufacturing. Arguments about whether Hess had enough fuel for his flight to Glasgow make it worth recording that his particular version of the BF 110 was designed for bombing and had enlarged fuel tanks. The compatibility of the large drop tanks is also important. Such tanks could not simply be strapped under any aircraft. When filled drop tanks were heavy, and this weight constantly changed as fuel was used. For obvious reasons this meant the changing weight should be mounted at the aircraft's centre of gravity. The contents had to be fed into the fuel system and the tanks had to be pressurised if they were to continue feeding when atmospheric pressure reduced at higher altitude. There also had to be a way for the pilot to drop the tanks in an emergency.

When we consider the range of the plane Hess flew we have to bear in mind his requirements. Nowadays international regulations ensure that a passenger plane has fuel enough to fly to its destination, can then divert to an alternative landing place if needs be, and remain in the sky over it for several hours. The dictionary definition of 'range' is the total distance a vehicle can travel without taking on fresh fuel. Military aircraft have to have enough fuel to fly to their target and return to base. For Hess the fuel requirement was simple: he needed only enough for the one-way trip.

Hess obtained a map of Scotland and marked the mountains in red. He had the map on the wall of his bedroom so that he could spend time committing the features to memory. He also obtained a radio so that he could tune into the radio station at Kalundborg, Denmark. This was on virtually the same latitude as his destination: the estate of the Duke of Hamilton. He planned to tune his aircraft's radio compass to that transmitter.

With a 900-litre tank under each wing, and 1,200 litres in the internal tanks,[8] Hess made a flight on Saturday 21 December. Munich suffers a severe winter, as I know from personal experience. On this day Augsburg was under 40 centimetres of snow and the runway had to be cleared for him to take off. After three hours Hess returned with the vertical stabiliser jammed. The landing would have been as demanding on his pilot's skills as the heavily laden take-off over ice. An inspection of the plane found that his flare pistol had fallen on to the floor and jammed some of the control cables.

Hess made many flights from the Augsburg field: he told his wife that they provided 'recreation'. It is difficult to know when his practice sessions ended, and which one marked his first attempt to fly to Britain. Helmut Kaden – the Messerschmitt test pilot responsible for the aircraft Hess used – said the first attempt was on 21 December, followed by another on 18 January. Hess's son says there was no attempt in December but there was one on 10 January (and this was the date given by Karlheinz Pintsch, Hess's adjutant at the time). In custody Hess said the first attempt was on 7 January.

The flight on 18 January lasted about four and a half hours. Hess returned to say that his radio compass had not picked up the signal from the transmitter at Kalundborg. This was because the aircraft radio – an FuG 16 – had insufficient range. He was told the normal practice was to use the nearest transmitter, in this case Munich, until the next station came close enough.

Hauptmann Karl-Heinz Pintsch[9] said that it was on the day of this January attempt that he discovered what Hess intended to do. Hess had given Pintsch two sealed letters and told him to open the first of them four hours after his departure. Pintsch opened it after four and a quarter hours. He was shocked to read that Hess had flown to Britain in an attempt to negotiate a peace. Pintsch confided what he knew to Hess's driver and his personal detective. As they were talking, Hess's plane reappeared and landed. After Hess landed he admitted to Pintsch what he was trying to do. There is no way of knowing to what extent the three men kept their master's secret.

Nearly three months later, on 30 April, Hess was sitting in the cockpit waiting for clearance to take off when Pintsch brought him an urgent message. It said that Hitler would not be able to attend the ceremony at Augsburg on 1 May at which the Messerschmitt works was to be honoured with the title Nationalsozialistischer Musterbetrieb – a model Nazi operation. Hess, in his role of Deputy, should attend the ceremony in place of Hitler. Hess climbed out of the plane and prepared to do as ordered.

*

At the centre of many conspiracy theories is the choice of the estate of the Duke of Hamilton as a place to land. Although Hess once claimed otherwise, there is no evidence that he and the Duke had ever met. Neither was Hamilton associated with men such as R.A. Butler, Sir Samuel Hoare or Lord Halifax, the sort of high-ranking politicians who believed it would be best to make peace with Germany. The only connection comes through the Haushofer family who were friends of both Hess and Hamilton.

And yet when we take into account Hess's aspirations as an aviator the choice of Hamilton and his estate is not so strange. Hess had been so moved by Lindbergh's solo eastward transatlantic flight that he had written to the American car manufacturer Henry Ford to ask for funding that would enable him to attempt the far more difficult westward crossing. He did not receive a reply. In 1933 the Duke of Hamilton (then Marquis of Douglas and Clydesdale) had made a record-breaking flight which some found as remarkable as Lindbergh's crossing. The Duke had flown over Mount Everest. For aviators the flight demonstrated a significant step forward, most particularly in British supercharger design. The supercharger, needed to counter the thin air at high altitude, was the heart of the engine and gave greatly increased power. It was a British lead, which, even by 1945, German piston-engine technology had failed to narrow. For those less interested in engine technology, the flyers brought back magnificent photographs of Mount Everest from above, together with film footage that was shown in cinemas all over the world.

The Duke of Hamilton was the sort of man Hess admired. And Albrecht Haushofer, who had been a house guest of the Duke, had seen that in the grounds of Dungavel House there was a grass airstrip where aircraft could land. By the time of the flight the Duke held the rank of wing commander and was the station commander (commanding officer) of the RAF Spitfire fighter base at Turnhouse near Edinburgh.

For Hess's purposes the weather on 10 May 1941 could not have been better. The meteorological office at Hamburg predicted solid cloud at 500 metres covering the North Sea. There was a large anticyclone creating high pressure and perfect weather over Britain except for the possibility of brief showers along the east coast. The winds would be light. Sunset in Glasgow would be at about 22.00 hours and the moon would rise at about 20.45 hours. Predicted clear skies would mean enough moonlight for Hess to see the Scottish coastlines, lakes, rivers and perhaps railways.

Hess spent the day in a normal routine. At his Munich-Harlaching home his luncheon guest was Alfred Rosenberg, one of the founders of the Nazi Party. A light lunch of cold meat and salad was laid out in the dining room of the Hess home. With no servants present the two men conversed in private. After the meal Rosenberg drove from Munich to Hitler's mansion at Berchtesgaden. That afternoon Hess's wife Ilse, who had a head cold and was not feeling well enough to join the two men for lunch, shared tea with her husband in her bedroom. She noticed that he was wearing blue. She thought blue was the colour that suited him best, an unfortunate burden for any member of the Nazi Party. He pretended that he was wearing blue to please her but this was in fact the Luftwaffe uniform in which he would fly to Scotland. Ilse Hess remarked that after his departure she found the tailor's bill for a Luftwaffe uniform, with the customer's name cut away. 'Unfortunately not paid,' added Frau Hess. She told James Leasor that her husband had noticed that her bedside reading was *The Pilot's Book of Everest*. This book had been co-authored by the Duke of Hamilton, the man Hess was on his way to see. Hess picked it up. Looking at a photograph of the Duke, Hess said, 'He's very good-looking.' That Saturday Hess kissed his wife goodbye and said farewell to his small son.[10] He promised to be back by Monday at the latest. He got into the front seat of his Mercedes SSK beside the driver. Pintsch carried a small suitcase containing some of Hess's personal needs including a Leica camera and homeopathic medicines. Some people believe that Ilse Hess knew all about her husband's planned trip: she admitted seeing the map of Scotland on the wall of his bedroom but denied recognising it as Scotland. Sceptics say that the letters Hess wrote were cleverly contrived to make her sound innocent of the whole affair.

The airport was quiet when they arrived. Hess borrowed the flying suit belonging to Helmut Kaden, as his own was being repaired. Hess gave his destination as Norway. As before, he gave Pintsch an envelope to be opened four hours after departure. When the four hours had passed Pintsch opened it; he found letters for

Hitler, Ilse Hess, Willy Messerschmitt and Helmut Kaden. The last was an apology for taking Kaden's flying suit without permission.

Willy Messerschmitt did not escape criticism for helping Hess. Goering sent for him on 12 May and asked how he could have let a lunatic like Hess have an aeroplane. Messerschmitt said: 'How am I supposed to believe that a lunatic can hold such a high office in the Third Reich?' Goering laughed and said, 'You are incorrigible, Messerschmitt!'[11]

Hess said his route took him over Mainz, Cologne, Amsterdam and then along the islands before heading north across the North Sea. Helmut Kaden believes Hess invented this route to avoid revealing the way in which he was able to avoid the German defences. He says that Hess's real route was over Hanover and Hamburg. A prudent course would have brought Hess to the one he describes: heading north, well out in the middle of the North Sea. The promised solid cloud at 500 metres failed to materialise; instead, the night was 'crystal clear'. Using his radio compass he flew on until the transmitter at Kalundborg was due east of him and then he turned due west. Some accounts say Hess deliberately flew backwards and forwards until he had the light he required. Whether this detour took place or not, his radio compass would provide a track that would take him almost exactly over Dungavel, the house and estate of the Duke of Hamilton.

Some theories say that Hess's aircraft was fitted with one of the intersecting beam guidance systems which German pathfinder aircraft flew to pinpoint a target. The Knickebein system has been mentioned. By 1941 the Germans were using rather better devices, such as the X-Gerät and the Y-Gerät. By the time of his flight RAF countermeasures experts were jamming the Knickebein system. It had therefore been realigned to become a network over the Midlands and southern England. The German bomber crews used it for general navigation but not for precision bombing.

By May 1941 the Germans had the finest military guidance systems available anywhere in the world but it is unlikely that Hess used any of them. The British were by that time energetically seeking more information about the beams. The technicians of RAF AI 1(g) Branch were examining the radio equipment of German aircraft brought down in Britain, but there is no record of any special radio equipment on the plane that Hess flew. Only selected Luftwaffe units used any of these devices, and the aircrews had to be trained in their use. Only experienced crews could be sure of distinguishing the German beams from the British retransmitted ones that sounded almost identical.

There was a technical reason why Hess would not have used the guidance systems. A radio guidance beam moved in a straight line. Curvature of the earth created a need for a receiver to go higher and higher the further it was from the transmitter. To employ them as far north as Liverpool on 12 March 1941 the Heinkels of KG 26 using the Y-Gerät had to climb to at least 16,000 feet, and some went to 19,000 feet, to get the signal. On the same operation pathfinder aircraft of K Gr. 100 using the X-Gerät failed to receive the beamed signals at 12,000 feet and had to bomb visually.[12]

Kampfgruppe 100, the most experienced and renowned of the German pathfinder forces, bombed Greenock, near Glasgow, on 7 April 1941. A history of this unit records that they found their target by DR (dead reckoning), 'Greenock being well out of X-Verfahren range.'[13]

Engine technology of that time prevented aircraft going high enough over Scotland to receive the German beams. Certainly no BF 110 was equipped to do so. Finally we have to remember that to be guided to Dungavel, Hess would have needed Luftwaffe technicians and operators to align the intersecting beams for him. It was a lengthy and difficult task. This would have meant considerable loss of confidentiality for Hess and, after the war, one of those in the know would surely have made this public. Lastly and most persuasively for me, there is the character of Hess himself. This flight was to be Hess's 'Everest'. It was to be one noted not only for bringing peace to two warring nations but also for being the remarkable feat of airmanship that it certainly was. Hess never intended asking anyone to line up radio beams over Dungavel to help him find his way there. This was to be a solo triumph.

The flight plan that Hess had so carefully created worked almost perfectly. Having turned westwards, using the radio compass and the signal from Denmark, Hess says he crossed the coast at 22.00 hours flying at 6,500 feet. 'A veil of mist hung over England', he told his wife, and he dived to fly low enough to find his whereabouts visually. The sun had set and the moon was rising. He continued west across Scotland but passed more or less over Dungavel without spotting it. When he reached the west of Scotland at West Kilbride he recognised the coastline and turned to head back. Some accounts say that he abandoned his drop tanks over the River Clyde (presumably the Firth of Clyde) and that a British drifter recovered one of them the next day. But German drop tanks had been found from previous aircraft, and this tank has not been positively identified as being one of Hess's.

Heading back eastwards, Hess recognised Dungavel from the curve of the railway line and identified a small lake to the south of it (this would have been the L-shaped Glengavel Water).

Having made no preparations for a parachute descent, Hess must have been dismayed to discover that he could not land on the Dungavel airstrip. This small field, used by the Duke and his friends for flying tiny sports biplanes in daylight hours, would bring almost certain death to the pilot of a large, heavy aircraft trying to land on unknown terrain at night. The Messerschmitt's wingspan was 53 feet. Two powerful Daimler-Benz engines that provided high speeds in the air inevitably meant a high landing speed.

Hess climbed to 2,000 metres, switched off the engine ignition and set the pitch of the airscrews to zero. One of his engines had overheated to a point that it created combustion in the cylinders. It continued to turn over. Hess waited until the engine had stopped, discharged the cockpit cover and tried to climb out. But with the whole cockpit open to the airstream he was pinned to his seat. The cruising speed of a BF 110 is 300 mph.

At this moment, said Hess, he remembered advice from Robert Ritter von Greim, a fighter group commander.[14] To abandon a fighter in a hurry it is best to roll the machine and let gravity assist. Whether by accident or design, Hess pulled up, and started a loop. He blacked out, recovered and then tumbled from his seat, hitting his right foot against the tail as he left the aircraft. The parachute opened so that he landed close to Floors Farm on Bonnyton Moor, about ten miles south of Glasgow's city centre, and commendably close to Dungavel. He probably hurt his ankle again as he landed. A parachutist hits the ground with considerable force: the sensation is rather like jumping from a 20-foot wall. A report by

Lieutenant-Colonel Graham of the RAMC said that Hess complained of back pain, and X-rays revealed a chip fracture of the twelfth dorsal vertebra.

The Messerschmitt crashed into a field next to the farm where Hess was captured by a ploughman who took him inside the farmhouse. He was offered a cup of tea but Hess said he didn't drink tea in the evening and would prefer water.

The activities of the British defences have come under close and suspicious scrutiny by those who believe there was a conspiracy to which the British defences were a party. But the way in which the flight by Hess was detected and monitored was rather efficient and the records correspond with the account given by Hess. His plane was 'seen' by the radar when approaching the coast of Northumbria near Holy Island. It was designated 'raid number 42', estimated as being only one aircraft, and logged at 22.10 hours. The radar sets could only look out to sea, so after he crossed the coast reports depended upon men with binoculars, or sometimes upon no more than the sound of engines. Despite the poor light the defences kept track of Hess as he headed west to the Clyde and then back again. The final report said that raid 42 had crashed in flames on Bonnyton Moor.

Two Spitfires of No. 72 Squadron were in the air and were directed towards the Hess plane. They failed to intercept it but Hess was still not safe. At the time he baled out, a Boulton Paul Defiant from 141 Squadron at Ayr was close to him. There was no radar apparatus in the Defiant or in any of the fighters that sought him. AI (air-interception radar) was still a rarity at the time but 141 Squadron was doing very well without it. Hess almost became an addition to the squadron's score of night victories. It didn't all go perfectly of course but the mistakes were minor ones of the sort common at the time, and mostly due to technical errors. One radar station reported Hess as being three aircraft, and one station misidentified the Spitfires as incoming enemy aircraft.

My contribution to this book is confined to the flight. Everything I have learnt about it confirms that Hess was capable of planning it and carrying it out. I have found nothing in his activities up to the day of the flight that suggests that he was deranged or dysfunctional. On the contrary, Hess could have taught Bomber

Command planners a thing or two about night navigation (although we have to allow for the way that, by luck or by judgement, Hess enjoyed perfect weather conditions for his flight).

One final question remains: did Hitler know that Hess was planning his flight to Scotland? Normally this would be outside my brief but in one respect it is not. Immediately after the war, throughout 1946 and into 1947, Lieutenant-General Adolf Galland, probably the Luftwaffe's most experienced fighter pilot, worked with the Historical Division of the US Forces to provide an extensive overview of the German air force. In Argentina in 1953, using material provided by Captain John M. Whitten, one of the Historical Division interrogators, Galland wrote his autobiography: *Die Ersten und die Letzen*. Galland's long career in aviation meant that *The First and The Last* became a standard work for anyone studying the history of the Luftwaffe. In 1989 Galland gave his approval to a biography written by two American historians, which he said was more complete and accurate than his own book. Photographs from Galland's private collection illustrated it. So I must accept Galland's recollections in *Fighter General: The Life of Adolf Galland* as being memories carefully considered over many years.[15]

Galland says that on the evening of 10 May 1941, with only a few minutes of daylight remaining, he had a phone call from Goering. He was told to take off with his whole Geschwader: 'With your whole Geschwader, understand?' said Goering. 'The Deputy of the Führer has gone mad and is flying to England in an Me 110. He must be shot down. And, Galland, call me personally when you get back.' Goering then gave Galland the time of Hess's departure from Augsburg, and his probable route.

Galland did not do as ordered. He feared midair collisions and landing accidents, and he had no idea how any of his men would distinguish Hess's Messerschmitt from all the others flying over Germany. Galland sent a token force into the sky and then told Goering that his men had failed to find Hess.

Nazi Germany's intricate system of police spies and informers would have made it difficult (although not impossible) for Hess to keep his preparations secret, but that does not mean that he was acting on Hitler's instructions or with his blessing. Moreoover, because of the anecdotal ring and lack of any independent corroboration of Galland's undoubtedly intriguing claim, it fails to undermine any of the vital facts.

Hess had always been an introvert, something of a loner. I conclude that his flight was not assisted by German electronic guidance systems, or by secret instructions from Whitehall to the RAF defences. Hess may have been of unusual mentality but this did not affect his skills as an aviator. And the sort of person who flies over Everest or across the Atlantic is of unusual mentality, too.

Notes and References

I must thank the Imperial War Museum, London, in particular the Department of Printed Books. They found twenty-three books devoted to Hess and made them available to me at short notice. The books mentioned below are selected because they provided material about Hess and his aviation activities. They do not reflect my valuation of them, or of their contribution to the story of Rudolf Hess.

Information on the type of plane Hess flew (a BF 110E–1 rather than the BF 110D usually described) is taken from *The History of German Aviation. Willy Messerschmitt Pioneer of Aviation Design,* as is the description of the long-range tanks and details of the aircraft flown and registered in his name. From this book I have also taken Helmut Kaden's descriptions of the flight preparations. Where this account varied with other sources I have noted this in the text.

Hess's own descriptions of the flight came from his post-war writing, mainly letters to his family. See *Rudolf Hess: Prisoner of Peace* by Ilse Hess and *My Father Rudolf Hess* by Wolf Rüdiger Hess.

Roy Conyers Nesbit has studied the flight. His account *The Flight of Rudolf Hess* (written with Georges Van Acker) (Stroud, 1999), and his contribution to James Douglas-Hamilton's book, *The Truth About Rudolf Hess,* was especially useful, as was Hamilton's text, of course. Nesbit also wrote about the flight in a previous work, *Failed to Return.*

That Hess suffered a chip fracture of the vertebra is taken from *The Case of Rudolf Hess* by Dr J. R. Rees (London, 1947). In the absence of a personal copy of this interesting book I was grateful to have it quoted in *After The Battle Number 58,* which remains the most concise and accurate overall account of the Hess flight. It is also the best illustrated account.

An excellent map showing the radar stations and observer posts can be found in *Hess: The Führer's Disciple* by Peter Padfield (London,

1993). Padfield also gives information about the flight. I have also found James Leasor's *The Uninvited Envoy* a useful reference because in 1962 Leasor was able to speak to many of the participants.

1 S. Pope and E. A. Wheal (eds.), *Macmillan Dictionary of the Second World War*, 2nd edn. (London, 1995).
2 'True psychosis' was the description used by Colonel Rees, the British army's Consultant in Psychological Medicine, in a report on 19 June 1941. In an interrogation that was probably preparing material for Hess's trial at Nuremberg, Karl Haushofer said, 'He was not very intelligent.' This is not easily reconciled with the academic post that Haushofer had offered him.
3 Peter Padfield quotes the correspondence in *Hess: The Führer's Disciple* (London, 1993).
4 Wulf Schwarzwäller, *Rudolf Hess: The Deputy* (London, 1988).
5 Joachim Fest (trans. Richard and Clara Winston), *Hitler* (New York, 1975). See also Wulf Schwarzwäller, *Rudolf Hess: The Last Nazi* (Bethesda, MD, 1988). He says, 'It would not be exaggerating to call Hess the co-author of *Mein Kampf.*'
6 Ian Kershaw, *Hitler 1889–1936: Hubris* (New York, 1999).
7 Some accounts say that the initial instruction flights were made alongside Bauer, Hitler's personal pilot, and that his name was enough to persuade Messerschmitt that the Hess flights had Hitler's approval. For some of his practice flights Hess arrived wearing a Luftwaffe uniform. This might have been a tacit way of suggesting that his flying activities were both approved and official.
8 We have to assume the tanks were full. Roy Conyers Nesbit, a most reliable historian who has made a study of this flight, calculates that this would provide fuel enough for about 2,000 miles. The route Hess probably took is about 1,300 miles. These details of Hess at the Messerschmitt airfield are taken from an account by Helmut Kaden, an engineer and test pilot employed by Messerschmitt. It appears in Hans J. Ebert, Johann B. Kaiser and Klaus Peters, *Willy Messerschmitt: Pioneer of Aviation Design* (Atglen, PA, 1999). The book is a translation of *Willy Messerschmitt: Pionier der Luftfahrt und des Leichtbaues*.
9 Pintsch spoke with James Leasor, a writer preparing a book, *Rudolf Hess: The Uninvited Envoy* (London, 1962). Hess had several adjutants.
10 In contradiction to Leasor's account, Wulf Schwarzwäller's biography says the conversation with Frau Hess about the Everest book took place before lunch. Neither author found reason to disbelieve the coincidence of Frau Hess reading the book on the day of the flight.
11 Messerschmitt gave this account to a newspaper after the war. With no

better provenance than that it would not have been worth including here but the story was repeated in *Willy Messerschmitt: Pioneer of Aviation Design*, which is a serious history of Messerschmitt's work.

12 Alfred Price, *Blitz on Britain 1939–1945* (London, 1977). Price is a noted expert on the history of electronic air warfare.

13 Kenneth Wakefield, *The First Pathfinders: The Operational History of Kampfgruppe 100, 1939–1941* (Somerton, 1992).

14 In the final days of the war Hitler appointed Greim to succeed Goering as commander of the Luftwaffe.

15 Colonel Raymond F. Toliver and Trevor J. Constable, *Fighter General: The Life of Adolf Galland* (Atglen, PA, 1999).

ROY CONYERS NESBIT

Hess and Public Records

My first knowledge of Rudolf Hess's arrival came from a wireless announcement by the BBC on 12 May 1941, two days after he parachuted into Scotland. At the time, I was a nineteen-year-old officer serving in an RAF squadron. We assumed that Hess had arrived with peace proposals, but this surprising event was soon eclipsed by other news of the war, while our operational flying against enemy targets tended to concentrate our minds on bombing and survival tactics.

It was not until many years later, after retirement from private enterprise, that the subject cropped up again. By this time I had written several books and articles on the subject of RAF history. The editor of *Aeroplane Monthly*, Richard Riding, requested an examination into the technical background of Hess's flight. The research brought me into contact with Flugkapitän Helmut Kaden, the former chief test pilot at the Messerschmitt works at Augsburg, who had supervised the modifications to Hess's BF 110 without knowing the true purpose of the flights the Deputy Führer was making. The information he provided included details of the machine, its range, and some of the special equipment installed. Among these was the radio compass (Peilgerät V) which provided an essential aid for his pilot-navigation to the coast of Northumberland. Inevitably this research also involved an examination of documents at the Public Record Office, principally those in the AIR, WO and PREM classes. These gave additional details of the flight, including a record by the Royal Observer Corps, Hess's interrogation, the reaction of the Duke of Hamilton and some details of Hess's subsequent imprisonment.

The resulting article was published in two parts by *Aeroplane Monthly*, in its issues of November and December 1986. Although these were not intended to discuss the various conspiracy theories which surrounded this matter, a stream of letters from readers concerning these was sent to me. Most had been inadequately researched and some proposed various fantasies. As an example, one writer asserted that Hess could not have made such a flight but was hiding in a barn at Floors Farm at the time the aircraft crashed, when he popped out to reveal himself. Inspired by Stella Gibbons's book *Cold Comfort Farm*, my response was, 'It sounds like something Nazi in the woodshed.'

Hess committed suicide unexpectedly at Spandau prison on 17 August 1987, prompting renewed public interest into his bizarre behaviour. In advance of the fiftieth anniversary of his flight, I was invited by BBC *Timewatch* to act as consultant in a programme about Hess. This was shown on 17 January 1990 under the title of *Hess: An Edge of Conspiracy*. I was astonished to see that much of the filming of facts was deleted from this programme. In my opinion, viewers were left with a very imperfect idea of the truth.

Up to this time, certain Foreign Office documents concerning Hess had not been transferred to the Public Record Office. They were expected to be released in 2017, under the seventy-five-year rule for sensitive material, thus giving the conspiracy theorists ample opportunity to air their views without official contradiction. In October 1991, I was introduced to Lord James Douglas-Hamilton (now Lord Selkirk of Douglas), the second son of the Duke of Hamilton who was the unwitting person Hess wished to contact in Britain. Some documents had been released unexpectedly at the PRO and it was expected that many more would become available in the following January. Lord James, who at the time was Member of Parliament for Edinburgh West, required assistance in perusing these documents and in updating his book *Motive for a Mission*, first published in 1971.

The new releases were included in the FO class and proved voluminous. None of their content supported any of the conspiracy theories and indeed could be used to refute most of them. The document which interested me most was in FO 1093/1, a long letter Hess wrote to his son Wolf Rüdiger (nicknamed 'Buz') between 10 and 15 June 1941, shortly after his landing. The boy was only four years old at the time and thus unlikely to have understood its content, but there can be little doubt that Hess wished him to have a record of his flight and purpose. Translations of parts of it are as follows:

> Take-off from Augsburg went smoothly. I made a wide turn east of the River Lech to verify that everything was in order. Then I steered a course of 320 degrees in the direction of Bonn. At first, I could make few pinpoints to check if the machine was on the correct course for this north-east direction set earlier. A railway line junction enabled me to check that I was exactly on course. After a while Darmstadt loomed up on my right. A short while later, I spotted the point where the Main flows into the Rhine – I was a few degrees off course, and adjusted the automatic pilot accordingly. The Rhine disappeared on my left, only to reappear after a while. Already the Siebengebirge [Seven Peaks] came in sight – Godesberg of childhood memories, and recollections of staying there with the Führer and later during our frequent night stops there, the last time when the fall of France was imminent . . .

Hess then continued his letter with times, courses and turning points, enabling an aviation researcher to plot his entire flight with some accuracy on a Mercator chart. Moreover, the distances and times worked out precisely in accordance with the performance of the Messerschmitt, including its fuel consumption when running to dry tanks. Hess's long letter concluded with a homily addressed to his son, evidently for him to read in his later years:

> Buz! Take notice, there are higher, more fateful powers which I should point out to you – let us call them divine powers – which intervene, at least when it is time for great events. I HAD to come to England [*sic*] to discuss an agreement and peace! Often we do not understand these hard decisions immediately. In days to come their meaning will become clearly understood.

The Foreign Office files also revealed that Hess spent much of his time writing letters. These were in his own hand and, lest any readers should hold the eccentric belief that the prisoner was an imposter, the handwriting is identical with that of his pre-war letters. A letter addressed to the Duke of Hamilton appears to have been the only one which was deliberately prevented from reaching the addressee. Many others were sent to his wife, discussing intimate family details. Another, dated 14 June 1941, was sent to his idol, Adolf Hitler. A translation is as follows:

My last salute concerns you, for in the last two decades you have fulfilled my life. After the 1918 collapse you made it worth living again. For you and also for Germany, I have been reborn and able to start once more. It has been a rare privilege for me, as well as your other subordinates, to serve such a man and to follow his ideas with such success. My heartfelt gratitude for all that you have given me and meant to me.

I am writing these lines in the clear knowledge that there is no other way out, however difficult the end may be. I commend my relatives, including my aged parents, to your care. Through you, my Führer, I salute our Greater Germany, which has expanded to an unexpected size. I am dying in the conviction that my last mission, even if it ends in my death, will somehow bear fruit. Maybe my flight will bring, in spite of my death or even through my death, peace and understanding with England.

If this letter reached Hitler it does not appear to have made a favourable impression, for his propaganda minister, Josef Goebbels, recorded in his diary that Hitler believed Hess should be shot. Two days after writing this letter, Hess anticipated Hitler's wish with a first attempt at suicide by jumping over some banisters, although he achieved no more than a fracture of his left femur. Details of this event, followed by descriptions of his medical treatment and unbalanced mental state, are recorded in the files.

During his recovery from this self-inflicted injury, Hess wrote on 15 August 1941 to his principal adjutant, Karl-Heinz Pintsch, who was the person with prior knowledge of his intended flight to Britain. He had been arrested, interrogated, imprisoned for a while, and sent to the Russian Front. A translation of this letter is as follows:

Among other rumours I have heard that you were arrested in

connection with my flight. I hope and assume that this is not correct, but if it is the case – which would be very painful to me – I beg you to look upon it as a decision of destiny and as part of an endeavour which I am convinced had to be made.

Whatever the case, I thank you for your loyalty and for your silence – otherwise I should not have been able to carry out my flight.

I wish you well especially if, I assume, you are at the front.

To our meeting in good health.

It was amusing to witness the discomfiture of some of the conspiracy theorists when these Foreign Office files were released, although most of them stuck to their views and expressed the belief that dark secrets were still being withheld. However, Lord James Douglas-Hamilton's book was revised from a study of these new releases at the Public Record Office. It was published in 1993 under the title *The Truth About Rudolf Hess* and received acclaim from critics in the national press.

There the matter appeared to have been put to rest, at least so far as I was concerned. Meanwhile, during the previous few years, I had been in touch with the air historian Georges Van Acker in Belgium concerning certain technical details of aviation matters. It is not uncommon for air historians to exchange information with those in other countries, and Georges Van Acker was one of several like-minded enthusiasts. Not only was he an acknowledged expert on the wartime Luftwaffe and its machines but he was fluent in English, German and French, in addition to his native Flemish. He was the person who translated the letters listed above from German into English, and accompanied the results with many discerning comments.

A particular problem for air historians remained at this stage – the identification of the exact variant of the Messerschmitt BF 110 which Hess had flown to Britain. With a remarkable piece of aviation detective work, Georges Van Acker identified this as a BF 110E-2/N, fitted with extra tanks for both petrol and oil. Although of little interest for general readership, this information seemed worth submitting to an aviation magazine.

However, Georges continued his researches into a wider field. From the Bayerisches Hauptstaatsarchiv in Munich, he obtained a copy of Hess's official records in the First World War. These amount to no fewer than forty pages, written in old German which is difficult to read. One of the documents is Hess's original and personal *Kriegs-Rangliste* (wartime service record). In part of this Hess wrote '*Für richtig befunden*' (found correct) and signed it. Other documents are records of the wounds Hess sustained and their treatment in hospital. The last of these wounds, from a rifle bullet on the Romanian front on 23 July 1917, is of particular interest since it has been stated by a conspiracy theorist that it must have been 'massive', as part of a contention that the pilot who flew to Scotland was not Hess but an imposter. In fact this official document records that the bullet entered the front of the chest near the left armpit, leaving a pea-sized hole. Then it passed through the lung and exited near the spinal column by the fourth vertebra, leaving a hole the size of a cherry stone. Hess recovered completely from this wound and was back on active service by 15 December 1917.

This document and other discoveries by Georges Van Acker, coupled with my further researches, seemed worth including in a joint book. We began work but my participation was limited at first owing to requests from publishers for books on other aviation subjects. Even after we had completed most of a draft manuscript, deferment was required in the knowledge that SOE documents from the Foreign Office would be released via the Public Record Office; these were expected to include more information about Hess.

The SOE files were released in July 1998, in the HS class. They concerned Operation Foxley, plans to assassinate Hitler and Himmler in late 1944. Hess was part of a plan recorded in file HS 6/625, since it was thought that he could be hypnotised into believing that Himmler was the only person preventing a negotiated peace between the Allies and Germany and thus might be sent home to kill him. However, these wild proposals were abandoned, partly because it was deemed inadvisable to make martyrs of the Nazis and partly because Hitler's ineptitude as a supreme commander was helping the Allies to win the war.

Following these releases, we learnt that some MI5 files would be transferred from the Foreign Office. They became available in January 1999 in the KV class and are extremely important, although their significance seems to have been missed by the newspaper reporters who throng the Public Record Office on such occasions. It is possible, of course, that they were ignored since they merely confirm the common sense view that the decision for the flight to Scotland was made solely by Hess.

There are five files in this KV class. They include numerous letters written to Hess while in British hands, sent from all over the world. Most of these were sent from sympathisers, with some from religious fanatics. Presumably they were retained for such a long time in order to conceal names and addresses until after the writers had died. However, within the files there are several letters of significance. One of these in KV 2/34, dated 19 May 1941, is an official letter sent to the Central Department of British Intelligence. Part of this is as follows:

We have learned by trustworthy means in Finland that a Baron von Engelhardt, of the German Intelligence Service, who arrived in Helsingfors from Germany, on the 18th May, has told a friend the following. Whether or not this was the version he had been instructed to give if asked about Hess, is difficult to say.

(i)   Hess was educated in a British school in Alexandria and has always well disposed towards the British.

(ii) He was particularly depressed by the war with England, which he regarded as fratricidal.

(iii) He flew to England to prove that the continuance of the war was senseless and to stop the war.

(iv) An aircraft, which he could fly himself, was always at Hess's disposal.

(v)   By nature Hess is an idealist and a fanatic, with an imaginative strain.

(vi) Hitler was very upset at Hess's flight.

(vii) The first reports regarding the flight caused commotion in the German General staff and were disbelieved.

Another document in the same file is dated 17 May 1941. It is a copy of an intercepted telegram sent three days earlier by the Japanese ambassador in Rome, General Hiroshi Oshima, to the Foreign Minister in Toyko and the Japanese ambassadors in Vichy, Moscow, London, Berlin, Ankara and Washington. Part of this reads:

The Foreign Minister RIBBENTROP arrived in Rome on the afternoon of the 13th, and I called on him at his request in the forenoon of today. RIBBENTROP prefaced his remarks by saying that his coming to ROME had become necessary in order to discuss with MUSSOLINI and CIANO the HESS incident, the IRAQ question and questions relating to the three Powers, and I am telegraphing it at once just as he said it.

Hess has been suffering for some years past from an illness of the gall bladder and in order to forget this pain had become full of fanciful ideas from credence in horoscopes. Although he had achieved a high position in the Party as the Fuehrer's deputy, he has not in fact had much hand in questions of policy. Having been a leading light for a good many years he was greatly trusted, but he has worried over the fact that he was cutting little ice in the present war . . . Investigations of letters left behind by him, interrogation of his adjutant, etc. show that he had no treasonable intention whatever. Although his action has been eccentric it is clear that his intentions were excellent. Although this incident has provided first class material for Anglo-American anti-German propaganda, in the extraordinary nature of the circumstances the whole thing will die down in a short while.

Perhaps the most important document in this collection of releases is an investigation made post-war by the British Secret Service into the reasons for Hess's flight. This is in KV 2/38 and is dated 12 March 1946. It is the result of an interrogation of Standartenführer (Colonel) Friedrich Hermann Rang of the SS, and reads:

a) Investigation by Amt IV [the German Secret Service]
In May 1941, after the flight to the UK, a group of Amt offrs were selected to investigate the case under the direction of SANDERS and STAGE.
b) Immediate Action
The following personalities from Hess's entourage were arrested, together with a number of others whose names Prisoner has forgotten:
    (i)   Reichsamtsleiter LEITGEN (Adjt to Hess)
    (ii) Krim Rat Lutz (" " ")

(iii) Prof HAUSHOFER, Karl (Geopolitics)
(iv) Prof HAUSHOFER, Albrecht (")
(v) Reichsamtsleiter Dr SCHULTE-STRATHAUS
     (Astrologer)
(vi) Prof Dr GERL-HINDELANG

c) Results of investigation

It transpired that HESS had flown to UK on his own initiative, notwithstanding HITLER'S orders to the contrary. HESS had written a letter to HITLER explaining the object of his flight, which LEITGEN had passed to the Führer after HESS' departure. HESS had stated that he hoped to obtain a last-minute understanding with BRITAIN before the projected date of the offensive against USSR, 22 Jun 41.

Both KARL HAUSHOFER and his son Albrecht had great influence with HESS, and Prisoner is of the opinion that their geopolitical theories weighed considerably in HESS' calculations.

SCHULTE-STRATHAUS had plotted horoscopes for HESS on many occasions; in the last instance (end Apr 41) the signs had proved propitious for HESS' personal activity for beg May 41; HESS had apparently accepted this prognostication and acted accordingly.

d) Disciplinary Action Taken

Both LEITGEN and LUTZ had been 'in the picture' concerning HESS' preparation for the flight. They both knew of the trial flights undertaken over the countryside in the vicinity of REGENSBURG and near the MESSERSCHMITT factory at AUGSBURG; they were also fully aware of HITLER'S categoric orders forbidding HESS'S project. Both Adjts were arraigned and sentenced to imprisonment in SACHSENHAUSEN, whence they were eventually discharged and sent to the fighting front (1942).

SCHULTE-STRATHAUS was also sent to SACHSEN-HAUSEN for a period; both the HAUSHOFERS and GERL-HINDELANG were released after being kept under arrest during the investigation.

e) Further Measures against HESS

Referat 'Partei' censored all mail leaving the Reich for HESS, especially letters from his wife. Progress reports were sent to RF SS and a final report on the case was submitted to HITLER.

f) Fate of the HESS Case-file

The Case-file was still in the possession of Referat IV 5 A 5b (Sachgebeit Partei) on arrival in HOF (Mar 45). Prisoner believes that it was burned together with other documents, by order of PIER [indistinct] (Apr 45).

There is an error with one of the names in this report. Dr Gerl-Hindelang was in fact Dr Franz Gerl, who lived in Hindelang. An important witness who could not be present during the investigation was Hess's chief adjutant, Karl-Heinz Pintsch, who had been captured by the Russians. He was not repatriated to Germany until 16 December 1951, where he remained until his death on 1 May 1965. Hess had told him of his intention to fly to Britain and presumably he had passed this information on to the two subordinate adjutants. But there is no evidence that Hitler was aware of Hess's plan, although he must have known that his Deputy was amusing himself with flying from Augsburg-Haunstetten.

Of course, these MI5 documents released by the Public Record Office will not stop conspiracy theorists writing books on the subject of Hess. It is likely that more will be published to satisfy the public appetite for such theories. A frequent practice is to assert that the author has a special knowledge of information which has never been released by the British Secret Service, although he cannot disclose the source. Provided this is surrounded by enough genuine facts, possibly with the misinterpretation or rejection of other facts, the conspiracy theory can assume a spurious authenticity.

Notes and References

The book written by Georges Van Acker and myself was entitled *The Flight of Rudolf Hess: Myths and Realities* and published in October 1999. Some of the content has formed the basis for this essay. The files at the Public Record Office were included in our Bibliography and are repeated here. Permission to quote verbatim extracts from the KV class was kindly granted by the Public Record Office, provided they are accompanied by the following standard notice:

Public Record Office Sources

AIR 16/235	Fighter Command Intelligence Summary, Jan–Dec 1941.
AIR 16/365	Order of Battle, Fighter Command, Jun 1940–Apl 1942.
AIR 16/519	Feb–May 1941. Hitler: Proposed abduction to England by his private pilot.
AIR 16/698	War Room Log, Mar–Jly 1941.
AIR 16/1266	Royal Observer Corps: Flight of Rudolf Hess.
AIR 19/564	Duke of Hamilton: allegations concerning Rudolf Hess, Jan–Jly 1941.
AIR 22/73	War Room Daily Summaries, Oct 1940–Feb 1941.
AIR 22/78	War Room Daily Summaries, Apl–Sep 1943.
AIR 22/116	Air Ministry and War Room Summary, May 1941.
AIR 25/233	13 Group operations Record Book, Jun 1941–Dec 1943.
AIR 27/442	43 Squadron Operations Record Book, Jan–Dec 1941.
AIR 27/460	46 Squadron Operations Record Book, Apl 1916–Dec 1943.
AIR 27/624	72 Squadron Operations Record Book, Jly 1917–Dec 1942.
AIR 27/969	141 Squadron Operations Record Book, Oct 1939–Dec 1941.
AIR 27/1706	317 Squadron Operations Record Book, Feb–Dec 1941.
AIR 27/2075	602 Squadron Operations Record Book, Jan–Dec 1941.
AIR 27/2079	603 Squadron Operations Record Book, Sep 1925–Dec 1943.
AIR 28/40	Ayr Operations Record Book, Jan 1941–Sep 1944.
AIR 28/219	Drem Operations Record Book, Oct 1929–Apl 1945.
AIR 28/624	Ouston Operations Record Book, Mar 1941–Jly 1942.
AIR 28/861	Turnhouse Operations Record Book, Aug 1936–Dec 1940.
AIR 28/864	Turnhouse Operations Record Book, Appendices, Jan–Nov 1941.
AIR 29/1019	63 MU Operations Record Book, Sep 1939–Dec 1946.
AIR 40/195	Messerschmitt Aircraft, Apl 1939–Mar 1945.
AIR 41/17	*Air Defence of Great Britain* Vol. III, *Night Fighter Air Defence.*
CAB 118/56	Correspondence concerning Hess, 1941.
DEFE 1/134	Rudolf Hess: censorship of mail, 1941.
FO 115/3544	British Embassy, Washington files: flight of Hess, 1941.

FO 181/969/12   Moscow Embassy: Correspondence concerning Hess, 1942.
FO 371/26565   Flight of Rudolf Hess to Scotland, 1941.
FO 371/26566   Flight of Rudolf Hess to Scotland, 1941.
FO 371/30920   Parliamentary statement on Rudolf Hess, 1942.
FO 371/30941   Nazi explanation of the mission of Herr Hess, 1942.
FO 371/33036   Soviet criticisms of British policy towards Hess, 1942.
FO 371/34484   Rudolf Hess, 1943.
FO 371/50976   German War Criminals, 1945.
FO 371/50986   German War Criminals, 1945.
FO 371/50993   German War Criminals, 1945.
FO 371/51001   German War Criminals: minutes of Nuremberg trials, 1945.
FO 371/57564   War crimes: Trial of Hess, 1946.
FO 371/93535   Germany general (C). Treatment of War Criminals, 1951.
FO 371/93544   Germany general (C). Treatment of War Criminals, 1951.
FO 371/97970   Germany general (C). Treatment of War Criminals, 1952.
FO 371/103732   Conditions of War Criminals in Spandau Prison, 1953.
FO 371/118429   Consideration of cases of German War Criminals while in prison, 1955.
FO 371/124690   War Criminals in Spandau Prison, 1956.
FO 371/124691   War Criminals in Spandau Prison, 1956.
FO 371/124692   War Criminals in Spandau Prison, 1956.
FO 371/130852   War Criminals in Spandau Prison, 1957.
FO 371/130853   War Criminals in Spandau Prison, 1957.
FO 371/146063   Publications of Federal German Republic, 1959.
FO 371/146064   Prisoners in Spandau Prison, West Berlin, 1959.
FO 371/154293   Inarceration of German War Criminals in Spandau Prison, 1960.
FO 1093/1   Conversations between Hess and various officials, May–Jun 1941.
FO 1093/2   Translations of personal correspondence, Aug–Dec 1941.
FO 1093/3   Translations of personal correspondence, Dec 1941–Dec 1942.
FO 1093/4   Translations of personal correspondence, Feb 1942–Dec 1943.
FO 1093/5   Correspondence between War Office and PoW Reception Station, Abergavenney, Jun 1941–Oct 1945.
FO 1093/6   Possible exploitation of Hess incident for propaganda purposes, 1942.
FO 1093/7   Memorandum by O'Neill on propaganda use of Hess, 1941.
FO 1093/8   General correspondence on Camp Z, 1941–1944.
FO 1093/9   Proposal to call Hess in libel action, 1941.

FO 1093/10   Conversations between Hess and various officials, 1941.

FO 1093/11   Conversations between Hess and various officials, 1940–41.

FO 1093/12   Conversations between Hess and various officials, 1941.

FO 1093/13   Conversations between Hess and various officials, 1941.

FO 1093/14   Correspondence between War Office and Camp Z, 1941.

FO 1093/15   Correspondence between War Office and Camp Z, 1942.

FO 1093/16   Correspondence with Swiss Legation, records of visits to Maindiff Court, translations of personal correspondence, 1942–1943.

FO 1093/17   Ibid., 1944.

FO 1093/18   Ibid., 1945.

FO 1093/19   Ibid., 1945.

FO 1093/20   Notes on personal correspondence, 1944.

HO 144/22492/ 863753   Rudolf Hess: public disquiet and rumours about his mission, 1941–1942.

HO 199/305   Auxiliary petrol tanks jettisoned from British and German aircraft, 1940–1945.

HO 199/482   Messages about Hess's landing in Scotland, 1941.

HO 201/9   Ministry of Home Security, Daily Reports May–Jun 1941.

HO 324/1   Register of Prison Burials 1834–1969.

HS 6/623   Operation Foxley: plan to liquidate Hitler and/or his satellites.

HS 6/624   Operation Foxley, undated.

HS 6/625   Operation Foxley, 1944–1945.

HS 6/626   Little Foxleys, 1945.

INF 1/912   Ministry of Information: Rudolf Hess, 1941–1945.

KV 2/34 MI5   Documents relating to Hess, 12 May 1941–20 May 1941.

KV 2/35   Ibid., 20 May 1941–07 Jun 1941.

KV 2/36   Ibid., 05 Jun 1941–30 Jun 1941.

KV 2/37   Ibid., 30 Jun 1941–08 Apl 1945.

KV 2/38   Ibid., 14 Apl 1945–28 Mar 1946.

PREM 3/219/1   Hess: Effect in USA, Jun 1941.

PREM 3/219/2   Hess: Medical Report, Aug 1941.

PREM 3/219/3   Duke of Hamilton's Libel Action, Jun–Jly 1941.

PREM 3/219/4   Hess: Public Statements, May 1941.

PREM 3/219/5   Hess: Interview with Dr Guthrie, Jun 1941.

PREM 3/219/6   Hess: Soviet attitude and report by Lord Privy Seal, Oct–Nov 1942.

PREM 3/219/7   Various, May 1941, Sep 1943, Apl–May 1955.

PREM 3/434/7   Records of Meetings and Conversations, Oct–Dec 1944.

TS 27/510   Question of whether Hess should be subpoenaed in Duke of Hamilton's libel suit, 1941.

WO 166/1260   War Diaries, Home Forces, Bedfordshire, Huntingdon-shire, Northamptonshire, Jun 1940–Dec 1941.

WO 166/1293   War Diaries, Home Force, North East London HQ, Apl–Dec 1941.

WO 166/2293   Headquarters 49 AA Brigade, Sep 1939–Dec 1941.

WO 199/3288A Scottish Command – The Capture of Rudolf Hess.

WO 199/3288B Scottish Command – The Capture of Rudolf Hess.

WO 208/4471   MI14 dossier on Hess, 1941–55.

HUGH TREVOR-ROPER

Rudolf Hess: The Incorrigible Intruder

The sudden and unconventional arrival of Rudolf Hess in Britain – his descent by parachute into Scotland on 10 May 1941 – was the most bizarre single episode of the Second World War. The news caused dismay in Germany, amazement in the world, and much needed hilarity in Britain. What could have brought him? Was he an emissary or a refugee, a secret agent or the victim of a power struggle in the Nazi jungle? Or was he, as the German radio declared, mad? The announcement that the Führer's Deputy had been, for some months, going mad caused further dismay in Germany and further hilarity in Britain. But the questions were never answered. The British government, as usual, was economical with the truth: the German profuse with varying explanations. Hess disappeared into prison in Britain and would reappear, four years later, in the dock at Nuremberg showing all the outward signs of a deranged mind.

Since then, some questions have been answered, others added. At least seven books on the problem have been published in Britain. The psychiatrists who attended Hess in Britain and at Nuremberg have uttered their observations. New ground was broken in 1971 when Lord James Douglas-Hamilton revealed the important part played in the story by the Haushofer family. Peter Padfield has accumulated a mass of incidental evidence. And there have been some ingenious conspiracy theories hardly less bizarre than the episode itself. In this paper I offer no new material: I merely seek to set the affair in its context, historical and political, as seen by those involved, British as well as German, and thereby, I hope, to reduce the mystery and suggest answers to some of the questions.

The episode, I shall suggest, was an attempt by Hess – whether with or without Hitler's knowledge and approval – to intervene in internal British politics: to unseat Winston Churchill and to replace him as Prime Minister by a politician committed to a settlement with Nazi Germany, thus leaving Hitler free to concentrate on the conquest of Russia. The drama is in two acts, linked together by the consistent war aims and illusions of Hitler and the character of Hess. The protagonists are Hitler, Hess, Professor Karl Haushofer and his son Albrecht. There are walk-on parts for an English widow in Cambridge, the Duke of Hamilton and British Secret Intelligence. There are several supernumeraries and some ghosts. I shall try to place the ascertained facts in the context of the war situation and to see that context as it was seen by the *dramatis personae*, beginning with the prime mover, Hitler.

Act One

In May 1940 Hitler had achieved two-thirds of the ambitious programme which he had set out in *Mein Kampf*. The Treaty of Versailles was in ruins. The client states created or re-created by it in Eastern Europe – Czechoslovakia and Poland – had been erased from the map. France, as promised, had been 'annihilated'. Politically and geographically the way was open for the conquest and colonisation of Russia which was to solve all the social problems of Germany. This last stage, Hitler insisted, must be completed 'by 1943 at latest' – while Russia was still weak and while he himself was there, and in full vigour, to carry it through.

There was only one hitch. In *Mein Kampf* Hitler had blamed 'the men of 1914' for a grave error, their failure to neutralise Britain. By their irrelevant and unnecessary colonial and naval policy they had challenged Britain and Britain's entry into the war had saved France, leading to a long war on two fronts and catastrophe. He himself, he said, would never commit that error. Here, however, he had been proved wrong, and now, unless he could end the war with Britain before launching his attack on

Russia, he would be exposed to the reproach which he had levelled at his predecessors. In the summer of 1940 he therefore sought by all means to drive Britain out of the war.

At first it seemed easy. With France destroyed and the British Expeditionary Force surrounded at Dunkirk, Britain seemed to have no alternative to surrender. But later, with the rescue of the British army (though not its arms) and the victory of the RAF in the Battle of Britain, Churchill's view prevailed: the war was to go on. On 19 July 1940 Hitler went as far as he thought he could go towards soliciting peace with Britain without compromising his status as victor. In a broadcast speech he promised that if the British government would see reason and seek a settlement, it would find him a magnanimous and generous enemy. But the British government was unmoved. Hitler's promises by now had lost all credibility, and the reply was a firm rebuff. To emphasise its firmness, it was delivered, also in a broadcast, by Lord Halifax, a former 'appeaser'. Thus rebuffed, Hitler decided that there was only one way to shake off his last enemy in the West and free his hands for a new war in the East: Churchill must go; he must be deposed by an internal coup in Britain, organised from Berlin.

How was it to be done? Hitler probably consulted Ribbentrop, who, though always wrong in his prophecies, could be assumed, as former ambassador, to know the mechanics of British government. The essential figure in the plot was the King. As ambassador, Ribbentrop had confidently assured the Führer that in order to marry Mrs Simpson, King Edward VIII would dismiss Stanley Baldwin as Prime Minister and appoint a more amenable (and more pro-Nazi) government. If Edward VIII could have dismissed Baldwin, surely George VI could dismiss Churchill. But how was he to be persuaded to do so? The threat of armed invasion was of course one powerful argument, and Hitler had ordered that the preparations for the invasion must be complete by 15 September. But internal pressure was also necessary. For this Hitler relied on a supposed 'peace party' whose aristocratic leaders, having access to the royal court, would be able to circumvent the Machiavellian Churchill and win over the King.

Did such a party exist in Britain? Certainly neither the British people nor any British government wanted war, from which they had nothing to gain and much to lose. Chamberlain's policy of 'appeasement', disastrous and ineffective as it was, had enjoyed massive support at the time. How could Hitler fail to be influenced by the enthusiasm with which Chamberlain had been greeted when he returned from Munich waving his worthless piece of paper? And certainly the traditional and possessing classes, who had most to lose, were apprehensive of the financial and social implications of a long war. But since March 1939, when Hitler had cynically repudiated his solemn pledges and seized Czechoslovakia, all the arguments for appeasement had been destroyed. The desire for peace itself might be as strong as ever in Britain but no responsible British politican could advocate another treaty with Hitler. He was a wolf in politics. This point, however, was unlikely to be emphasised to him by his cronies and he continued to believe that the party and the policy of appeasement were still alive and, by a palace coup, could be restored.

When Hitler planned an operation which might discredit its author either by criminality or by failure, his practice was to entrust its execution to one of his cronies while reserving final decisions to himself. Thus, before and after the outbreak of war, Goering was licensed to seek to soften up the Chamberlain government through his Swedish friend Birger Dahlerus, and in 1943 Ribbentrop would be allowed to angle for a separate peace with Russia through his agent Peter Kleist, while the 'Final Solution' of the Jewish question was entrusted to Himmler. These commissions were not officially recorded: they were given orally, as 'the Führer's wishes', which had the force of law. The commission to organise the deposition of Churchill was entrusted to Hess.

Why Hess? But why not? Was he not rather mad? No, that was a retrospective charge, made after his flight to Scotland. He was certainly eccentric, but who, in that gang, was normal? He had dietary and medical fads. So did Hitler. He believed in astrology and Tibetan magic. So did Himmler. He believed that Hitler was a genius unparalleled in centuries. So did Bormann, Goebbels, Himmler and Hitler himself. He also had some virtues. He was not greedy and corrupt like Goering, or violent and shrill like Goebbels. He was a modest man who lived simply and was regarded as the conscience as well as the secretary of the Party. Above all, he was the Führer's oldest and most intimate friend, the scribe of *Mein Kampf*, who (as he would claim in England) knew the Führer's mind and thinking better than anyone. He did not know much about the English mind, but he had sources of information, for he headed the Auslandsorganisation, which watched over Germans abroad and was associated with the Abwehr, the German secret intelligence service.

What distinguished Hess was the naïve absolutism of his Nazi faith. He was a man born to believe, a Nazi *devot* who simplified his religion in order to swallow it whole. His was a Manichaean universe in which the forces of good, the Aryan and particularly the German race, were constantly at war with those of evil, the Jews; and Hitler, to whom his loyalty was no less absolute, was not merely a political leader but a Redeemer sent by Providence. If this grand antithesis ran into particular difficulties, he found a way round them. If otherwise sound Aryans, as in Britain, rejected the Führer and his gospel, then it was clear that they were victims of long-range hypnotism by 'the forces in the background', the Satanic Jews. He knew this because when he preached the saving doctrine to such persons, their eyes became 'glazed' and their knees wobbled; they had become 'zombies'. These are certainly odd views, but they do not denote madness or practical incapacity. Many a devout Mormon or Jehovah's Witness may be a perfectly competent accountant or engineer – though not perhaps politican.

This Aryan fundamentalism marked a latent difference between Hess and Hitler. Hitler was a gangster politician of genius: a realist and a cynic. He had no love of humanity, of Germans, or of peace: he positively liked bloodshed. The British quest for peace, to him, showed the decadence of a sated power, to be exploited by him. Hess, on the other hand, was an idealist, not a politician. He deplored the Anglo–German war not merely because it interfered with Hitler's plan of eastern conquest but as an Aryan civil war, and he regarded the British King and nobility not as feeble enemies to be manipulated but as sound pure-blooded allies in the common cause.

Hitler summoned Hess to give him his 'wishes' in late July 1940. In a serious discussion lasting nearly two hours he no doubt set out the problem and the proposed solution. That it was Hitler himself who defined the problem was stated by Hess himself, and is confirmed by two parallel incidents. The first is the attempt to seduce or, if necessary, forcibly abduct the ex-King Edward VIII, now Duke of Windsor, in Spain, to which he had escaped from France. Hitler personally gave this commission to Ribbentrop, who assigned the execution of it to Walter Schellenberg. The Duke was to be taken to Germany and there set up in appropriate state, as 'king across the water' in case his brother proved unamenable. But here Churchill got in first, sending the ex-King across the water in the opposite direction, to govern the Bahamas. The second episode is the segregation of certain captured British officers, known as the *Prominente*, from other prisoners of war. The cause of this segregation was never stated, but the timing and the distinguishing character of the prisoners suggest that they were pawns in the same game. All were from aristocratic or otherwise influential families: they included Lord Lascelles, afterwards Earl of Harewood, a cousin of the King, and the Master of Elphinstone, a nephew of the Queen. They also included Lord Cromwell, perhaps as a long-stop, in case the House of Windsor should be uncooperative and have to be replaced; the Germans could not be expected to know that he was unconnected with the great Protector. The order to segregate these officers must have been political and could have come only from Hitler. When the occasion to use them had passed, they remained aimlessly segregated: the order remained though its purpose had been forgotten. These three episodes – the order to Hess to mobilise the British 'Peace Party', the order to Ribbentrop to secure the Duke of Windsor, and the order to the army to segregate the British *Prominente* – illustrate the coherence of Hitler's aims.

But how was Hess to succeed where Ribbentrop had failed? Faced with so grave a responsibility, Hess decided to consult the man on whom he had a fixation second only to that on Hitler, his old teacher at Munich University, Professor Karl Haushofer. Haushofer was a distinguished scholar who had been a general in the First World War. He was professor of geography and a man of some importance in Munich, founder and Director of the Institute of Geopolitics, a new science according to which the interest, survival and policy of nation states was determined by their quest for *Lebensraum*, or 'living space'. It may have been through Hess that Hitler adopted this principle, which he transformed to his own purposes.

In an eight-hour session and long walk Hess set out Hitler's problem to Haushofer. Haushofer's reaction was to consult his son Albrecht, who, for his father's sake, had been given a post, and protection, by Hess. He needed protection because his mother, the professor's wife, was half-Jewish. He was now Hess's representative in the German Foreign Office, used by his patron to check, if possible, the follies of Ribbentrop. As such he had been in the German embassy in London and had many British friends.

Thus Hitler's plan to engineer the overthrow of Churchill was delegated, in effect, to a kitchen cabinet consisting of Hess and the two Haushofers, father and son. Our knowledge of its activity comes from the correspondence of the father in Munich and the son in Berlin.

The views on the war held by the four men who shared the secret were not identical. Hitler only wanted to end the war with Britain in order to begin another against Russia. Hess agreed with that aim because it was Hitler's, but also deplored the fratricidal war against Britain. Karl Haushofer, a Bismarckian conservative, would have deplored the impending war against Russia. Albrecht Haushofer, the half-Jewish Anglophile intellectual and poet, deplored Nazi policy and war altogether. But all were, if with differing emphasis, eager to end the war with Britain and agreed that, for this purpose, it was necessary to depose Churchill.

To achieve this it would be necessary to make secret contact with the supposed British 'peace party'. How could such contact be made? On 8 September 1940 Hess summoned Albrecht Haushofer, as his expert on Britain, to a discussion lasting two hours. The subject was thoroughly ventilated and Haushofer wrote an account of the conversation immediately afterwards. Three points made by him are important. First, having asked and obtained permission to speak freely, he told Hess the unpalatable truth that by now no person of any influence in Britain regarded a treaty with Hitler as anything but 'a worthless piece of paper'. In other words, a settlement with Britain required the removal not only of Churchill but also of Hitler. To this terrible suggestion he recorded no reaction by Hess, but Hess, the idolator of the Führer, must have been shocked by it. Secondly, asked to name men of influence opposed to the war, he named three, all of whom were by now ambassadors abroad and therefore unusable. As an afterthought he added a fourth name, the Duke of Hamilton, whom he described as a close personal friend. Thirdly, among the qualifications of the Duke he mentioned that he not only knew everyone of importance but had direct access at all times to the King.

Direct access to the King! Was not this precisely what was wanted? But how was the Duke to be reached? By a remarkable coincidence, just at this time, Professor Haushofer had received a card or letter of greeting from an English friend, Mrs Violet Roberts, the widow of a professor of geography in Cambridge, expressing her regret that this war had occurred and her hope that it would not interrupt their (anyway long intermitted) correspondence; after which she obligingly cited a post office box number in Lisbon to which a reply could be sent. The professor was excited by this timely accident: surely this letter was providential. He at once reported it to his son in Berlin, and Albrecht reported it to Hess. Hess was delighted too; and between them they decided to use Mrs Roberts and the Lisbon post-box as a channel to Hamilton. By this route Hess would secure the overthrow of Winston Churchill. That would bring peace in the West, triumph to the Führer, glory to himself, and one in the eye for the hated Ribbentrop.

A personal letter to the Duke was duly drafted by Albrecht Haushofer, approved by Hess, and sent, together with a covering note, to Mrs Roberts through the post-box at Lisbon. The language was deliberately opaque, but the import was clear enough. The writer, who gave his address as Berlin but concealed his identity from the profane under the monogram 'A', was inviting the Duke, a serving officer in the RAF, to meet him in a neutral country, preferably Portugal, for unspecified but serious discussion, and he gave him a new postal address in Lisbon for reply. No reply ever came. The letter had been spotted by the British censorship and diverted to MI5.

Interlude

The period of six months between 6 November 1940, when Albrecht Haushofer's letter to the Duke of Hamilton arrived in MI5, and 10 May 1941, when Hess flew to Britain, is the seedbed from which all the conspiracy theories about the Hess affair have sprung. These theories are not without a rational base. Hess's lone flight from Germany to Scotland in the middle of the war was an act so heroic, so quixotic, and charged with such danger in itself and such tragic consequences for him, that if he was not mad – and there is nothing in the reports of either Karl or Albrecht Haushofer to suggest that they saw him as anything but a responsible paladin of the Führer taking seriously a serious duty – then he must have been either pushed by an irresistible force or pulled by an irresistible lure. The irresistible force could only be a direct wish of the Führer; the irresistible lure could only be a Machiavellian plot by the British Secret Service. I shall face these two questions in turn, beginning with the second, the theory of the British conspiracy. This requires us to examine the reception of the material by British Intelligence.

When Albrecht Haushofer's letter to Hamilton was sent to MI5, copies of it were forwarded, for information, to the Foreign Office (which disclaimed interest) and, since the Duke was an officer in the RAF, to Air Intelligence; but responsibility for action, since it was a matter of internal security, was left to MI5. Two British subjects had been named. What was Mrs Roberts up to, acting as a conduit for secret communication with the enemy? Why was Hamilton thought likely to accept an invitation to go abroad and conspire with the enemy? These two persons were at least identifed; but who was the mysterious 'A' in Berlin, the organiser of the conspiracy? The easy and obvious way to answer this question was to put it to the Duke, who could have given a full account of his friend. But this was not done. The letter was neither shown nor mentioned to the Duke. For five months he was left completely in the dark about it. Why? The answer is easy and obvious. He was under observation.

I recall a somewhat similar case later in the war. A collaborating French aristocrat informed the Abwehr in Paris that a certain English lady, well known in high society in London and Paris, might be willing to serve as a German agent in England. When this was revealed by a deciphered message, MI5 took action. Measures unacceptable except in wartime were adopted. The lady's movements were closely but secretly observed. In the end she was completely cleared, and would never know that she had been spied upon. I have no doubt that similar steps were taken in respect of the

Duke. Indeed, MI5 would be failing in its duty if it did not take them.

What would those steps be? MI5 would have begun by sending for a 'trace' – a summary account of the Duke's career and contacts, where relevant. That would have shown that he had been a member of the Anglo-German Fellowship; that he had visited Germany for the Olympic Games in 1936 and been officially entertained there; and that he had publicly advocated sympathy for genuine German grievances. All this was open and innocent, but invited caution and further enquiry. In the end, like the lady, he would be entirely cleared; Albrecht Haushofer's letter, of whose existence he was unaware, would be given to him; and the five months' delay in its transmission would be tactfully explained away: the document, it would be said, had been 'lost in MI5'. That may have been partly – but only partly – true.

How then did MI5 discover, as it soon did, that 'A' was Albrecht Haushofer – a name of which, we are told, no one in that department had previously heard? Most probably from Mrs Roberts. She had exposed herself by acting as 'A's agent and could therefore be questioned on the basis of evidence. She probably was.

Mrs Roberts is still, as far as I am aware, a mystery. What was her motive, or who her motivator, when she wrote, apparently spontaneously, to Professor and Frau Haushofer? Was she really just an innocent old lady anxious to correspond with old friends in spite of this regrettable war? The Haushofers did not think so. And how did she furnish herself with a post-box in Lisbon? Perhaps she was a genuine pacifist, a member of some pacifist organisation. If so, she was probably discharged with a warning and told to keep her mouth shut, which she evidently did. Or was she perhaps prompted, and her pen guided, by some member or some freelance on the fringe of secret intelligence, eager to use her known friendship with the Haushofer family to open not a way to peace but a source of intelligence? This explanation, which, if true, would have saved her further trouble, cannot be discounted. The subterranean rivulets of secret intelligence trickled quietly through the groves of academe and the connection of the Roberts family with the Haushofers must have been known in Cambridge. But if so, that channel would have been blocked by the response. The message from Mrs Roberts had been tentative and exploratory.

The sender would have expected an equally tentative reply, addressed to Mrs Roberts from Professor or Frau Haushofer in Munich. Instead there had come a compromising proposal from the mysterious 'A' in Berlin, addressed to the Duke of Hamilton. Evidently the link had been hijacked, in its infancy, by some third party, and could not safely be used. Who was now in command? Who was controlling whom? The matter, and the document, were anyway now in the hands of MI5; so we are back in MI5.

What use could or would have been made of it by MI5? Theoretically it could be used to deceive the enemy. The policy and practice of such deception was, at this time, by a historical accident – because it had grown out of the capture of German radio spies in Britain – directed, through the specially created inter-service 'XX Committee', by a particular section (Section B1A) of MI5. However, this mechanism could not be used so long as the Duke was being investigated. He could not be impersonated without his consent in communications with a personal friend in Germany. That situation changed in mid–March 1941 when the Duke had been cleared and shown the letter. It then became possible, at least in theory, to make use of the link. It seems that this idea occurred to Air Intelligence and was at one time seriously discussed, for on 25 April 1941 there was a meeting in the Air Ministry between Air Intelligence, the Duke and Major T.A. Robertson, the head of Section B1A.

T.A. Robertson (always known from his initials as 'Tar') was the genius of the deception policy which would lead to the great successes of operations Mincemeat and Fortitude, by which German forces were diverted from Sicily to Greece in 1943 and from Normandy to the Pas-de-Calais in 1944. I had known him personally since January 1940, when I had worked in a cell in Wormwood Scrubs prison, then the headquarters of MI5, only a few yards from his. We became close friends from then till his death in 1996. So when I read, in James Douglas-Hamilton's book in 1971, of this meeting I knew at once what had been discussed; and I then asked 'Tar' about it. His reply was summary: the project, he wrote, was, from the beginning, a 'non–starter'. The reasons were obvious enough: the long delay, which was bound to arouse suspicion; and the question of control. To use the link at this stage would be positively dangerous. B1A anyway by this time was using its own double agents, including the famous Tricycle, and had no need for so risky a venture.

Thus for the whole period from September 1940 to May 1941 the mechanism proposed by Mrs Roberts and adopted by the Haushofers simply did not work. Mrs Roberts received no answer from the Haushofers in Munich. Albrecht Haushofer in Berlin received no answer from the Duke. Although Air Intelligence continued to toy with it, the idea of a meeting in Lisbon soon evaporated, and meanwhile, on 10 May, Rudolf Hess, a man never mentioned by any of the parties, descended by parachute into Scotland. To account for this sudden and remarkable development we must return to the sole place of its origins: Germany.

Act Two

If Hess was not pulled to Britain by an irresistible British lure for which no rational purpose can be imagined – even to the 'peace party' (if it existed) his personal presence would have been an embarrassment, not an asset – we are faced with the question: was he pushed by an irresistible force in Germany – a command or 'wish' of the Führer? This has been seriously argued and deserves serious consideration. I believe that evidence and probability alike dictate the answer 'no'.

First the evidence. The most direct evidence of Hitler's position in the matter is his reaction to the letter in which Hess informed him of his flight. This letter was delivered to him by Hess's adjutant Karl-Heinz Pintsch at the Berghof on the morning of 11 May. Hitler, on reading it, had one of his famous *Wutausbrüche*, or tantrums. He denounced Hess as a traitor and ordered the arrest of Pintsch as an accomplice. The courtiers echoed the denunciations, the propaganda machine was cranked up, and a witch-hunt was declared against astrologers, who were said to have encouraged Hess in his follies: whereupon fashionable astrologers fled for protection to Himmler's more sympathetic court. This scene is well documented, as is Hitler's genuine shock at the news. But those who wish to believe that Hitler had secretly prompted Hess's flight insist that the tantrum was simulated: that the whole affair was an elaborate charade previously concerted with Hess in order to conceal Hitler's responsibility if the project should fail.

For this speculation there is no evidence and, in my opinion, it can be disproved. The disproof lies in the timing. Hitler's tantrum took place before he could have known what had happened to Hess, for the British government disclosed nothing for a further two days. Hess himself, in spite of his forced landing, believed that he was still on course. He had met the Duke of Hamilton, had delivered his message, had stated his programme. But his credibility depended on his status as the Führer's Deputy and confidant. Why then should the Führer, if he had sent him, thus prematurely sabotage his mission? Peter Padfield, the most diligent and erudite advocate of the charade theory, is aware of this difficulty and seeks to circumvent it. He suggests – and then assumes – that a telegram, which Hess dictated and asked to be sent to his aunt in Zurich, was a coded message to the Führer to inform him of his failure and thus authorise him to declare him mad. This is a desperate hypothesis. Padfield gives no reason to suppose that the telegram was sent. Hess was an enemy officer who had entered Britain secretly and under a false name in very suspicious circumstances. No British officer would send or authorise a dictated telegram at his request; and anyway Hess, at that time, did not believe that he had failed.

Evidence is supported by probability. Hitler was a politician of genius, quick to grasp and exploit the implications of events. He might commission his Deputy to feel the way, through secret conversations in Lisbon, towards a purely internal coup in Britain, but is it conceivable that he would send him, a political *ingénu*, alone and unprepared, into the heart of the enemy country to waste his naïve rhetoric on unknown politicians in that enigmatic island?

Hess was a brave and skilful aviator and a competent organiser, but no politician. It is instructive to compare the detailed care with which he prepared his hazardous flight to Britain with his apparent indifference to the problems which awaited him there. In the six months in which he prepared the flight, studying weather reports, securing and equipping a plane, working out the route, concealing his intentions, he did not discover whether the airstrip at Dungavel was fit to to take his Messerschmitt (it was not) or whether the Duke was residing there (he was not). He had made no contacts in Britain, no contingency plans in case he should miss the Duke.

Without the co-operation of the Duke, which he simply assumed, he would be helpless and alone, captive in a strange and hostile land.

What did he expect to happen if he had landed smoothly at Dungavel? Presumably, having left his Messerschmitt on the airstrip to be admired by the wondering peasantry, he would have walked to the house in his Luftwaffe uniform and rung the front door bell. After a conversation with a surprised footman, he would ultimately meet the Duke. To him he would make his prepared speech on the generous terms which the Führer would offer to Britain. The scales of Churchillian censorship which had hitherto blinded him would thereupon fall from the Duke's eyes. He would see the light. He would summon the leaders of the 'peace party'. From castle and grouse moor they would come, dukes and earls, obedient to the call, and soon they would converge on Buckingham Palace or Windsor Castle. It would be 1688 come again. The King, not unwillingly, would yield. The hated Churchill would be deposed, and a new government would at once begin negotiations for peace. Hess would fly home, his Messerschmitt refuelled by the RAF, bringing peace with honour, like Chamberlain from Munich, and the Führer would be free to conquer Russia without fear of an enemy in the west.

An absurd scenario! But not incredible, for Hess in fact acted thus, even though he had fallen into the wrong hands, and said these things, even if to the wrong people. When he met the Duke, he embarked on a 'long eulogy of Hitler'. He asked to be introduced to 'your party'. The Duke replied that there was now only one party in Britain, but Hess was undeterred and kept to his script. To the Duke and Sir Ivone Kirkpatrick of the Foreign Office, who was sent by the government of Britain to interrogate him, he would end a two-hour rant with a calm statement, added as an afterthought, that of course the Führer's generous terms of peace would not be available to a government which included 'Winston Churchill or any of his men': they were not acceptable treaty partners. The new British government must be approved by Hitler.

What was the British government to do with this incorrigible intruder? Hess had come uninvited, so he was not an envoy; in uniform, so he was not a spy; unarmed, so not an assassin.

Churchill decided that, as an enemy officer who had strayed into British territory, he was a prisoner of war, but, in view of his status, a prisoner of very high rank, meriting special treatment: in fact the equivalent of the British *Prominente* in German captivity. This was clearly rational, but Hess did not see it so. He acted and spoke as if there were no war, as if he were outside or above it: an arbiter or *deus ex machina*, who had descended from the clouds to judge and settle the problem of Britain.

What had come over him? Was this the same man to whom Hitler, in a long interview, had entrusted the task of mobilising the British 'peace party', and with whom the hard-headed professor and general, Karl Haushofer, had spent eight hours, and the intelligent and sceptical Albrecht Haushofer two hours, exploring the practical possibilities: the same man whom even the waspish Dr Goebbels, in October 1940, had described as 'a good dependable man . . . calm and rational'? Surely not. Surely something had happened to him since then.

Consider the predicament of Hess in October 1940, when he had to face the fact that Albrecht Haushofer's letter had elicited no response from Hamilton. To him the Führer's commission had been a great honour but also a great challenge. Success in it would be a triumph, failure a disaster in the politics of the court. In the circumstances, the letter of Mrs Roberts and the identification of the Duke must have seemed providential and he must have felt confident and excited as he waited for the Duke's reply. When no reply came, euphoria would have been succeeded by questioning. What had gone wrong? Had Albrecht's letter, or the Duke's reply to it, gone astray, or been intercepted? Could Mrs Roberts be trusted? Was her Lisbon post-box secure? And what about Albrecht Haushofer? Was he the right intermediary? Was he really as intimate with the Duke as he supposed? Even if he was, had he sufficient status? Why should the Duke fly to Lisbon to conspire with a mere underling in the German Foreign Office? And how far could Albrecht himself be trusted in such a conspiracy? How could Hess forget those shocking remarks on the total untrustworthiness of the Führer's solemn pledges? All these questions pointed in the same direction. If the plan was to be put back on course all intermediaries must be dispensed with. The hazards of the postal service must be avoided. The Duke must be visited in Britain by an emissary whose status and authority were unquestionable, who could speak for the Führer: in fact, himself. For whatever his doubts about others, Hess evidently never doubted the central position of the Duke.

In the five months from December 1940 to May 1941 Hess made three attempts to fly to Britain. In those months his mind must have been preoccupied by the adventure: the practical difficulties to be overcome, the technical problems of the flight, the necessity of keeping the plan secret even from his closest collaborators. He did not tell Hitler because he feared refusal, but he was convinced – as he would say in his letter to be delivered to him after his departure – that he was acting within his general instruction: to make contact, by whatever means he could, with the 'peace party', and so to achieve the Führer's wishes. It was a gamble, a great risk to himself, but what a rich reward for the Führer if it should succeed! As he planned the adventure and contemplated the risks, his sense of his own importance must have been revived. He was no longer merely a secretary directing action from his office in Berlin: he was a hero, like one of those missionaries who, in the sixteenth century, had set out, fortified by faith and prepared for martyr- dom, to an infidel country to convert the ruler – the Emperor of China or the Great Mogul – and thereby bring a whole nation to the true religion, and perhaps also an empire to their own sovereigns. Like them he carried protective talismans – a Tibetan elixir supplied by that other Aryan geopolitician Sven Hedin – and he was encouraged by the prayers and visions of the faithful: Professor Haushofer had seen him in a dream walking at ease through a royal palace in England. By commissioning him Hitler had sought to end one war merely in order to begin another, but by the time he arrived in Britain Hess ascribed to himself a much higher role: he was an angel of peace in a warring world, and he used messianic language. Naturally he was impatient of the mundane rules and usages under which he was categorised and locked up as a prisoner of war.

Throughout his imprisonment in Britain Hess was nothing but a burden and a nuisance to the British government. He was a burden to himself too: for a second time his high hopes had ended in failure, and now the Führer had declared him a traitor. Isolated, cut off from the stronger personality on whom he had previously depended, he sank deeper into depression and behaved in a mad way, amply recorded by the psychiatrist who attended him. But there was method in his madness, or pretended madness: it saved him from further interrogation and from revealing any secrets that he knew. The same painful farce was continued at Nuremberg. I watched him there as he sat in the dock, ostentatiously ignoring the proceedings, pretending to read a novel, and occasionally drawing attention by idiot grimaces and gestures. He claimed to have lost his memory and to recall nothing of the past. But then at the very end of the trial, when no more questions could be asked, he seized his opportunity. Miraculously recovering his memory he made (till he was stopped by the president of the court) a prepared speech. It was his credo, for in it he expressed both his fundamental faith in Nazi ideology – the Jewish conspiracy to destroy the Germanic Aryan race (including the long-range hypnotism, the glazed eyes and wobbling knees) – and his own unconditional loyalty to the Führer: 'the greatest son whom my country has brought forth in its thousand-year history'.

Epilogue

If this interpretation of the facts is correct we can say that the plan implicit in Hitler's commission to Hess in July 1940, was – within its own limits – rational and coherent. Against the background of actual or imminent invasion, the old party of 'appeasement', still strong in Parliament – it was, after all, the same Parliament which had welcomed Chamberlain so jubilantly on his return from Munich – was to be persuaded to put pressure on the King, demanding that he dismiss Churchill and restore 'good old Chamberlain', who would then accept the generous terms of the Führer. Freed from the fear of a two-front war, Hitler could then throw the whole weight of his armies against Russia which, without allies and war supplies from the West, would collapse and the new German Empire would be established.

However, the plan rested on false premises. First, there was no British 'peace party'. Whatever the desire for peace, however distant the prospect of victory, peace with Hitler was simply not an option. Appeasement was dead. Chamberlain himself had now joined the war party. Secondly, there was no invasion. When Hitler commissioned Hess, he assured him that the invasion was being prepared: he had 'only to press the button' and everything would go off. But on 15 September – the date by which the invasion force was to be ready to act – Hitler postponed the whole operation, and a week later effectively cancelled it. The Royal Navy and the Royal Air Force had proved too strong. When Albrecht Haushofer wrote to Hamilton on 23 September, the invasion was already off.

It is useful to cast an eye back into history. On two other occasions in the last four centuries the most powerful rulers in Europe, in order to complete their hegemony, have sought, like Hitler, to promote an internal coup d'état in England. In the 1580s Philip II of Spain, seeking to complete the reconquest of the Netherlands, decided to depose Queen Elizabeth I. He had a veteran and victorious army in Flanders and a 'peace party' – the English Catholics – in England. But the defeat of the Armada, which was to cover the invasion, wrecked the plan and the English Catholics did not lift a finger. A century later Louis XIV wished similarly to detach England from his enemies by deposing William III and restoring the golden days of appeasement under good old James II. He too had a formidable army at hand and a 'peace party' – the Jacobites – in England. But like Hitler he funked the Channel crossing. Without an invasion to concentrate their minds, peace parties in war lie low. The Jacobites did not stir. It would be different in Italy in 1943: then the grandees of the Fascist peace party would play their part, pressing King Victor Emmanuel to dismiss Mussolini; but by then there had been a successful invasion: the Allied army had landed in Sicily.

When Hitler cancelled Operation Sealion he had probably forgotten his commission to Hess, as he had forgotten the Duke of Windsor, now out of reach in the Bahamas, and the imprisoned British *Prominente*. It was clear to him by now that Churchill could not be deposed. In that case his immediate task was to block any possibility of a return by British forces to the Continent during the brief Blitzkrieg which was to destroy Russia in a single campaign. So in November he planned the capture of Gibraltar – only to be defeated by the obstinate Spanish patriotism of General Franco. Then, in the spring, he forced the British out of Greece. That left the way open for the crowning adventure. Britain would be powerless to create a second front, and once Russia had collapsed would have no option but to contract out of a pointless war. In such circumstances the exploit of Hess was not only irrelevant but also damaging. The farcical relic of a policy which had already failed, it suggested that the Führer was not granting but soliciting peace; and that, of course, would never do.

Notes on Contributors

Len Deighton is the bestselling author of spy novels beginning with *The Ipcress File* (London, 1962). In *Bomber* (London, 1970) and *Goodbye Mickey Mouse* (London, 1982) he produced stories of the air war, while his non-fiction historical studies include *Blitzkrieg* (London, 1979), *Fighter* (London, 1977) and *Blood, Tears and Folly* (London, 1993).

James Douglas-Hamilton, an historian and Member of the Scottish Parliament, is the younger son of the Duke of Hamilton whom Hess fruitlessly sought out on his mission to Scotland. He read History at Balliol College, Oxford, won a boxing blue, and was President of the Union. He is the author of *The Truth About Rudolf Hess* (Edinburgh, 1993).

John Erickson is Professor Emeritus at the University of Edinburgh and the author of several distinguished books on the Soviet Union, including *The Soviet High Command* and his two-volume history of the Soviet–German war, *The Road to Stalingrad* (London, 1975) and *The Road to Berlin* (London, 1983). He is also co-editor of *Barbarossa: The Axis and the Allies* (Edinburgh, 1997).

Lothar Kettenacker is Deputy Director of the German Historical Institute in London and co-editor, with Wolfgang Mommsen, of *The Fascist Challenge and the Policy of Appeasement* (London, 1983) and, with Gerhard Hirschfeld, *Der Führerstaat:*

Mythos und Realität. Zur Struktur und Politik des Dritten Reiches (Stuttgart, 1981). His book *Germany since 1945* was published in 1997 (Oxford).

Warren F. Kimball has recently retired as Robert Treat Professor of History at Rutgers University. He is the distinguished editor of the definitive three-volume *Churchill and Roosevelt: The Complete Correspondence* (1984) and author of *The Juggler: Franklin D. Roosevelt as Wartime Statesman* (Princeton, N.J., 1991) and *Forged in War: Churchill, Roosevelt, and the Second World War* (London, 1997).

Peter Longerich is Professor of Modern German History at Royal Holloway College, London. He is the author of several books on Nazism, including *Politik der Vernichtung* (Munich, 1998) and *Hitlers Stellvertreter* (Munich, 1992), a study of Hess and Bormann's Nazi Party staff. He has also acted as a consultant to the Crown Office, War Crimes Investigation, Edinburgh.

Roy Conyers Nesbit is the co-author, with Georges Van Acker, of *The Flight of Rudolf Hess: Myths and Reality* (Stroud, 1999). A Second World War veteran of Coastal Command, he is an aviation historian closely familiar with files in the Public Record Office.

Hugh Trevor-Roper (Lord Dacre of Glanton), a graduate of Oxford University, was a member of the Radio Security Service (RSS) and the Secret Intelligence Service (SIS) during the Second World War. While still in the SIS he was ordered to find out what had happened to Hitler and his report became the basis for his bestselling book, *The Last Days of Hitler* (1947). He then returned to Oxford, where he became Regius Professor of Modern History (1957–80). From 1980 until 1987 he was Master of Peterhouse College, Cambridge. Among his many books is *The Philby Affair* (1968), which also includes an essay on Admiral Canaris, head of the German Abwehr.

Index

Abwehr 157
Acker, Georges Van 143–44
Aeroplane Monthly 139, 140
Air Intelligence 163–64
Atlantic Conference 68
Atlantic Summit Conference 9
Augsburg 39, 127, 128

Bahamas 158
Baku oil fields 54
Baldwin, Stanley 155
Balfour, Michael 19
Barbarossa, Operation 4, 9–10, 45, 56
Barros, James 45
Bauer, Captain Hans 137 n. 7
Beaverbrook, Lord: interviews Hess 23, 24, 30, 41, 52, 70
Beneš, President 80
Beria, Lavrenti 48
Berlings, Orests 51
Bernadotte, Count Folke 98
Bethge, Eberhard 98
Bevin, Ernest 43
Bird, Colonel 100
Bismarck 68
Blunt, Sir Anthony 40
Bohle, Gauleiter 96
Bonnyton Moor 133, 134

Bormann, Martin 25, 106, 107, 108, 111, 124
Bracken, Brendan 33
Burckhardt, Carl 46, 85, 93–95
Burgess, Guy 40
Butler, R.A. 51, 92

Cadogan, Sir Alexander:
    diaries 27, 68
    disinformation and 7–8, 29
    Welles and 9
Censorship Department 21
Chamberlain, Neville 155–56, 169
Chichayev, Colonel Ivan A. 40–41
Churchill, Winston:
    coup against 12, 155, 156, 159, 166
    Eisenhower, talks with 61
    Foreign Office and 11
    Hess:
        attitude to mellows 33–34
        Stalin's accusation concerning 6, 42
    Hess's arrival, reaction to 1–2, 4, 7, 20, 22, 26–27
    peace, refusal to make 14, 155
    Roosevelt and 66–67

War Crimes and 31
Ciano, Count 146
Clarke, Lieutenant 22
Clydesdale, Marquis of see
    Hamilton, Duke of
Costello, John 5
Cripps, Stafford 29–30, 44, 54
Cromwell, Lord 158
Croneiss, Theo 124, 126
Czechoslovakia 80, 156

Dahlerus, Birger 156
Daily Herald 63
Dekanozov, V.G. 42–44
Dilks, David 27
Douglas-Hamilton, Lord James
    140, 143, 153, 163
Dunglass, Lord 92
Dunkirk 155
Dupree, Tom 41

Eckart, Dietrich 123
Eden, Anthony:
    disinformation and 45
    German–Soviet agreement and
        53–54
    Hamilton reports to 22–23
    Hess, visits 41
    Hess's mental state and 32
    statement on Hess's arrival 20,
        39, 44
Edward VIII, King 155, 157
Eisenhower, General Dwight D.
    61
Elizabeth I, Queen 170
Engelhardt, Baron von 145

Fath, Hildegard 127
Fest, Joachim 123
Finland 145
Fleming, Peter 62
Floors Farm 1, 133

Ford, Henry 129
Foreign Office:
    Churchill and 11
    documents 140–41, 144
    MI6 and 7
Foxley, Operation 144
France 155
Franco, General 171
FSB 49

Gerl, Professor Franz 147, 148
German–USSR Non-Aggression
    Pact 6
Gibraltar 171
Gibson, Harold 47
Gibson, Hugh 65
Goebbels, Joseph 19, 28, 29, 91,
    142, 167
Goering, Hermann 110, 124,
    126, 131, 135, 156
Gorodetsky, Gabriel 29, 50, 52
Gorske, Anatole (A. V. Gorsky);
    'Vadim'/'Henry' 5, 40
Graham, Lieutenant-Colonel 134
Gregor, Richard 45
Greim, Robert Ritter von 133,
    138 n. 14

Hague Convention 32
Halifax, Lord 62, 63, 72, 82, 92,
    95, 155
Hamilton, Duke of:
    airstrip 129
    Everest flight 15, 80, 129
    Haushofer's letter to 11, 13,
        15, 21, 22, 88–89, 160, 162,
        163
    Hess correspondence (spurious)
        48, 49
    Hess's admiration for 129
    and Hess's capture 22, 39, 89,
        166

MI5 observation of 161
The Pilot's Book of Everest 130
US trip vetoed 71
Hamilton, General Sir Ian 83
Harewood, Earl of 158
Harris, John 10–11
Harrison, Ted 21, 24
Hassell, Ulrich von 82
Haushofer, Dr Albrecht:
  Britain, liking for 13, 80
  Britain, peace with 80, 81, 84,
    89
  British contacts 21
  execution 99
  expert on Britain 21, 97
  Foreign Office, sacked from 97
  Hamilton (Duke of):
    friendship with 13, 80–81
    letter to 11, 13, 15, 21, 22,
      46, 81–82, 86–88, 160, 162,
      163
  Hess and 12–13, 21, 80, 83-84,
    85-86, 88–89, 90–91, 96,
    137 n. 2, 158, 161
  Himmler and 97-98
  Hitler and 80, 91–92
  Hitler opposition and 82
  imprisonment by Gestapo 13,
    91, 95, 97, 98
  imprisonment in Dachau 99
  Jewish ancestry 91, 159
  peace: prospects of doubted by
    13
  report on English connections
    92–95
  The Sonnets of Moabit 97–8
  'Thoughts on a Peace Plan' 97
Haushofer, Heinz 100
Haushofer, Martha 79, 99, 100
Haushofer, Professor Karl:
  background 79, 158
  disillusionment 99

geopolitics 13, 79, 85, 123
  Hamilton and 80, 83
  Hess and 79, 82, 99–100, 105,
    159
  Hitler and 85
  Nuremberg and 99
  suicide 13, 100
  wife half Jewish 79, 99
Hedin, Sven 168
Heinkel, Ernst 124
Hess, Alfred 88
Hess, Ilse 122, 130, 137 n. 10,
  147
Hess, Rudolf:
  alternative medicine, interest in
    114
  anti-Semitic beliefs 4, 116–17
  assassination fears 24
  as aviator 121–36
  background 104–5
  Britain, misperception of 14,
    26, 46, 78
  British peace party and 46
  as bureaucrat 111
  business and 123
  cabinet minister 109, 124
  Church and 117–18
  death 56
  decline of 111, 114, 125
  diet, interest in 114
  family and 115–16
  First World War 122, 144
  and flying 15
  Führer myth 112–13
  Hamilton correspondence
    (spurious) 48, 49
  Haushofer (Albrecht) and 13,
    21, 80, 83–84, 88–89,
    90–91, 147, 159, 161, 167
  Haushofer (Karl) and 79, 82,
    85–86, 99–100, 105, 147,
    167

Hitler:
  admiration of 1, 25, 105, 106,
    112, 123
  Deputy to 79, 106, 107,
    107–10
  flying forbidden by 125
  letter to 19–20
  letter to from prison 142
  rejected by 125
  secretary to 79, 105
  as idealist 157
  identification 121, 142
  imprisonment in Landsberg 1,
    79, 105, 123
  imprisonment in Spandau 3,
    100
  intelligence low 25, 78, 79,
    114, 137 n. 2
  letters from prison 16–17, 141,
    142–43, 145
  living space doctrine 123
  Mein Kampf and 25, 79, 105,
    156
  mental state 24–25, 72, 142,
    153, 157, 160, 168
  in Munich 124–25
  naivety 157
  National Socialist Party,
    control of 107–10, 113
  Nazi Party member 1
  neo-Nazis and 3, 33
  Nuremberg Trials 3, 55, 70,
    100, 169
  obsessions 122–23
  Operation Barbarossa and
    45–46
  Party Central Commission
    headed by 105
  party rallies 113, 117
  peace terms 23
  personality 114–15, 124
  pilot training 122

  pilot's licence 123
  as politician 115, 118, 165
  public function 111–12
  public records and 139–52
  role as Deputy 107–10, 111–12
  SA and 106
  state, control of 109–10
  suicide 140
  USSR, Germany's invasion
    and 45–46, 110–11
  virtues 156
  as war criminal 3, 27
  Second World War's effect on
    status 110
  Zugspitze air race won by 125
  see also following entry
Hess's flight to Scotland:
  aircraft flown 20, 39, 89, 126,
    139, 143
  aircraft obtained 126
  bails out 133–34
  British disinformation
    campaign over 8, 11, 43, 44,
    45, 53, 56
  British press release 20, 39, 50
  British propaganda and 25,
    27–28, 29
  British response to 7, 19, 26,
    27, 44, 53, 153
  conspiracy theories 2–12, 16,
    28, 153, 161
  controversy over 2
  diplomatic fallout 30
  first attempt 128
  flying suit 121, 130, 131
  flying's impact 15
  fuel tanks 127
  Horn, Captain: calls himself 1,
    22, 39
  interception attempt 134
  interviews after 23–25
  letters left by 131

London bombing and 20
motives for 12–17, 19, 154–55
parachute jump 133
planning 127
practice flights 127–28
as prisoner of war, treatment of
    27, 31
radio 127, 132
radio compass 139
route 131, 132–33
stage of war 4, 6
story of 22, 39
substitute aircraft theory 121
tracked by defences 134
vertebra fractured 134
weather 129–30, 131
Hess, Wolf Rüdiger (RH's son)
    3, 141
Hesse, Fritz 84
Heydrich, Reinhard 2, 96–97
Hildebrandt, Rainer 90
Himmler, Heinrich 42, 45, 96,
    97–98, 156, 164
Hitler, Adolf:
Anglo-German understanding
    85, 97
assassination, plans for 144
Britain:
    misperception of 14
    as possible ally 25
British Empire and 27
German resistance to 82, 84
Haushofer (Albrecht) and 80,
    91–92, 95
Haushofer (Karl) and 85
Hess denounced by 3
Hess's flight:
    knowledge/ignorance of 12,
        19–20, 30, 40, 85, 136, 148,
        164, 170
    reaction to 3, 91, 142, 164
imprisonment 1

Mein Kampf 1, 13, 14, 25, 100,
    105, 154, 156
peace offensives 20, 82, 155
Rhodes admired by 25
SA and 107
Second Book 25
supreme commander,
    ineptitude as 144
USSR and 29
Windsor and 49
Hoare, Sir Samuel 88, 92
Hoover, J. Edgar 71
Hoover, President Herbert 65
Hopkins, Harry 8, 67, 70

Intelligence services:
conspiracy theories and 5–8,
    10–12, 22
see also MI5; MI6
Iraq 43, 54
Irving, David 46
Italy 171
Izvestiya 56

Junkers, Professor Hugo 124

Kaden, Helmut 128, 131, 139:
    flying suit borrowed 121, 130,
    131
Kerr, Sir A. Clark 32
Kershaw, Ian 3, 123
KGB 5, 49
Khrushchev, Nikita 47, 50
Kirkpatrick, Sir Ivone:
    identifies Hess 40
    interviews Hess 23, 24, 28, 41,
        48, 166
    Nuremberg Tribunal, report
        for 70
Kleist, Peter 156
Knickebein system 131
Krupp 117

Langbehn, Carl 82
Lascelles, Lord 157
Leasor, James 130, 137 n. 9
Lee, Brigadier-General Raymond E. 10
LeHand, Missy 68
Leitgen, Reichsamtsleiter 146, 147
Lindbergh, Charles 12
Lippmann, Walter 62
Lisbon 11, 22, 88, 160, 164, 167
Livingstone, Consul General 95
Lloyd George, David 52
Lothian, Lord 93
Louis XIV, King 170
Luftwaffe 124

MacLean, Donald 40
Macmillan Dictionary of the Second World War 121
Maisky, Ivan 31, 45, 51–52, 53, 54
Marshall, General George C. 61
Menzies, Sir Stewart 10
Messerschmitt, Willy 124, 125, 126, 131, 137 n. 7, 138 n. 11
MI5:
  conspiracy theories and 2, 11, 12, 16, 20–21, 22, 44, 48
  disinformation spread by 44
  Haushofer's letter to Hamilton 46, 160, 161, 162–63
  Hess's flight, investigation into 146–48
  records 144–45, 148
  USSR's suspicions about 47–49
  XX Committee 163
MI6:
  conspiracy theories and 2, 10

Foreign Office and 7
Milch, Erhard 124, 126
Molotov, Vyacheslav Mikhailovich 48
Moravec, Colonel František 47, 48
Morton, Desmond 10, 25
Mueller, Gestapo Chief 95–6, 98
Mussolini, Benito 91, 146, 170

National Socialist Party:
  Akten der Partei-Kanzlei 104, 108
  Bavaria as spiritual home 124
  experts 108–9
  finances 123
  Party Central Commission 105
  special representatives 108–9
  structure 107–8, 123
  Second World War and 110
neo-Nazis 3, 33
Nesbit, Roy Conyers 137 n. 8
New York Herald Tribune 62, 63
New York Times 62, 63
NKVD 5, 45, 47, 48, 50
Northumberland, Duchess of 92
Nuremberg rallies 1, 15
Nuremberg Trials 33, 39, 55, 70

O'Neill, Con 28, 29
Oshima, General Hiroshi 16, 145–46

Padfield, Peter 5, 153, 165
Pätzold, Kurt 33
peace party 12, 20–21, 64, 155, 159, 168, 170
Percy, Lord Eustace 92
Philby, Kim:
  Hess as trump card 43–44
  Hess's arrival, report of 5–6, 39, 40, 41

Hess's letter to Hamilton 41
Philip II, King 170
Pintsch, Captain Karl-Heinz 128, 130, 142–43, 148:
  Hess's letter to Hitler 91, 128, 164
  interrogated by NKVD 45
Political Warfare Executive 11
Popitz, Johannes 82
Pravda 30, 32, 55
Primakov, M. 39
Pröhl, Ilse 122
Prominente 158
Public Record Office (PRO) 139, 140, 141, 144, 145, 148, 149–52
Putsch 1923 1, 79

radar guidance systems 131–32
Rang, Standartenführer 146
Rees, Colonel 137 n. 2
Reinhardt, Fritz 109
Rhodes, Cecil 25
Ribbentrop, Joachim von 49, 80, 81, 97, 146, 155, 156, 159:
  disinformation about 45
  foreign policy 42, 80–1, 109
  on Hess 16
Riding, Richard 139
Roberts, Mrs Violet 11, 13, 21, 86, 160, 162, 163, 167
Roberts, Walter 11
Robertson, Major T.A. 12, 163
Röhm, Ernst 106, 107
Roosevelt, F. D.:
  Hess's arrival:
    briefings about 9, 28, 64–65, 66, 67, 68
    reaction to 1–2, 4, 6, 8–9, 64, 68–69
    uninterest in 9–10
Rosenberg, Alfred 117, 123, 130

Rowe, James 66
SA (Sturmabteilung) 106, 107
Schellenberg, General Walter 45, 49, 157
Schirach, Baldur von 3n
Schlie, Ulrich 19
Schmidt, Rainer F. 20, 21, 29
Schroedel, Laura 16
Sealion, Operation 171
Security Service see MI5
Semler, Rudolf 28
Sherwood, Robert 68, 69
Schulte-Strathaus, Reichsamtsleiter Dr 147
Simon, Sir John 10, 53, 54
  interviews Hess 23, 24–25, 45, 70
Simpson, Mrs 155
SIS (Secret Intelligence Service) see MI6
SOI 11, 12
SOE 144
Sonnchen see Philby, Kim
Sorge, Richard 45
Spain 82, 157
Speer, Albert 123:
  on Hess 14, 16, 91, 109, 121
  Hess's identity and 121
  imprisonment 3n 121
Stalin, Joseph:
  Britain, mistrust of 30, 54–55
  conspiracy theory and 5, 6, 7, 8
  Germany, collaboration with 30
  Hess's arrival, reaction to 1–2, 4, 6, 41, 42, 43–44, 46–47, 49–50, 55
  prisoners of war and 32
  war criminals and 32–33
Stalingrad 31

Stauffenberg, Colonel Claus
Schenk Graf von 98
Stimson, Henry 61
Stör, Willi 126
Strasser, Otto 123

Thümmel, Paul 47
Thyssen, Fritz 123
Timoshenko, S. 50
Trow, M.J. 10–11
Tsarev, Colonel Oleg 39, 40, 44,
48–49

Udet, Ernst 125–26
Union of Soviet Socialist
Republics:
archives 39
German attack on 4, 10, 24, 45
German military build-up on
border 6, 50, 55
Germany, collaboration with
29, 30
Germany, negotiations with 52
Great Britain's relationship
with Germany and 31–32,
44, 53, 67
Hess's flight and 29–33, 38–56,
67
Intelligence Services 39–40,
45, 46, 47, 48
Red Army 50
war criminals and 32–33, 55
United Nations Commission for

the Investigation of War
Crimes 31
United States of America:
anti-interventionists 65, 69
British need for 62
Hess's flight and 61–72
interventionists 68, 69
isolationists 64, 68, 69
press 62–64
public opinion 65
see also Roosevelt, F.D.

Victor Emmanuel, King 170
Vorontsov, M.A. 43

War Crimes Commission 31
Washington Post 62, 63, 64
Wednesday Society 82
Weissbecker, Manfred 33
Weizsaecker, Ernst von 97
Welles, Sumner 8–9, 65, 68, 114
Wheeler, Senator Burton K. 69
William III, King 170
Winant, Gilbert 64, 65
Windsor, Duke of 49, 71,
157–58, 171

X-Gerät system 131, 132

Y-Gerät system 131, 132
Yakovlev, A.N. 39

Zhukov, General G. 50